D1877756

HARNESSING CHILD DEVELOPMENT

HARNESSING CHILD DEVELOPMENT

(In 3 Volumes)

Volume 1

(Children and the Culture of Human Rights)

Editor

O.P. Narayan

ISHA

ISHA BOOKS

Delhi-110033

Harnessing Child Development
(Children and the Culture of Human Rights)

Rs. 2500 (Set)
Rs. 835 (Each Volume)

ISBN : 81-8205-202-5 (Set)
ISBN : 81-8205-300-5 (Vol. 1)

© O.P. Narayan

All rights reserved. No part of this book may be reproduced in any manner without written permission.

Published in 2005 in India by
Isha Books
D-43, Prithviraj Road,
Adarsh Nagar, Delhi - 110033
e-mail : ishabooks@hotmail.com

Laser Typesetting at : Global Printers, New Delhi
Printed at : Chawla Offset Press, Delhi

Contents

Preface

Childhood is the time for children to be in school and at play, to grow strong and confident with the love and encouragement of their family and an extended community of caring adults. It is a precious time in which children should live free from fear, safe from violence and protected from abuse and exploitation. As such, childhood means much more than just the space between birth and the attainment of adulthood. It refers to the state and condition of a child's life, to the quality of those years. Yet childhood remains under threat all over the world. There is no way to thoroughly enumerate the various ways in which children around the world are economically exploited and physically mistreated. But the numbers are great — and the suffering widespread. Behind the hideous imagery — of children beaten or sexually abused by parents; ravaged beyond their years by hard living and drug abuse on the streets; maimed by landmines or turned into killers by war; stricken with AIDS — are the all-too-common struggles against disease, hardship, and family or social traditions that compromise children's humanity or subject them to physical and emotional suffering.

While victims of injustice and poverty have always had trouble being heard, none have had more trouble, historically, than children. Whether exploited as child labourers or prostitutes, drafted as young teenagers into armed forces, forced as young girls into a lonely life as domestic workers, deprived of an education to work on the family farm, or denied adequate nutrition and health care, children need help and protection from an adult world that perpetrates most of the abuse. According to figures compiled by UNICEF , there are now well over a dozen countries in which conditions for children are far below the norms to be expected for their levels of economic development. This includes such gauges as malnutrition levels; under-five mortality rates; percentage of children reaching the fifth grade of primary school; and low literacy rates for women. In many poor countries, children work to supplement meagre family income or otherwise to help the family business. Although they may not always work under the most desirable conditions, most are not being intentionally exploited by their families. The real issue in such cases is not whether the children work or not, but whether the conditions under which they work are just, and whether they are being denied other basic rights because of their work — such as the right to education, to freedom from abuse, and to proper health care.

Prior to the 20th century, children were for the most part regarded as inferior and subordinate to adults, and childhood was a period of life that was often brief and regarded as a stage of passage to adulthood. Now, in the 21st century, childhood is regarded as a relatively sacred part of life among many of the more affluent. Children have been included, either directly or indirectly, in most of the nearly 80 treaties and decrees on human rights in this century. The first major step on behalf of children taken by the United Nations was UNICEF's creation in December 1946. Two years later, the Universal Declaration of Human Rights was adopted by the General Assembly. The provisions of that Declaration and its two International Covenants on human rights, adopted in 1966, recognised that child rights need protection. The 1959 Declaration on the Rights of the Child is devoted exclusively to the rights of children. However, besides all these initiatives to protect and promote the rights of children, it is still a period of great struggle and deprivation for most of the children around the world.

A child that grows up protected from violence and abuse is more likely to grow up physically and mentally healthy, confident and self-respecting and less likely to abuse or exploit others. By contrast, when children are left unprotected and vulnerable to exploitation and abuse their childhood and their rights are fundamentally undermined. Ensuring a protective environment is the responsibility of governments, international organizations, civil societies, families and individuals.

The present compilation constitutes a trilogy under three specific heads—*Children and the Culture of Human Rights; Children and the Right to Education* and *Children and the Access to Information*. The first volume *Children and the Culture of Human Rights* provides a comprehensive analysis of the human rights issues of children and the international initiative to foster their rights. The second volume *Children and the Right to Education* focuses on the educational rights of children and the importance to protect these rights to achieve the millennium development goals. The third volume *Children and the Access to Information* deals with the indispensable role of information in children's developmental process. This work examines the key issues in all areas of child development and offers a comprehensive action agenda to combat them, and calls on all stakeholders to reaffirm and recommit to their moral and legal responsibilities to children. It will be an indispensable reference tool for social workers, sociologists, child welfare agencies, civil liberty groups, policy-makers, researchers, and all who interested in child development.

Editor

1

Children and Human Rights

As human beings, children are entitled to all the rights guaranteed by the Universal Declaration on Human Rights (UDHR). Children also need special protection and care. They must be able to depend on the adult world to take care of them, to defend their rights and to help them to develop and realize their potential. Governments pay almost universal lip service to this ideal, yet have signally failed to ensure that the rights of children are respected. Children's human rights are the blocks with which we build a human rights culture in societies and secure human rights for future generations. Take action to protect and promote the human rights of children around the world. To guarantee the human rights of children is to invest in the future. Children's rights are the building blocks for a solid human rights culture, the basis for securing human rights for future generations.

Children suffer many of the same human rights abuses as adults, but may also be targeted simply because they are dependent and vulnerable. Children are tortured and mistreated by state officials; they are arbitrarily or lawfully detained, often in appalling conditions; in some countries they are subjected to the death penalty. Countless thousands are killed or maimed in armed conflicts, many more have fled their homes to become refugees. Children forced by poverty or abuse to live on the streets are sometimes detained, attacked and even killed in the name of social cleansing. Many millions of children work at exploitative or hazardous jobs, or are the victims of child trafficking and forced prostitution. Because children are "easy targets", they are sometimes threatened, beaten or raped in order to punish family members who are not so accessible.

The international community has long recognised the need to protect children from such abuses. The 1959 UN Declaration on the Rights of the Child set out ten principles which provided a powerful moral framework for children's rights, but which were not legally enforceable. The Convention on the Rights of the Child (the CRC) was adopted by the UN General Assembly in 1989, and entered into force the following year. The CRC elaborates rights according to the special needs and perspectives of the child. It is the only human rights treaty that covers the full spectrum of civil, political, economic, social and cultural rights, stressing their indivisible and interdependent relationship. By virtue of its comprehensive nature and near-universal ratification, the CRC stands as a landmark for the international consensus on the basic principles of the universality and indivisibility of all human rights. According to the CRC, every human being under the age of 18 is a child, unless majority is attained earlier under national law.

This stipulation poses important challenges for the application of the CRC, especially in countries where the age of majority is linked to puberty, often different for boys and girls. Under the CRC, all states are required to establish a minimum age of criminal responsibility, which according to the Beijing Rules(1), should "not be fixed at too low an age level bearing in mind the facts of emotional, mental and intellectual maturity". And even though a state may set the age of criminal responsibility below 18, the rights in the CRC still apply, especially those governing the child's treatment at the hands of law enforcement and judicial authorities.

One of the guiding principles of the CRC is that the "best interests of the child" should be a primary consideration in all decisions or procedures related to the child. Children have the right to be heard and to have their own opinions on matters affecting them taken into account, "in accordance with the age and maturity of the child". Very young children rely on others to express their views and protect their best interests, as they grow older, they become more and more able to speak for themselves and to engage in decision-making on their own behalf.

It is up to governments to ensure that all children enjoy their rights. No child should suffer discrimination. The rights of the CRC apply, "regardless of race, colour, sex, language, religion, political or other opinion, national, ethnic or social origin, property, disability, birth or other status". The essential message is equality of opportunity. Girls should be given the same opportunities as boys. Poor children, disabled children, refugee children, children of indigenous or minority groups should have the same rights as all others, the same opportunities to learn, to grow, to enjoy an adequate standard of living.

The rights contained in the CRC fall into four broad categories

— subsistence rights, including the rights to food, shelter and health care;

— development rights, which allow children to reach their fullest potential, including education and freedom of thought, conscience and religion;

— protection rights, such as the right to life, and to protection from abuse, neglect or exploitation;

— participation rights, which allow children to take an active role in community and political life.

The CRC deals not just with child rights, but with the responsibility of the child to respect the rights of others in their family and community. It recognises that all children should be able to grow up in a happy and loving family environment, and stipulates that the family has a duty to help children understand both their rights and their responsibilities, in order to prepare them to live "in the spirit of peace, dignity, tolerance, freedom, equality and solidarity". While the CRC emphasizes that the family is the natural environment for nurturing the child, it places the primary obligation on the state to protect children from all forms of abuse, neglect and exploitation, even where these are not carried out directly by state agents. In this way, the CRC challenges the traditional perception that states are not responsible for abuses committed within the family or the community.

Domestic violence, bonded child labour or child prostitution, for instance, are usually perpetrated by private individuals, but governments can be held accountable for failing in their responsibility to protect children from such abuses.Implementation of the CRC is overseen by the Committee on the Rights of the Child. The Committee comprises ten experts "of high moral standing and recognised competence in the field". They are elected by secret ballot of all State Parties, each of which may nominate one national expert. Because the CRC is so wide-ranging, covering social policy as well as law, the Committee usually includes people from a wide variety of professional backgrounds, such as human rights and international law, juvenile justice, social work, medicine, journalism and governmental and non-governmental work.

Governments are obliged to report to the Committee within two years of the treaty coming into effect in their country, specifying the steps taken to bring national laws, policy and practice into line with the principles of the CRC. The Committee examines the facts and hears a wide range of evidence relevant to the government's report, often from non- governmental organizations (NGOs), and meets with each government to discuss its child rights record. The Committee advises governments on the implementation of the CRC, and engages them in substantive policy discussions on the resolution of specific children's rights issues. At the end of the process, the Committee adopts "concluding observations", which provide a series of recommendations on how states can improve their implementation of the provisions of the CRC. Governments must submit progress reports every five years.

The only regional treaty on children's human rights, the African Charter on the Rights and Welfare of the Child (the African Children's Charter), was adopted by the Organization of African Unity in 1990. The Charter is rooted in other human rights treaties, such as the UDHR and CRC, but it emerges out of the social and cultural values of Africa, including those relating to family, community and society. In some respects the African Children's Charter strengthens the protections afforded by the CRC, it stipulates that everyone below the age of 18 is a child, without exception; it enjoins states parties not to recruit children to military service; and internally displaced children are accorded the same rights as refugees. In addition, the Charter seeks to eliminate harmful social and cultural practices, in particular those that are discriminatory or that put the health of the child at risk.

Amnesty International (AI) has often highlighted individual cases of children who have been the victims of human rights violations such as torture, ill-treatment or extrajudicial execution. But too often, AI's work on children has been incidental to its core research and campaigning. As a result, children have often been invisible in AI's coverage of human rights violations in the adult sphere. In recent years, AI's membership forums have recognised the need for AI to increase its work on children and adapt its research and campaigning strategy so that we can play a wider and more constructive role in promoting and protecting children's rights. In the process, AI is hoping to forge closer links with other institutions and NGOs working in this field.

Guided by the framework of the CRC, AI is seeking to develop its work on children around three key themes juvenile justice; children in armed conflict; and children in the community and family. Which combine our traditional strengths with new fields of work, we can develop our work in a holistic way and address abuses across a range of social and economic, as well as civil and political, rights. Although the CRC provides a comprehensive baseline for children's rights, AI will continue to remind states of their obligations under other human rights treaties to protect the rights of the child. In so doing, it hopes to engage other children's rights organization in concerted action in support of human rights protection more generally. The CRC may be the most widely ratified human rights treaty in the world, but it is still a long, long way from universal acceptance to universal observance.

Juvenile Justice

The rights of the child to special care and assistance are being disregarded by the very institutions that should be protecting them. Children often suffer neglect, abuse and violence in the administration of juvenile justice. When children are picked up and questioned by police, they are frequently beaten and humiliated. Their legal rights are often ignored their parents are not informed of their whereabouts; they are held in degrading conditions, and often have to share cells with adults. Some are denied their right to fair trial, and are given sentences that disregard the key objectives of juvenile justice the child's rehabilitation and reintegration into society. For the vast majority of children, the reality is not rehabilitation and special care, but punishment, intolerance and greater marginalization.

Yet when children come into conflict with the law, it is most often for minor, non-violent offences usually theft and in some cases their only "crime" is that they are poor, homeless and disadvantaged. Children forced to live on the streets are particularly vulnerable to arbitrary arrest and ill-treatment. Many survive on begging, petty crime or prostitution, activities which bring them regularly to the attention of the police. Some are detained and ill-treated simply because they are easy prey; others are arrested under laws which make destitution, vagrancy and begging criminal offences.

Poor children and those from indigenous and ethnic minorities are far more likely to be detained than other children. The CRC sets out the fundamental principles which should guide the treatment of all children who come into contact with the law. In common with the laws of most countries, the CRC prohibits torture and cruel, inhuman or degrading treatment or punishment. Yet legal safeguards are not enforced. In many countries, young women and girls taken into custody by the police are vulnerable to rape and sexual abuse.

Provision for girls in custody is often arbitrary or improvised. Because girls are much less likely to come into contact with the law than boys, their specific needs are rarely taken into consideration. The authorities in many countries have argued that the number of young female offenders is comparatively low, and does not justify the provision of dedicated custodial facilities. As a result girls are more likely to be detained a long way away from their families and to be held together with boys or adults, putting them at risk of sexual abuse and even rape. The reality is that many children in detention are not accorded even basic minimum safeguards. Children are detained without charge or trial, denied access to lawyers and relatives, and tortured and ill-treated to obtain confessions. Where children are held without access to relatives or legal counsel, the risk of physical abuse increases dramatically.

In Turkey, torture in police custody is common; the perpetrators make little distinction over the age of their victims, and are rarely brought to justice. Turkish children as young as 12 have reportedly been subjected to torture - including electric shocks, hosing with cold water and beating. Testimony of sexual torture has been received from children as young as 14 who describe being stripped naked, sexually assaulted and threatened with rape. In many cases, the torture testimony of children and juveniles is supported by medical evidence.

In the USA, there have been many reports that staff in juvenile facilities have punched, kicked, shackled, sprayed with chemicals and even used electro-shock devices against children in their care. In some countries, however, administrative detention has been used as a means of controlling children who have not even been accused of a criminal offense. If children are detained, they have the right to have contact with their families, to be held separately from adults, and to be treated with due respect for their age. Yet in many countries, young offenders are not separated by age or by the seriousness of their offence — steps which should always be taken in order to minimise the possibility of children being abused or influenced by others.

In at least 33 US states, children who are tried and convicted as adults may be sentenced to imprisonment in adult prisons and housed with adult inmates. In September 1998, more than 4,000 such children were in custody. Their welfare was of grave concern because of their extreme vulnerability to physical and sexual abuse by adults. The prohibition of the death penalty for juvenile offenders is widely accepted in both law and practice. The CRC, like the International Covenant on Civil and Political Rights

(ICCPR), unequivocally forbids the imposition of the death penalty for crimes committed before the offender turned 18. Yet in the 1990s AI has documented 18 executions of juvenile offenders in Iran, Nigeria, Pakistan, Saudi Arabia, the USA and Yemen. Ten of these were carried out in the USA.

Children are sometimes detained under conditions that pose a serious threat to their health and well-being. Several thousand children accused of genocide and murder are still being held in prisons and local detention centres in Rwanda, where overcrowding is rife and conditions extremely harsh, amounting to cruel, inhuman or degrading treatment. Children in the Russian Federation charged with minor non-violent crimes are kept in pre-trial detention centres for lengthy periods in conditions described as "torturous" by the UN Special Rapporteur on torture.

The "best interests of the child" must be the guiding principle behind all procedures and justice systems affecting children. Their overriding aim must be to protect and promote children's fundamental rights and to give young offenders the greatest possible chance of reintegrating into society. Juvenile crime has specific causes. Tackling these causes through social policy before children come into contact with the law is clearly in the best interests of the child, and indeed of society as a whole. The principles of juvenile justice emphasize preventive measures, such as alleviating the social and economic exclusion of children, providing educational opportunities, and ending race and gender discrimination.

System of Justice

The rights of children in custody and before the law are inextricably and indivisibly linked to other basic rights set out in the CRC, such as the right to education, to the highest standard of health and well-being, and to protection from abuse and exploitation. Any meaningful attempt to prevent juvenile crime must involve promoting and protecting all rights for all children. A system of justice adapted to the special needs of children and adolescents, and respecting their fundamental rights as set out in the CRC, is needed to achieve these aims. Such a system must include a realistic age of criminal responsibility which takes into account the maturity of the child; a juvenile penal law based on children's rights; sanctions for juveniles which prioritize education and training over detention and retribution; specially trained judges and lawyers; special training for the police and military; separate detention facilities for children, including rehabilitation centres; and proper follow-up and coordination with social services.

First steps are being made towards creating equitable systems of juvenile justice. Although practice often lags behind legislation, many countries are using the provisions of the CRC to help protect the rights of children in custody. Viet Nam, France and the Philippines are among the countries that have trained judges and law enforcement professionals on how to apply the CRC. El Salvador and Peru have enacted new justice codes for children, while Pakistan has modified criminal laws regarding minors. Brazil's progressive Statute of the Child and Adolescent of 1990 incorporates most of the CRC's principles. In Rwanda, the United Nations Children's Fund (UNICEF) and the International Committee of the Red Cross (ICRC) have used provisions of the CRC as the basis of their program to transfer some of the children accused of genocide and murder out of the desperately overcrowded adult prisons and into rehabilitation centres.

At the end of 1998, however, several thousand children, some under the age of 14, were still being held in prisons and detention centres across Rwanda. So despite the advances made in the ten years since the CRC came into force, international standards for the treatment and protection of juveniles in custody continue to be flouted on a massive scale. Ultimately, this is because governments have not had the political will to ensure that these standards are put into practice. AI and other organizations working on behalf of children must ensure that governments are not allowed to cite good intentions in place of decisive action — we must put pressure on governments to promote and enforce the highest possible standards of juvenile justice. War is an everyday reality for millions of children.

Some have never known any other life, they have grown up in the midst of civil wars, guerrilla insurgency, or long-term occupation by a foreign army. For others, the world is suddenly turned upside down when invasion or ethnic cleansing forces them onto the road as refugees or displaced persons, often separated from their families. Untold thousands have been killed, disabled or orphaned. Many more have died or suffered from starvation or malnutrition, or lack of clean water, sanitation and medical care. Many are traumatized by witnessing brutal deaths and being surrounded by violence, fear and hardship. And hundreds of thousands of children around the world are obliged to participate in the killing.

Children are not always the accidental victims of the carnage. Some are killed deliberately by security forces and armed opposition groups, either in retribution or to provoke outrage in each other's communities. Some, mainly girls, are singled out for sexual abuse. Many are killed and tortured because of where they live, or because of the politics, religion or ethnic origin of their family.

Young people are sometimes picked up without charge, on the assumption that they participate in, or sympathize with, armed opposition groups. It is frightening enough for an adult to be held in secret detention, to be cut off from the outside world, from the support of family and the advice of a lawyer, at the mercy of the detaining authorities. It is even worse for vulnerable children. In

Manipur state in India, children, especially boys, are targeted by soldiers who believe that these boys might be supporters or future members of armed opposition groups. Under a Special Powers act, the security forces enjoy virtual immunity from prosecution, and have attempted to block judicial inquiries into many cases.

Child Soldiers

Children are singled out for recruitment by both armed forces and armed opposition groups, and exploited as combatants. Many children have been forced to join by intimidation, including threats against their families, or abduction. Others volunteer, sometimes because they want to fight, sometimes because their families are destitute, and sometimes because they themselves are homeless and seeking food, shelter and security. Most get only minimal training and equipment before being thrown into the firing line of an adult war. Casualty rates among children are generally high, because of their inexperience, fearlessness and lack of training, and because they are often used for particularly hazardous assignments, such as intelligence work or planting landmines. In Colombia, child soldiers are sometimes called "little bees", because their size and agility enables them to move quickly and "sting" their enemies.

More than 300,000 children under the age of 18 are thought to be fighting in conflicts around the world, and hundreds of thousands more are members of armed forces who could be sent into combat at any time. Although most child soldiers are between 15 and 18 years old, significant recruitment starts at the age of 10 and the use of even younger children has been recorded. AI has drawn attention to human rights abuses in the context of child recruitment both by governments and armed opposition groups in countries such as Angola, Burundi, Colombia, Democratic Republic of Congo, Rwanda, Sierra Leone, Sri Lanka and Uganda.

In northern Uganda, thousands of boys and girls have been abducted by the Lord's Resistance Army (LRA), and forced to fight the Ugandan army. The children are subjected to a violent regime. Those caught trying to escape are killed or tortured, and both boys and girls are brutalized by being made to kill other children. Abducted children are owned by LRA commanders, with girls allocated to commanders in forced marriages and effectively held as sexual slaves. All children are sent to fight. LRA commanders force children to take part in the ritualized killing of others soon after they are seized, apparently to break down resistance, destroy taboos about killing, implicate children in criminal acts and generally to terrorize them.

Reintegration is difficult, with children haunted psychologically and facing an immense struggle to rebuild shattered lives. The medical and social consequences are particularly bad for girls, almost all of whom are suffering from sexually transmitted diseases, and face the social stigma of having been raped.

Concern for child soldiers is now becoming higher on the international agenda. The CRC currently sets 15 as the minimum age for recruitment into armed forces and participation in hostilities, but NGOs and many governments have been arguing for an end to the use of child soldiers and have campaigned for a minimum age of 18 years for both recruitment into armed forces and participation in hostilities.

Strong support for this position has also come from the International Red Cross and Red Crescent Movement, UNICEF, the Office of the United Nations High Commissioner for Refugees (UNHCR), and the Expert of the UN Secretary-General on the Impact of Armed Conflict on Children. The UN itself no longer allows under-18s to serve as peacekeepers. There are a number of reasons why under-18s should be excluded from military service. In most countries, 18 is the legal voting age, and the age which marks the formal transition from childhood to adulthood, with the assumption of adult legal and moral responsibilities. Children who become combatants before they gain emotional maturity can suffer devastating psychological effects as the case of Uganda so graphically illustrates.

Casualty rates among child soldiers who are intrinsically less cautious than adults tend to be high, and children are less likely than adults to survive battlefield injuries. Girl soldiers are generally expected to provide sexual services as well as to fight, and so suffer the additional risk of sexually transmitted diseases, pregnancy, childbirth or abortion. Participation in armed conflict is necessarily "hazardous" work, which jeopardizes the health, safety and moral development of child soldiers, and as such would be contrary to Article 32 of the CRC. However, efforts within the UN to agree an optional protocol raising the age to 18 have been blocked by the USA and a handful of other countries. In response to the failure of these negotiations, AI and five other international NGOs formed the Coalition to Stop the Use of Child Soldiers.

The Coalition, launched in 1998, is campaigning for a protocol to the CRC to stop the recruitment of anyone under 18 into both government and opposition armed forces. It also urges that all peace agreements should specifically address the need to demobilize and reintegrate child soldiers back into society, in line with Article 39 of the CRC. In June 1999 the International Labour Organisation's (ILO) 174 member States unanimously adopted a Convention aimed at ending the worst forms of child labour. The new Convention applies to all people under the age of 18, and includes a ban on forced or compulsory recruitment of children for use in armed conflicts. While AI welcomes the Convention, it believes that the most effective means of preventing children from participating in hostilities is to stop all forms of recruitment of under-18s, both voluntary and forced.

Each year, armed conflicts force many thousands of children to flee their homes in search of refuge. Sometimes they go with their families, sometimes alone; many get separated on the way. Children have not been spared the atrocities of the conflict: many have been killed, deliberately mutilated or maimed, others abducted and forced to fight with the rebel forces. Girls have been raped and forced into sexual slavery. Many of the refugees and displaced are unaccompanied children, who became separated from their parents after being abducted by rebel forces, or after their parents were killed or abducted in attacks on their towns or villages. Following the rebel incursion into Freetown in January 1999, UNICEF registered some 3,400 children as missing by mid-May 1999 only about 500 had subsequently been traced and reunited with their families.

Many children flee because of abuses directed at them in their own right. Children may engage in political activities, such as joining demonstrations, distributing leaflets or attempting to organise in their schools and workplaces. This is often enough to get them detained and tortured. In many countries, just being a student is dangerous, as schools and colleges are suspected of being hotbeds of radical opposition to the government. Cases where girls seek asylum in order to escape the practice of female genital mutilation are beginning to appear.

In Colombia, internal warfare has displaced nearly a million and a half people, mostly women with children, over the last 12 years. Some are casual victims caught up in the hostilities, some are fleeing guerrilla reprisals, but displacement is often a deliberate strategy used by army-backed paramilitary forces to "cleanse" the civilian population from areas of guerrilla influence. The displaced have to start from scratch, having lost their homes, possessions, livelihood and, in many cases, the family's main breadwinner. Many of the children are thus trying to cope with the loss of their home and community as well as the recent and violent death of a parent, usually their father.

They are seldom welcomed by their new community, which may view them with suspicion or resentment, and they are usually relegated to squalid camps or shanty towns. Many thousands of displaced children have lost both parents, and are left in charge of families and households. Children in displaced persons' camps inside their own country are seldom able to carry on with their schooling, and are often subjected to forced recruitment to the armed forces, exploitation and sexual abuse. Often the camps where they have sought security are themselves in the line of fire.

In April 1996 over a hundred civilians, including children, were killed in Qana, a UN compound in south Lebanon, when the compound was recklessly shelled by Israeli long-range artillery. Those children who are forced to flee across international borders, and are thus recognized as refugees, have far better formal guarantees of protection: government parties to the CRC and to the 1951 UN Convention (UN Refugee Convention) and the 1967 Protocol relating to the Status of Refugees are obliged to give them protection and security. Unfortunately these guarantees do not often translate into better treatment. States that should be able to offer security are increasingly trying to keep refugees out.

In developed countries, restrictions include visa requirements that are in practice impossible to fulfil, coupled with punitive fines on transport companies that carry passengers who do not have valid travel documents. Some countries, particularly those that lack the resources for sophisticated preventative measures, or that face a large-scale influx that would overwhelm any procedures in place, simply close the border.

Convention on the Rights of the Child

The Convention on the Rights of the Child (CRC) puts the best interests of the child as the primary consideration in all actions concerning children. AI calls on governments, opposition groups and all other actors who exercise control over children to adhere to this principle in all matters concerning the treatment of children. AI calls on governments to follow these concrete steps to protect children at risk of human rights abuses in custody, in the community and in situations of armed conflict

— Pass legislation guaranteeing the rights set out in the CRC and make available adequate resources to implement these rights. Cooperate fully with the Committee on the Rights of the Child, by submitting timely reports and ensuring that the Committee's recommendations are implemented fully and disseminated widely.

— Ensure that children in detention or in the care of public or private institutions are protected from torture or cruel, inhuman or degrading treatment or punishment, including rape and sexual abuse. Recognise that girls are particularly vulnerable to rape and sexual abuse and take appropriate measures to protect them.

— Ensure that all children who come into contact with the justice system are subject to special procedures based upon the fundamental principles for juvenile justice set out in the CRC.

— Enforce the worldwide ban on the imposition of the death penalty for crimes committed when the defendant was under 18 years of age.

— Provide adequate redress, including compensation, to child victims of human rights violations, aimed at their rehabilitation and reintegration into society.

— Ensure that children are detained only as a last resort, and for the shortest possible time. Children should never be detained solely for being relatives of "wanted" political or criminal suspects. The detention or imprisonment of children along with their mothers must never be used in such a way as to inflict torture or ill-treatment on either.

— Investigate impartially and thoroughly all reports of "disappearances", extrajudicial executions or other human rights violations committed against children.

— Prohibit the compulsory or voluntary recruitment of anyone under the age of 18 into government armed forces, and ban people under the age of 18 from participating in armed hostilities.

— Protect the rights of refugee and internally displaced children, including protection against recruitment and sexual exploitation. Facilitate the return or resettlement of displaced people in safety and dignity.

— Take immediate steps to end hazardous and exploitative forms of child labour, including bonded labour, commercial sexual exploitation and any other work that threatens the health and welfare of the child. Ensure that all child workers are protected from abuse or exploitation.

— Develop comprehensive programs of action to promote non-discriminatory treatment of girls and boys and to eradicate harmful traditional practices.

Around the world today, children are increasingly not only war's victims, but also its combatants An estimated 300,000 children under the age of eighteen are currently participating in armed conflicts in more than thirty different countries on nearly every continent. While most child soldiers are in their teens, some are as young as seven years old. The rights of the child are the fundamental rights. The first step to implement children's rights is training educators to solve children problems and prevent the formation of psychopathologies during a child's developmental stage. If the child is not given an education which respects those rights, he/she will not be able to know what it means to be respected and to respect.

Community and Family

In ratifying the CRC, governments committed themselves to protecting all the rights of the child social and economic, as well as civil and political. Under the CRC, children are not only protected from abuses of state power, but from all forms of physical or mental violence or abuse while in the care of "parents, legal guardians or any other person who has the care of the child," including schools. The CRC affirms that every child has the right to an adequate education and standard of living. It establishes the right of the child to be free from sexual abuse and exploitation, and the illicit use of drugs. It commits states to protecting children from economic exploitation and work that may interfere with education or damage their health.

Delivering on this commitment is an enormous challenge. Some governments have taken worthwhile initiatives, ranging from legislation against bonded labour to human rights education programs, with varying degrees of implementation and success. But this cannot excuse the way state officials help to perpetuate a wide range of abuses against children in the community and family, either through active collusion and complicity or through tacit toleration and acquiescence. The spectrum of abuses faced by children in the family and community ranges from ill-treatment in institutions to violence in the family, from child trafficking to child bonded labour. The vulnerability of children to such abuses often depends on other aspects of their identity, such as gender, ethnicity or economic status.

This is a powerful reminder of the indivisibility of human rights. The denial of one set of rights leads to the abuse of others. Children denied an education because they are girls or because they are poor and forced to work are condemned to a cycle of marginalization, poverty and powerlessness that involves further violations of their civil, political, economic, social and cultural rights. AI has been campaigning for nearly forty years to focus the world's attention on civil and political rights, but we are now engaging in broader human rights debates. We are working towards raising awareness of the full range of human rights in our promotional activities, and are attempting to address the underlying economic and social causes of human rights violations in our reporting.

We will be looking more closely at human rights abuses by non-state actors, including businesses and private institutions, and at the state's role in failing to prevent such abuses. Children's rights are at the nexus of state, family and community responsibility, and therefore demand new strategies for research and action. AI is taking its first steps in this direction, with a series of pilot projects exploring different areas of state responsibility for private abuses, and hopes to move further in a way that will complement the efforts of other NGOs and organizations working in the field of children's human rights.

Many children are abused in the care of institutions, such as schools and orphanages, that are supposed to look after their needs. Even when the abuses become widely known, the authorities appear unwilling to take decisive action to protect the children. Many poor parents in Pakistan send their children to the country's 13,000 or so Islamic seminaries or madrasas, which provide free food and lodging. They are often run by religious organizations, parties or sects, and offer a religious education, although some also provide intensive political and armed training. Investigations by the Human Rights Commission of Pakistan in 1994 showed that in some seminaries, children in groups of four or five were locked in iron chains to a heavy wooden block to prevent them escaping. Several children were found to have been continuously chained for up to one year.

The authorities are aware of the abuses children suffer in some madrasas, no effort has been made to outlaw the beating, chaining or abduction of children from such schools. Leaders of religious parties resent official probing into the functioning of the madrasas and threaten retaliation if they are more closely controlled.

Child Labour

Children all over the world are hard at work -- in fields and sweatshop factories, in mines, brick kilns or brothels, and especially in private homes. They often work in dangerous and unhealthy environments and are deprived of rights promised them in the CRC such as health, education, recreation – even childhood itself. They grow up illiterate, unskilled and prone to crime. Many are sold or forced into labour by their parents or families. In other cases, the state itself forces children into dangerous or inappropriate work. Over the past three years, the army in Myanmar has been forcibly relocating hundreds of thousands of civilians from Shan State. Some of them, including children, have been forced into heavy labour, including building roads, cutting and transporting teak logs, building military shelters, and even building a Buddhist temple.

Shan refugees reported that children from eight to 15 years of age were often used for this project, and that children also worked in place of their parents, who were busy earning money to support the family. Child labourers are often employed in rural communities, many as bonded labourers. Some are sold to a rural landlord to work against a debt incurred by the family. Others are born into bondage, simply by being the children of bonded labourers who work in the family unit to pay off a family debt. Most of the world's 250 million child workers do domestic labour. For many children, this is the only work they can find, while in some societies children from poor families are placed in another home by their parents in return for cash.

Child domestics may be forced to work long hours for little or no salary, often endure permanent or long-term isolation from their families and friends, and rarely have the chance to attend school. An unknown number suffer rough treatment at the hands of their employers, sometimes including severe beatings. In Jakarta, the capital of Indonesia, there are an estimated 700,000 child domestic workers. In Brazil, domestics account for 22% of all working children Although child domestics can be as young as five years old, most are teenage girls, who are especially vulnerable to sexual abuse. In Haiti, rural poverty forces many families to send their children, some as young as seven or eight, to work as unpaid domestics in the cities.

The parents generally receive no cash payment, they simply hope that the child will be fed. Most of these "restaveks" work in poor households, only slightly above them on the economic ladder. According to a UNICEF study, most work for families with incomes of less than US$250 a year. They work long hours at very heavy labour, cleaning, cooking and fetching water and food from long distances in scorching heat. They usually eat no more than the family's meagre leftovers, and have no time to play or to make friends. Many are beaten and mistreated, and those who try to run away face severe punishment. Even though this abuse occurs in private households, the CRC, which Haiti has ratified, obliges the country to protect the child "from all forms of physical or mental violence, injury or abuse, neglect or negligent treatment", including sexual abuse.

The issue is complicated, not all child workers are abused, and there is an ongoing debate about the degree to which children should be allowed to contribute to their families economically. Some argue that prohibiting child labour completely would increase the economic deprivation of extremely poor families who often depend on money brought in by children for their basic needs. Others say that removing children from some industries will only force them onto the streets or into more dangerous and exploitative forms of work. There are no easy answers to this. Under the CRC the "best interests of the child" should be the primary consideration in all decisions affecting them. Child labour can often involve a violation of more than Article 32 of the CRC, which deals with protection from economic exploitation. Children who work are often denied their rights to education, health and physical integrity, and child labour often becomes a critical link in the cycle of deprivation and disadvantage that feeds other abuses.

As a minimum, governments must ensure that child workers are protected: including by regulating children's working conditions, eliminating small children from the workplace and ensuring that those who abuse child labourers are brought to justice. In June 1999, the ILO adopted an international Convention obliging member states to end the worst forms of child labour, including all forms of slavery or practices similar to slavery, such as the sale and trafficking of children, debt bondage, forced labour, commercial sex work, or work likely "to harm the health, safety or morals of children."The Convention requires states to "design and implement programmes of action" to eliminate the worst forms of child labour, and to establish mechanisms for monitoring implementation of the Convention, in cooperation with employers and workers organizations. It also obliges states to provide education and rehabilitation to children removed from exploitative work, and to take into account the special situation of girls.

Every day, across the world, a miserable cargo of women and children is being trafficked across well-beaten paths. The illegal and highly profitable transport and sale of human beings for the purpose of exploiting their labour, is a human rights abuse with global dimensions. In any given year many thousands of women and girls around the world are lured, abducted or sold into forced labour, forced prostitution, domestic service, or involuntary marriage. On just two established routes, from Nepal to India and from Bangladesh to Pakistan, an estimated 9,000 girls a year are trafficked. Organized groups kidnap girls and sometimes boys, often very young, and sell them into prostitution, domestic servitude or bonded labour.

Smugglers take advantage of the economic vulnerability of young women from disadvantaged and marginalised groups, luring them with the promise of jobs or acquiring them from their impoverished families. The youth of the victims makes it difficult for them to escape or retrace their families. The number of very young children being sold into prostitution is on the increase, apparently because of the preference for virgins and fear of AIDs. A significant number of trafficked children end up being detained by the authorities on grounds such as prostitution. Many remain in detention for indeterminate periods as they have no money for bail or to make the return journey.

Female Genital Mutilation (FGM)

FGM, the surgical removal of all or part of the genital organs, is generally performed by a traditional practitioner with crude instruments and without anaesthetic it is painful, terrifying and traumatic. Most of the victims are young girls, usually between the ages of four and ten, although in some cultures FGM is carried out in infancy or on newly-married women. The long-term physical effects include permanent damage to the genital organs and mild to severe impairment of normal body functions, including sex and birth. The psychological trauma is impossible to quantify.

FGM is practised in some 29 countries in Africa and in minority communities in other parts of the world. It is estimated to have afflicted well over 100 million women and girls. In some countries, FGM is prevalent in all sectors of society. In Sierra Leone the practice is carried out by all ethnic groups, apart from the Creoles, and all classes, including the educated elite. FGM is similarly widespread in Ethiopia, Eritrea, Mali and Somalia. In Côte d'Ivoire FGM affects about half of all women, and in some communities is performed on baby girls less than 40 days old. Some two million African girls are believed to undergo FGM each year. There is a complex web of interrelated cultural factors behind FGM. It is seen by its practitioners as a necessary rite for initiation into womanhood and integration into the culture, without which a woman cannot marry. But it is increasingly opposed by women and men in Africa and elsewhere as a systematic form of violence against women and girls and a denial of their fundamental rights.

In December 1997 the Supreme Council in Egypt upheld a Health Ministry decree banning female circumcision from being carried out in state hospitals. By rejecting arguments that FGM is a religious requirement and that medicalization makes the practice acceptable, the court's decision gave a major boost to eradication efforts worldwide. Some 90% of Egyptian girls have reportedly undergone FGM, usually between the ages of three and six. States are obliged to respect and to ensure the protection and promotion of all human rights, including the right to non-discrimination, the right to physical and mental security and the right to health.

An estimated 100 million children live and work on the streets -- begging, peddling fruit, cigarettes or trinkets, shining shoes, often resorting to petty theft and prostitution to survive. Some of them have family links, but many others have been abandoned, rejected or orphaned, or have run away from home because of abuse or poverty. These children sleep in parks or doorways, under bridges or in abandoned buildings. Many are addicted to drugs; in Central America, street children often use inhalants, such as glue, which are cheap and easily accessible, but which cause irreversible brain damage, as well as a host of physical debilities. Very few street children enjoy the standard of living guaranteed by the CRC, which must be "adequate for the child's physical, mental, spiritual, moral and social development"

Street children often fall victim to "social cleansing" campaigns, in which local business owners pay to have them chased away or even killed. Many are victims of abuse, sometimes murder, by police and other authorities who are supposed to protect them. AI has documented violence against street children in many countries, including Bangladesh, Brazil, Guatemala, India, Kenya, Nepal and Uganda. What these attacks have in common is the almost complete impunity enjoyed by those who perpetrate them. Recent court judgments in Brazil have taken the first steps towards holding those who abuse street children accountable.

Parent/Child Relationships

Parent/child relationships are bounded by two extreme cases: i) an attitude of neglect, indifference and lack of attention; and ii) an overprotection and involvement which does not allow the child to develop a sense of autonomy and self-assurance. This behaviour expresses the adult's personality, and thus he/she cannot help transmitting these values and conditionings to the child. We should give the developing child not only rights, but also empowerment. If the child is not given an education which respects those rights which he/she inherently feels, he/she will never be able to know in the future what it means to be respected and to respect.

If the child is taught to express egoism, prejudice, racism (not only against different ethnic groups, but mostly against different ideas), if the child is offered psychological violence as a behavioural model and as a way of problem solving, if the child is taught to see interpersonal relationships as only an instrument for personal benefit, if the child is taught to achieve success in order to be considered "important" and so on, it means that we are educating the child to disrespect the rights of both itself and others.

The brain of a 4-5 year old child is already full of information which creates conflicts between what the child feels and what he/she is given as a behavioural model. A child "absorbs" the adults' misconceptions, which manifest themselves by anguish, distress and fears because the developing brain is not yet able to find many solutions. The ability for abstract thought is already established around 6-7 years of age, which theoretically could mean that children of this age are able, for instance, to willingly kill. In my opinion, it is not really a question of being able to think abstractly, but rather a matter of having absorbed misconceptions and conditionings from adults prior to having the chance of living a "normal" situation which would have given the child a frame of reference for comparison.

Violence, social climbing and the power of money are normal conditions to many children nowadays. They are able to want only what is in consonance with the conditionings they uncritically received from adults, and they don't even know that they could want something else. Only few parents are able to detect these signs of distress. It is not sufficient to check the child's progress at school, but it is also necessary to observe its way of reasoning, what makes it suffer and why, how it faces its problems, to what extent it participates in its environment and its level of understanding of other people's motivations.

The psychological wellbeing of the child during this crucial period risks grave problems, because to the parents every behaviour of their child is normal until something very tragic happens. In fact it is considered normal for children to tell their parents to "go to hell", to not accept people, to act polite with an ulterior motive, to hide their feeling to avoid consequences, while at the same time it is considered normal for a child to be rational and clever but insensitive and selfish.

Everything seems normal because we expect children to improve as they grow up, but we must realise that the respect for human rights stems from education, from the principles we instil in their young brains and from the abilities we nurture. In order to respect a child's rights we have to understand that age is not the main difference between an adult and a child, because nowadays children are confronted with an adult's perverse world which has an unlimited power of persuasion. As a consequence children show the limitations and conditionings of adults, yet their mental abilities are still those of a child.

Every child should have the right to play, to happiness, to the expression of one's own opinion and thinking and to the respect of one's own dignity. Parents can guarantee all this only with great difficulty, because they often find themselves alone in coping with the huge amount of information that the child has absorbed from other sources. Furthermore they have very few means to fight the highly suggestive power of this "pathological" information. The amount of news and images a child takes in nowadays is much higher than twenty years ago, Our children are no longer interested in an innocent game without "victims", but rather want a game capable of making them feel invincible, strong and capable of everything, a game which can give them strong emotions.

Even when children are playing traditional games we can see episodes of intolerance, discrimination, the incapacity to lose, aggression, the impossibility to say "I was wrong", and the need to overwhelm peers. This is undoubtedly an infringed right, since children cannot wish good for others or seek dialogue if they have not be taught to.

Respect Children's Right

On the basis of these data it is clear that parents and teachers often have to respect children's right without having the proper tools to educate them, that is to say to bring out unexpressed potentialities of a developing brain. To educate does not mean to instruct. By instruction we mean to condition the brain to learn human rights, whereas by education we mean to promote the experience of human rights, which then become inviolable for oneself and for others. It is the right of a child not to be conditioned by violence, power, force or pleasure associated with information not fit for his/her mental age, to be educated so that he/she can comprehend his/her surroundings, and to express his/her thinking while respecting the different ideas of others.

For this reason the first step to implement children's rights consists of training educators to solve children problems and prevent the formation of psychopathologies during a child's developmental stage. To this end the Centre for Human Evolution studies has developed the field of Neuropsychophysiology based on thirty years of multidisciplinary and integrated studies and research. This discipline is rooted in an understanding of the higher functions of the human brain, of how all levels of behaviour (rational, emotional, social) are produced, and of how the individual develops the awareness of both him/herself and his/her environment. It gives tools to the various institutions to substantially promote an education focused on the respect for, and spreading of, human rights.

According to neuro-psycho-physiology, a child's development includes not only so-called psychomotor development but also every cognitive and relational acquisition, thereby rendering the child progressively more autonomous, sure of him/herself and in growing interaction with the surrounding environment. Every child is a unique and unrepeatable subject, an original combination of many factors related to heredity (genetics) and education (environment). The instant of birth marks, in a way, the passage from the former to the latter. In fact education, habits and environment not only become predominant in determining the psychophysical development of the individual (genotype), but may even modify the trend of potential genetic components (phenotype). Developing a responsible society is surely a very ambitious task, as institutions and services typically intervene after a problem is encountered rather than searching for methods of prevention. An education towards prevention does not yet exist, even if this would clearly be more useful and cheaper.

Self-esteem and Motivation

A human being is born with a "basic education" determined by the genetic memories of around 14 billion neurons, which can potentially make him/her a "genius" and a "sage". One of the prerequisites needed to develop intelligence and wisdom is the creation of a "non-conditioned" motivation linked to the respect of genetic drives, that is the universal values valid for every individual regardless of his/her nationality, culture, religion or age. We can say that motivation is the motor of life, as it is at the root of learning, growth, planning and participation in life itself. Motivation must be born by the gradual awareness of the usefulness of what the child learns, and is linked to the drives promoting personality development.

The neuro-psycho-physiology of behaviour stresses that genetic drives represent the inborn aspect of motivation, as they push the child, since the first instant of birth, to explore the environment as if he/she was a little scientist moved by a "physiological" interest in everything that surrounds him/her. In this sense perceptive development witnesses the extraordinary competence and readiness of the child to notice every information, thereby allowing him/her to gradually acquire consciousness and awareness of the environment. But this "inborn motivation" may be extinguished or deformed when the child is induced to learn behavioural, ethical or social concepts and patterns for conditioning objectives.

A classical example of this is the child studying to get a prize or racing against other children to win. One could want the same things without conditioning objectives, such as studying because one wants to learn and acquire useful tools for his/her life within society or racing with friends for the pleasure of playing together, being active or improving one's physical well-being. At the base of the various motivations and objectives of a child, be they conditioned or not, there is the search for the assertion and respect of one's dignity, assertion and respect of the human being's genetic drives. It is these drives that determine behaviour, and if they are limited and repressed the individual, from the very first years of life, will develop endless strategies to try to satisfy such drives, including antisocial or deviant behaviour This is why no one accepts to obey, to be punished, mocked, rebuked or humiliated but we all desire to feel important, to feel that we have value.

Self-esteem must be grounded in the awareness and consciousness of the child's own "value" as a human being, of his/her own dignity and personality, not on external factors, while a number of studies made in this field show that at the present moment both self-knowledge and self-esteem largely depend on the way others perceive and react to our behaviour. When going to school children start to base their self-esteem on their cognitive and social competences. "Social confrontation" starts to establish if one is more or less competent than other children, if one makes more or less mistakes in an exercise, if one is faster or slower in a race. The tendency towards social confrontation, which can play a determining role in modelling self-esteem if an adequate education is not given, increases with age and becomes stronger if teachers create a competitive climate in the classroom or on the playground.

Furthermore it has been found that children with the highest self-esteem are generally those who do well at school and have many friends. From this it emerges that present educational methods induce the individual to base his/her self-esteem only on external factors, particularly related to the quality of interpersonal relations, the ability to control his/her surroundings, mastering emotional reactions, success at school, family life, physical skills and personal attraction and charm. As such one acquires value for what he/she does and not for what he/she is, i.e. one is measured on the basis of social dignity while personal human dignity is completely neglected. This is in spite of the fact that it is fundamental to the goals of education and the correct development of self-esteem that one has a clear awareness and understanding of the difference between these two kinds of dignity. Just by existing biologically a human being has in him/herself dignity.

While social dignity is acquired during life and depends on the social, cultural and political context, human dignity as a value of life is inborn and untouchable, has an endless value, cannot be traded or sold, is not subject to limitations in time and space, cannot be reduced or increased, and cannot and must not be questioned by anyone; instead it must be loved and respected. This must be the constant reference point for parents, teachers and everyone coming near a child love and respect for their human dignity. This means that every child must always be evaluated as a person independently from what he/she does.

For example if he/she hits another child we must discuss the action which is not right, without injuring his/her esteem, on the basis of the principle that we must fight against a person's action, and not the person. A child who always feels loved and respected will not have to waste energy looking for, often unsuccessfully, love and respect by pursuing aims which are not useful for his/her growth. He/she will instead be able to gradually develop a self-esteem based on his/her potentialities, and will be able to develop the will to verify the consequences of his/her actions and to continuously improve, without fearing to be wrong or to be judged and without having to depend on the approval of others.

Adults' Proposals

Children live in a world full of stimuli they do not understand

and do not know, which creates in them fears and uncertainties. Only after understanding them will they be able to cope and solve them, "choosing" their parents proposals and solutions. Up to that moment the greatest damage is caused by coercive stimulus, engendering only pain and very often aggressiveness. It is only a natural mechanism if a child rejects what makes him/her suffer. For instance, it is better to not bathe him/her and instead wash the child with a sponge if the imposition of a bath creates a situation of fear, tension and crying, for this also causes stress and worry in the parents, which are not useful for a serene education.

The child defends him/herself from everything he/she does not know and is not "normal" for his/he habits or familiar stimuli. Lights, sounds, attitudes, manipulations must be attentively modulated, according to the child's status and the aim we propose to ourselves. For instance, we have to stimulate with sweetness and persuasion in order to make the child accept a behavioural innovation, as this normally often provokes defence, uneasiness and pain. Great attention and identification with the child is therefore needed to understand the difficulties inherent in the adults' proposals.

Children's defences are a very important and serious problem. In fact a child's defences are an instinctive process which follow a stimulus/answer mechanism. It is the parent's duty to help him/her to control all his/her instinctive defences through intermediation and the development of both reason and the conscious act. Initially the child is unable to organize his/her intervention on the environment. His/her gestures are aggressive, often domineering and selfish, with the "desire" to do everything he/she likes and to submit everyone around him/her to his/her wishes. All that exists is a stimulus which results in an answer, thereby "leading" the child that is unable to select or choose them. He/she is used to be taken care of in all his/her needs, and thus cannot suddenly be worried by his/her mother, father, or surroundings. He/she cannot surely mediate between his/her needs and those of others. To consider others he/she will have to become a subject, that is all his/her answers will have to become deeds formed by conscious choice.

Instead of rebuking a child because he/she did not give something to another child we must serenely make him/her perceive the joy of making others happy. And every time this happens a gratification must be given. Gratification does not mean a prize in toys, but rather a gentle voice full of love in which he/she will recognize the confirmation of his/her right deed. Similarly it doesn't help to yell, punish or hit when facing wrong behaviour from the child, but rather it is enough to not "gratify" the child. The little one will notice the lack of gratification, will compare what he/she has experienced as joy with that which is not gratifying, and little by little will try to produce gratifying behaviour.

The problems of children and youths starts to build up in the first stages of development. Parents' lack of ability in gradually giving information to their child's brain in order to promote autonomy, as well as the perception and building of subjectivity is a serious threat to the shaping of a sensitive and aware human being. At birth the brain contains a wonderful developmental project that "unfortunately" can only be realised in conjunction with the family and the surrounding social environment. Society and family should take it upon themselves, as stated by the UN Convention on the Rights of Child, the responsibility for protection and care of the child to enable it to become the subject of its life and not an object of conditionings imported from adults. In this way we will eventually reach the psychophysical and spiritual wellbeing of the child.

2

Childhood Under Threat

Childhood is more than just the time before a person is considered an adult. Meaning much more than just the space between birth and the attainment of adulthood, childhood refers to the state and condition of a child's life: to the quality of those years. A child who has been kidnapped by a paramilitary group and compelled to bear arms or forced into sexual slavery cannot have a childhood, nor can a child put to hard labour in a garment workshop in the capital city, far from family and home village. Children living in abject poverty without adequate food, access to education, safe water, sanitation facilities and shelter are also denied their childhood.

What then do we mean by childhood? The quality of children's lives can vary radically within the same dwelling, between two houses on the same street, between regions and between industrialized and developing countries. The closer children come to being full-grown, the more cultures, countries, and even people within the same country differ in their views of what is expected of children and on the level of adult or legal protection they require. Yet, despite intellectual debates about the definition of childhood and cultural differences about what to expect for and from children, there has always been a substantial degree of shared understanding that childhood implies a separate and safe space, demarcated from adulthood, in which children can grow, play and develop.

Children's rights been so high on the public agenda; never before have children's voices been heard as clearly and distinctly by the international community as they were during the United Nations General Assembly Special Session on Children in 2002. Yet for hundreds of millions of children, the promise of childhood that undergirds the Convention already appears broken as poverty, conflict and HIV/AIDS threaten their lives and well-being. Though a childhood of love, care and protection, in a family environment, with ample scope to survive, grow, develop and participate is the right of every child, millions do not experience it. When they become parents, their own children also risk having their rights denied as the threats to childhood, particularly the ones highlighted in this report, replicate themselves from generation to generation. This is already evident in the lives of millions of youth - those aged 15 to 24 - who have grown up since the Convention was adopted and who are still living amid penury, conflict, violence, exploitation and disease.

To take but one example, more than 140 million youth were illiterate in 2000, over 60 per cent of them young women. It is hard to avoid the conclusion that we, the adults of the world, have failed these young people and are failing the children of today. But this does not have to be the case. We have an unparalleled opportunity to fulfil the rights of children. The intent is there, as evidenced by the near-universal ratification of the Convention and the endorsement of other international and national instruments related to children's rights and well-being. The resources - knowledge, money, technology, people - are available in abundance: by any aggregate measure, the world is richer than it has ever been. The targets are clear:

Achievement of the Millennium Development Goals, and fulfilment of the broad aims embodied in 'A World Fit for Children', though not a panacea for all childhood's woes, would do much to make the world a better place for children. Decades of human development research have fine-tuned our strategies: We now know, for example, that for development gains to be sustainable, the participation of all parties - including children and young people - is essential.

While poverty fuels conflict, which in turn creates more poverty in a destructive spiral - and both render people much more vulnerable to HIV/AIDS - the flipside of this coin is that a serious assault on poverty will also reduce both conflict and HIV/AIDS. And there is the optimism that infuses both the Universal Declaration of Human Rights and the Convention on the Rights of the Child. If every family, community and government lived by the principles and worked to realize the standards established by the Convention, which preceded all other current commitments to children by over a decade, the Millennium Development Goals would be met and 'A World Fit for Children' would become a reality.

The notion of will is pivotal to creating a world fit for children. It is will that translates intentions into action. The will of one woman, Eglantyne Jebb, inspired her to launch the Save the Children Fund in 1919, in response to the misery of thousands of children in Europe. The will of the international community led to the creation of UNICEF in 1946 to look after the needs of children in post-war Europe. That will has helped save millions of lives as UNICEF has expanded its work into every developing nation where children's lives are at risk. Not all of us will have the opportunity to launch a children's fund or to save the lives of millions of children. But we all have a part to play in ensuring that every child enjoys a childhood.

Children's rights are human rights, the rights that we all share. The fulfilment of rights implies responsibilities. It is the duty of each and every one of us - not just parents, guardians and relatives, educators and governments - to guarantee that the terms of childhood laid out in the Convention, which our governments have endorsed on our behalf, are upheld for every child. States and societies, communities and families, individuals and international agencies and, most importantly, children and young people themselves - are all duty-bound to fulfil children's rights. Each can make a different contribution, depending on their capacities and resources.

Children's rights, human development and moral considerations are increasingly intertwined. In a world that brings us televised or Internet images of suffering from the other side of the planet, we are as capable of being moved by the pain of someone 5,000 kilometres away as we are by that of someone next door. In this sense, we are increasingly becoming a global community in which we can no longer partition off our ethical responsibility along local or even national lines. No image is more likely to speak to us across continents, from beyond oceans, than that of a child in distress. A girl abducted from her village and forced into sexual slavery by a gang of armed rebels: the very idea is unbearable. It moves us to justified anger, to a desire to do whatever we can to ensure that it does not happen again.

The difficulty is to have the same response to - and the same sense of responsibility towards - all the hundreds of thousands of children who we do not see or read about, except as bald statistics: those, for example, who die for want of a simple hydrating formula that could counteract the ravages of diarrhoea; those who die from diseases that are preventable either by inexpensive vaccinations or increased access to basic health-care services; those who are orphaned by HIV/AIDS, without family or the comfort of even one caring adult.

Although some of these threats to children have existed since the dawn of recorded history, in a very real sense we live in a new world. Since 1990, we have committed ourselves, through the Convention on the Rights of the Child and its two Optional Protocols, the Millennium Declaration and its associated goals, 'A World Fit for Children' and other international, regional and national initiatives, to a conception of childhood that is profound in its implications and will stand for decades, even for centuries to come. It gives us a clearer vision than ever before of what a safe, healthy, active childhood should look like.

For governments, the message is unambiguous: Keep your commitments to your nation's children. Despite numerous treaties and pledges, despite the UN Special Session on Children, there is simply not enough being done to realize children's rights: They must be given the highest priority. A key starting point for many nations will be to make progress in the health and development of their children a priority. At present, it is estimated that approximately one third of the global burden of disease is borne by children. Without greater attention to providing basic health care and education services for children, it is clear that most of the Millennium Development Goals will not be met in full by 2015.

Of all the MDGs, it is widely acknowledged that progress has been slowest on reducing under-five mortality. This goal can be achieved: It is estimated that two thirds of the almost 11 million under-five deaths that occur each year could be averted if children would receive appropriate home care and if simple curative treatments for the common childhood illnesses were available. The interventions to prevent child deaths, such as immunization, exclusive breast-feeding and oral rehydration therapy, are well known and tested, and can be scaled up even in resource poor settings. Achieving the MDG for child survival is therefore a clear case of will, for while the financial investment will be fairly modest, massive efforts will be required in social mobilization and the development of innovative strategies for delivering the interventions.

Reaching every child with a basic package of essential, proven interventions will demand cooperation between governments, bilateral and multilateral agencies, non-governmental organizations, health professionals, professional associations and the private sector. Such a collaboration, including governments, UNICEF, the World Health Organization, and many others, has recently been formed under the auspices of the Child Survival Partnership to respond to the health crisis facing children and help countries scale up their interventions rapidly. The partnership provides a forum for coordinated action to enable governments and partners to agree on consistent approaches to child survival interventions and to ensure concerted efforts towards their implementation.

The Child Survival Partnership is not a fund-holding or fund-disbursing organization. It is an advocacy initiative for the increased mobilization of resources and support for child survival programmes by participating countries and organizations to meet a specific objective: attain the fourth Millennium Development Goal. The interventions it recommends and encourages will require substantial additional funding, however, from national, bilateral and multilateral sources, as will other initiatives designed to achieve the MDGs, and other rights-based and development targets. Donors, therefore, are also pivotal actors in ensuring that every child has a childhood. Promises made to children at the Special Session and enshrined in 'A World Fit for Children' cannot be forgotten. Pledges made following the Monterrey Consensus in 2002 to increase official development assistance by around $18.5 billion a year until 2006 must also be realized.

Though this may appear a substantial sum, in truth it is a minimal increment: A figure closer to $50 billion annually over the same period would be required to meet all of the Millennium Development Goals by 2015. The quality of aid also requires enhancement through improved harmonization of donor policies with recipients' priorities. Investment in essential goods, services and infrastructure that directly satisfy children's rights is crucial: without it, none of the other international development agendas will be realized.

By 1994, four years after the Convention's inception, nearly 170 nations had accepted the document as an internationally agreed standard for childhood. A decade has since passed and human rights have been elevated to the top of the international agenda. But few governments have been guided by human rights principles in all of their actions towards their citizens. The human rights-based approach to development is relatively new. It is based on a longterm process of investing in people as citizens and actors in their nation's destiny as well as supporting their capacity to hold their government accountable for its promises.

Placing rights at the heart of human development strategies allows countries to give attention to those children and vulnerable members of society living at its margins; to prioritize goods and services essential for children's survival, health and education; and to construct a protective environment to safeguard children from the rights violations that cannot easily be quantified: abuse, exploitation, violence, conflict, bonded labour, stigmatization and discrimination. Applying new concepts such as the human rights-based approach to development and the protective environment is not only important for governments: donors and international agencies also have much to gain.

Refinements in development thinking over the decades have broadened UNICEF's approaches to its own programmes. We now know, for example, that educating children caught up in armed conflict, which was previously not given a high priority among our core commitments to children in emergency situations, is actually vital for injecting stability into their lives. The threats to, and opportunities for, childhood are not static: they evolve with the changing of the world. Each new generation faces fresh challenges: for instance, polio, long a leading cause of child deaths, has almost been eradicated, but a new threat - HIV/AIDS - has emerged. On the brighter side, the leap in information technology achieved in the 1990s has allowed several developing countries, India among them, to make great strides towards closing the technology gap with the industrialized nations. The utilization of information technology is almost certainly destined to drive economic development in most countries.

But it is not without cost or concerns, including the danger posed to children by predators using the Internet, and the difficulty faced by parents in monitoring their children's use of the web. There is no excuse for ignorance. It is the responsibility of both governments and donors to be aware of how children are affected by poverty, discrimination, ignorance, labour and exploitation, life threatening diseases and the environment. Accountability and knowledge provide a firm basis for action and must be incorporated into policies and programmes to bring about change.

Governments must adopt socially responsible policies, keeping children specifically in mind. For any government hoping to promote and protect human rights and achieve sustainable development, especially in the areas of poverty reduction and lowering HIV/AIDS prevalence, pursuing measures with children specifically in mind is the most effective route. Applying human rights principles to child policies will bring rich rewards. Educating and supporting citizens to participate in civic affairs will enhance their capacity to support their children's development and ensure the protection of their rights. Abolishing school fees will encourage poor families to enrol their children in school, as it has done in Kenya, Malawi, Uganda and the United Republic of Tanzania, allowing millions of children to enjoy their right to an education.

Mechanisms that increase the transparency and accountability of state services will help ensure that these are of the highest quality possible and the least wasteful of human and financial resources. Empowering and directing resources to marginalized groups will assist in strengthening the social fabric and reducing potential social discord, conflict and disintegration. Provision of social and protection services should be mandatory, not optional, and citizens should be encouraged to participate and fulfil their own duties to children and to society. Donors and governments must invest additional funds in children. The resources are available to fund a global transformation of childhood, through both increased official development assistance and improvements in the quality of national public finances.

Implementing national plans of action for children with a set of specific, time-bound and measurable targets and goals, as agreed to at the UN Special Session on Children, would go a long way towards meeting the agenda of 'A World Fit for Children'. The monitoring and analysis of national budgets from the perspective of their impact on children is a promising approach to promoting increased resource allocation for children and maximizing their effective use. Better targeting of education, health and social assistance services towards the poor, addressing government-related impediments to service quality and effectiveness, increasing community participation and scaling up on the basis of successful programmes would help meet the requirements of the Monterrey Consensus for developing countries - and must be matched by increased donor funding.

Substantial additional resources could be freed up, for example, by diverting expenditure on weapons and other military equipment. If even a fraction of this expenditure were diverted to health or education, it would release millions - if not billions - of dollars. Everyone must fulfil their obligations to children. Individuals, families, businesses and communities: all are duty-bound to make the Convention a reality by using their resources and capabilities to promote and protect children's rights. An array of possibilities exists for participation in activities that will benefit children, from sitting on school councils or volunteering as a youth counsellor, to sponsoring a local football team or expressing outrage at violations of children's rights to politicians and other leaders. All that is required is commitment and willingness to get involved and to stay engaged.

Childhood is the foundation of the world's future. And though the future may look bleak now, we must not despair. Our optimism is rooted in history - the world has shown that it is capable of doing great things when it has the will to achieve them. Major feats have already been achieved. To take just one example, children are half as likely to die before the age of five today as they were 40 years ago, largely thanks to better access to healthcare services and increased knowledge of the causes of child deaths. Expert opinion is that the Millennium Development Goals can still be achieved if both donor and recipient countries increase their efforts.

Several countries are already putting in place the elements required to create a protective environment for children that will help meet the protection aims of 'A World Fit for Children'. Although idealistic in the context of past experience, these goals are realistic in the sense that the principal obstacle standing in their way is the lack of will and commitment to achieve them.

A new definition of childhood based on human rights is reflected in the Convention on the Rights of the Child, adopted by the United Nations General Assembly in 1989. The Convention is the first international human rights treaty to bring together the universal set of standards concerning children in a unique instrument, and the first to understand child rights as a legally binding imperative. The Convention represents the culmination of a process of recognizing the rights of children and the special status of childhood that gained significant momentum as the 20th century progressed. Work on the Convention began in earnest in 1979 and spanned a decade. It involved exhaustive negotiation and research into differing cultural interpretations of childhood. The process of negotiating, drafting and approving the Convention brought governments, international agencies and nongovernmental organizations to agreement around the moral necessity of protecting children's rights.

Impacts of Convention on the Rights of the Child

The impact of the Convention on the Rights of the Child on

the status of children has been as profound as its consolidation of the rights of children. The Convention defines childhood as a separate space from adulthood. Historically, the needs and obligations of children were not well differentiated from those of adults. Like adults, able-bodied children traditionally engaged in arduous labour and were often combatants in battle. But the Convention, citing the "special care and assistance" that children require, recognizes that what is appropriate for an adult may not be suitable for a child. This is why, for instance, it sets a minimum age for recruitment into the armed forces and participation in armed conflict. Its recognition of childhood as a 'separate space' means that even when children face the same challenges as adults, they may require different solutions.

The Convention asserts the role of the family in children's lives. The family is the fundamental unit of society and the natural environment for the growth and well-being of its members, particularly children. Under the Convention, countries are obliged to respect parents' primary responsibility for providing care and guidance for their children and to support parents in this regard by providing material assistance and support. States are also obliged to prevent children from being separated from their families unless the separation is judged necessary in order to ensure the child's best interests. The Convention declares that all children have rights regardless of their circumstances.

Children have often been considered the property of their parents; any inherent value was thought to derive from their potential economic productivity. Even when laws were passed that benefited children, they were often motivated by a desire to safeguard family property rights rather than children themselves. The Convention recognizes that children are the holders of their own rights. And because these rights are invested in the child's own person, the child is no longer a passive recipient of charity but an empowered actor in her or his own development. Children have the right to influence decisions that affect their lives - in accordance with their age and maturity. The Convention views the child as both an individual and a member of a larger community.

The Convention commits nations to guarantee individual rights: no child is more important than another, and children are entitled to freedoms "without discrimination of any kind. " Yet while children are uniquely vulnerable and deserve particular protection, they are also to be "prepared to live an individual life in society. " The Convention emphasizes the need to respect children's "evolving capacities. " Adults are expected to create spaces and promote processes designed to enable and empower children to express their views, to be consulted and to influence decisions in all matters affecting them in accordance with their age and development.

The Convention lays down the terms of childhood. As the most widely endorsed human rights treaty in history, the Convention effectively represents a global consensus on the terms of childhood. Although there is not absolute agreement on the interpretation of each and every provision of the Convention - some of the States parties have issued declarations and reservations clarifying their national positions on one or more aspects of the rights - there is substantial common ground on what the standards of childhood should be.

The Convention identifies obligations to the child. A child's experience of life - childhood - especially in their earliest years, is largely determined by the care and protection they receive, or fail to receive, from adults: from the family and also from the wider community, including States parties. It is the responsibility of all duty bearers for children - governments, international organizations, civil society, families and individuals - to ensure that children's rights are fulfilled and protected. When children are left unprotected and vulnerable to exploitation and abuse, their childhood is undermined. A protective environment is pivotal to governments' and societies' commitment to ensuring that no child is deprived of the material, spiritual and emotional resources needed to achieve their potential or participate as full and equal members of society.

Protective Environment

Children have the right to grow up in an environment that protects them. Successful protection increases children's chances of growing up physically and mentally healthy, confident and self-respecting, and less likely to abuse or exploit others, including their own children. Child protection is also closely linked to other aspects of a child's rights. The right to health is not enjoyed by an immunized child who is constantly beaten; a schoolchild taunted or abused for her or his ethnicity does not fully benefit from the right to an education; an adolescent sold into prostitution has the right to freedom criminally violated.

Despite the near universal ratification of the Convention on the Rights of the Child, and the addition of two Optional Protocols, both of which address protection rights, child protection is weak in much of the world. While governments appear to agree with the principle that children should not be abused, trafficked, exploited or exposed to hazardous labour, their commitment to creating and sustaining a protective environment for children is less clear. Creating a protective environment, based on the ideal childhood of the Convention, is not just about changes in laws and policies; it is also about altering attitudes, traditions, customs and behaviours that continue to undermine children's rights.

In the years since the Convention was adopted, the world has seen concrete results. For example, there have been substantial increases in the provision of essential goods and services, such as immunization, insecticide-treated mosquito nets and oral rehydration salts, that children require if they are to survive and remain healthy. Between the early 1990s and 2000, the global under-five mortality rate declined by 11 per cent; in the decade to 2000, underweight prevalence among children under five fell from 32 to 28 per cent in developing countries, and global access to safe drinking water rose from 77 to 82 per cent. Child deaths from diarrhoea, the foremost killer of children the beginning of the 1990s, declined by half during the decade, saving an estimated 1 million lives. The Global Polio Eradication Initiative, launched in 1988, helped reduce the number of polio cases from 350,000 that year to fewer than 700 at the end of 2003.

The 190 governments that convened at the UN General Assembly Special Session on Children in 2002 pledged to accelerate progress on child development. World leaders unanimously embraced a set of time-bound goals: promoting the best start and healthy lives for children; providing quality education; protecting children against abuse, exploitation and violence; and combating HIV/AIDS. These commitments were reflected in a new international compact - 'A World Fit for Children'.

The vision of 'A World Fit for Children' complements the Millennium Development Goals (MDGs), adopted just 20 months earlier at the UN Millennium Summit. The MDGs, which encompass eight primary goals to be achieved by 2015, have become central objectives for all countries, UN agencies, including UNICEF, and bilateral donors and international financial institutions. The goals have a strong focus on children and the realization of their rights.

Millennium Development Goals

Progress is behind schedule for almost all of the MDGs. UN agencies, the World Bank, the Organisation for Economic Co-operation and Development and others have repeatedly voiced their concern that nearly all of the MDGs - and therefore most of the goals in 'A World Fit for Children' - will not be met unless there is a concerted effort by donors and governments. Failure to achieve the MDGs will have tragic consequences for children, particularly those in developing countries. Millions will see their childhood violated through ill health or death from preventable diseases. Millions more will see their futures compromised because of governments' failures to provide them with an education, and the number of children orphaned or made vulnerable by HIV/AIDS will continue to rise.

The advent of the Convention on the Rights of the Child was a landmark in human history, and its subsequent ratification by all but two of the world's countries is a remarkable testament to the universally shared vision of what childhood should mean. The concept of childhood, then, has never been stronger, clearer or more detailed.

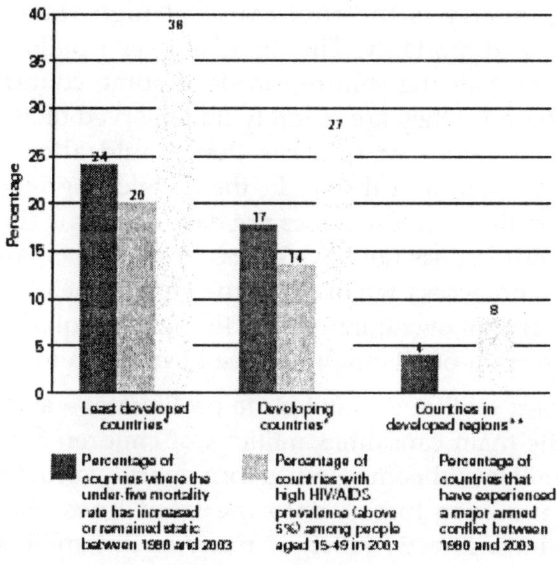

Figure 1. Poverty, armed conflict and HIV/AIDS threaten child survival

The powerful vision of children's rights set forth in the Convention and reinforced in 'A World Fit for Children' contrasts starkly with the actual childhood of most of the world's children. Around 29,000 under- fives die every day from causes that are easily prevented, such as diarrhoeal dehydration, acute respiratory infections, measles and malaria.

The lives of over 1 billion children are blighted by poverty, despite the wealth of nations.

Poverty, armed conflict and HIV/AIDS are grave threats to childhood. Worryingly, in several regions and countries some of the advances in fulfilling children's rights of recent decades - e. g. reductions in child mortality rates, increasing net primary school enrolment, and important strides in creating a protective environment for children - appear at risk of reversal from three key threats: poverty, armed conflict and HIV/AIDS (Figure 1). Other threats to children's survival and development persist largely because of poverty, armed conflict and HIV/AIDS.

Poverty: Poverty is the root cause of high rates of child morbidity and mortality. The rights of over 1 billion children - more than half the children in developing countries - are violated because they are severely underserved of at least one of the basic goods or services that would allow them to survive, develop and thrive. In the developing world more than one in three children does not have adequate shelter, one in five children does not have access to safe water, and one in seven has no access whatsoever to essential health services. Over 16 per cent of children under five lack adequate nutrition and 13 per cent of all children have never been to school.

Armed conflict: As civil strife proliferates - and civilians become its main causalities millions of children are growing up in families and communities torn apart by armed conflict. Many have been forced onto the front lines. Since 1990, conflicts have directly killed as many as 3. 6 million people; tragically, more than 45 per cent of these are likely to have been children. Hundreds of thousands of children are caught up in armed conflict as soldiers, are forced to become refugees or are internally displaced, suffer sexual violence, abuse and exploitation, or are victims of explosive remnants of war.

HIV/AIDS: AIDS is already the leading cause of death worldwide for people aged 15 to 49; in 2003 alone, 2. 9 million people died of AIDS and 4. 8 million people were newly infected with HIV. Over 90 per cent of people currently living with HIV/AIDS are in developing countries. In sub-Saharan Africa, HIV/AIDS has led to rising child mortality rates, sharp reductions in life expectancy and millions of orphans. Although the problem is most acute in this region, prevalence rates are also rising in other parts of the world.

Poverty, armed conflict and HIV/AIDS are not the only factors that undermine childhood but they are certainly among the most significant, with profoundly damaging effects on a child's chances of survival. The harm caused by each of these threats lingers well beyond the years of childhood and increases the likelihood that the next generation of children will be affected by the same threat. And as damaging as these three major threats are by themselves, when two or even all three coincide the impact on children's lives is devastating.

The vision of childhood that unites countries and peoples is at odds with the one that most children in the world actually experience. Into this gap between the ideal and the reality, between the Convention and convention, more young lives plunge with every passing day. And with each child that falls into this chasm, a little more of the world's shared future is compromised. Not one of the Millennium Development Goals - those idealistic objectives of the international community - will be attained if childhood continues under the current level of attack.

Faced with such assaults on children, it is worth refocusing on what the key terms of childhood should be as agreed to by the 192 States parties to the Convention on the Rights of the Child. Children have the right to survival, food and nutrition, health and shelter. Children also have the right to be encouraged and educated, both informally and formally, from birth. Children have the right to a loving, understanding family environment where the primary concern is their best interests, that provides guidance appropriate to their evolving capacities and prepares them to live an individual life in society in a spirit of peace, dignity, tolerance,s freedom, equality and solidarity.

Children have the right, and must be afforded the opportunity, to recreation and play, and to engage in sport and cultural activities rather than be subjected to violence and exploitation. Where they experience work, it should be as a positive contribution to the family and community that increases their own self-respect and sense of empowerment, and contributes to their learning rather than detracts from it. There are those who dismiss as impossibly utopian the conviction that the majority - let alone all - of the world's children could actually experience such a childhood. UNICEF is not among them.

3

Children Living in Poverty

Poverty inhibits the capacity of families and communities to care for children. It also poses a threat by exacerbating the effects of HIV/AIDS and armed conflict. Poverty in childhood is a root cause of poverty in adulthood. Impoverished children often grow up to be impoverished parents who in turn bring up their own children in poverty. In order to break the generational cycle, poverty reduction must begin with children. Foverty denies children both essential goods and services and opportunities Reducing child poverty means fulfilling children's rights to the goods and services necessary for their survival, normal growth and development. It also means improving the opportunities for disadvantaged children to participate in society. These two concerns support each other; together, they offer a platform for tackling child poverty as a human rights issue.

Without first meeting the survival, health and education rights of children, without providing essential goods and services such as access to safe water or adequate nutrition, it is impossible to talk about equal opportunities. Yet, even when these rights are met, children will still be relatively deprived if they are not able to take advantage of equal opportunities, and they will be at risk of exploitation if a protective environment is not in place. Lessons from countries that have made headway in reducing poverty suggest that a comprehensive approach is required, consisting of the following five key steps:

— Confront the issue of poverty conceptually

— Quantify poverty according to the conceptual definition

— Demonstrate the need and scope for action

— Mobilize stakeholders around clear goals

— Maintain awareness and build partnerships to sustain the attack on poverty and its underlying factors.

Understanding Poverty

Understanding how children experience poverty is essential to the design of effective poverty-reduction strategies. The Millennium Development Goals and 'A World Fit for Children' provide clear targets around which stakeholders - donors, governments, communities, international agencies · can structure national development plans or Poverty Reduction Strategy Papers (PRSPs), reflected in government budgets and external support. What is needed is higher political priority: better awareness of how children experience poverty and corresponding action from all stakeholders.

The United Nations views poverty as "a human condition, characterized by the sustained or chronic deprivation of the resources, capabilities, choices, security and power necessary for the enjoyment of an adequate standard of living and other civil, cultural, economic, political and social rights. "While poverty encompasses deprivation of basic goods and services, it also includes deficiencies in other vital elements of human rights - such as rest and recreation and protection from violence and conflict - that expand people's choices and enable them to fulfil their potential. Because children experience poverty as an environment that is damaging to their mental, physical, emotional and spiritual development, expanding the definition of child poverty beyond traditional conceptualizations, such as low household income or low levels of consumption, is particularly important.

Child poverty is rarely differentiated from poverty in general and its special dimensions are seldom recognized. UNICEF has long argued that children are often hardest hit by poverty. Since the best start in life - especially in the first few years - is critical to the physical, intellectual and emotional development of every individual, poverty in early childhood can prove to be a lifelong handicap. Children are disproportionately represented among the poor. Developing countries tend to be rich in children, and income-poor families generally have more children than wealthier families. Yet research dealing with child poverty has not progressed far enough, and many matters of definition and measurement have yet to be resolved.

As a step towards enhancing povertyreduction strategies, The State of the World's Children 2005 proposes the following working definition of children in poverty: Children living in poverty experience deprivation of the material, spiritual and emotional resources needed to survive, develop and thrive, leaving them unable to enjoy their rights, achieve their full potential or participate as full and equal members of society. This definition suggests that the poverty children experience with their hands, minds and hearts is interrelated. Material poverty - for example, starting the day without a nutritious meal or being forced to engage in hazardous labour - hinders cognitive capacity as well as physical growth. Living in an environment that provides little stimulation or emotional support to children, on the other hand, can remove much of the positive effect of growing up in a materially rich household. By discriminating against their participation in society and inhibiting their potential, poverty not only causes children suffering - it also disempowers them.

Highlighting the ways poverty prevents children from realizing their full potential and participating as equal members of the community is a key step towards reducing it.

Children living in poverty face deprivations of many of their rights: survival, health and nutrition, education, participation, and protection from harm, exploitation and discrimination. These deprivations cause suffering in the short term and hinder development in the long term. They tend to be associated with three underlying factors: low household income; poor physical infrastructure, often due to low levels of public investment; and weak institutions.

Poverty Measuring

The many dimensions of poverty - including mortality, morbidity, hunger, illiteracy, homelessness and powerlessness - are difficult to compress into a single measure. One of the most widely used measures of poverty is the $1 a day per person benchmark expressed in purchasing power parities, introduced in 1990 by the World Bank. Together with a measure on hunger, this is one of two targets employed in the Millennium Development Goals for measuring progress on poverty reduction. The UN Development Programme's human development index and its derivative poverty measure, the human poverty index, are powerful competitors to income measures of human well-being. They focus, respectively, on human capabilities and human deprivations. Attainment of the survival, health, education and gender-related targets of the Millennium Development Goals would significantly reduce poverty as measured by the human poverty index.

Comparisons between the human development index and income measures of poverty such as per capita gross domestic product (GDP per head) have shown that countries with the same level of per capita income can have very different levels of human development. This suggests that low-income countries have some scope for addressing illiteracy or poor health even if they fail to generate rapid economic growth. While important for measuring poverty in broad terms, neither the income measure employed by the World

Bank nor the UN Development Programme's composite indices have been specifically designed to assess child poverty. And, for all their merits, neither quantifies how many children live in poverty nor focuses directly on the deprivations of their rights.

The notion of deprivation focuses attention on the circumstances that surround children, casting poverty as an attribute of the environment they live and grow in. Household statistical surveys carried out since the mid- to late-1990s now make it possible to compare the levels of deprivation of essential goods and services that children experience across countries. The impetus for this investigation derived from the commitment of the 117 States attending the 1995 World Summit for Social Development to tackle poverty as a human rights issue.

A recent empirical study by the University of Bristol and the London School of Economics, commissioned by UNICEF, has looked at how children in developing countries are affected by severe deprivations in seven areas: adequate nutrition, safe drinking water, decent sanitation facilities, health, shelter, education and information. The study used a stricter interpretation of 'severe deprivation' than is normally employed in such investigations. For example, a child severely deprived of an education means here a child who has never attended school, rather than the more widely used concept of 'non-completion of primary education'. The researchers relied on these highly restrictive definitions to ensure that they measured deprivation at a level that undeniably undermines children's rights.

The study concluded that over 1 billion children - more than half the children in developing countries - suffer from at least one form of severe deprivation. The fact that every second child is deprived of even the minimum opportunities in life is alarming. Moreover, using these criteria, the study found that about 700 million children suffer two or more forms of severe deprivation.

— *Nutrition deprivation*: Over 16 per cent of children under five in the developing world are severely malnourished. Nearly half of these 90 million children live in South Asia. Many of these children are anaemic, weak and vulnerable to disease; most of them already had low weight at birth; some of them will have learning problems if they ever go to school. They will probably remain among the poorest of the poor throughout their lives.

— *Water deprivation*: About 400 million children - on average one in every five children in developing countries - have no access to safe water. The situation is particularly severe in sub-Saharan Africa: here, in countries such as Ethiopia, Rwanda and Uganda, four out of five children either use surface water or have to walk more than 15 minutes to find a protected water source. Rates of severe water deprivation are considerably higher in rural areas (27 per cent) than in urban ones (7 per cent). A lack of safe water is a major cause of disease, but also affects children's productivity and attendance in school. Children - mainly girls - who walk long distances in search of water are often in effect barred from attending school.

— *Sanitation deprivation*: One in every three children in the developing world - over 500 million children - has no access whatsoever to sanitation facilities; again, the problem is particularly pronounced in rural areas. Without access to sanitation, children's risk of disease rises dramatically, further jeopardizing their chances of survival and often reducing the likelihood that they will be able to take full advantage of schooling. For example, millions of school-aged children are infected by intestinal worms, which have been shown to sap learning ability.

— *Health deprivation*: Around 270 million children, or just over 14 per cent of all children in developing countries, have no access to health-care services. In South Asia and sub-Saharan Africa, one in four children either does not receive any of the six principal immunizations or has no access to treatment if they suffer from diarrhoea.

— *Shelter deprivation*: Over 640 million children in developing countries experience severe shelter deprivation, with those in sub-Saharan Africa clearly the most deprived. However, the lack of access to proper shelter is also widespread in both South Asia and the Middle East and North Africa; in the latter region, rural children are more than four times more likely than their urban counterparts to be shelter deprived.

— *Education deprivation*: Over 140 million children in developing countries - 13 per cent of those aged 7-18 years - have never attended school. This rate is 32 per cent among girls in sub-Saharan Africa, where 27 per cent of boys also miss out on schooling, and 33 per cent among rural children in the Middle East and North Africa. The gender gap is greatest in the latter region: 34 per cent of girls and 12 per cent of boys there have never attended school. In South Asia these percentages are 25 and 14 respectively, contributing significantly to the overall global disadvantage girls suffer. Worldwide,16 per cent of girls and 10 per cent of boys miss out on school completely.

— *Information deprivation*: Over 300 million children in developing countries are deprived of information, lacking access to television, radio, telephone or newspapers. Without access to information, children are deprived of education in the broader sense, including mechanisms enabling them to be informed of their rights and opportunities, as well as the ability to participate effectively in society.

A lack of sanitation pollutes the water that children use, and poor nutrition makes them vulnerable to sickness and diarrhoea which then go untreated, further reducing their body weight and resistance to disease. Children who are poorly fed, frequently ill or have no access to safe water, decent housing or adequate sanitation facilities are likely to encounter more problems in school. A child severely deprived of shelter, living in an overcrowded home and an impoverished neighbourhood, may not be able to absorb an education even if there is a school nearby.

Children in Rural Area

Children living in rural areas in the developing world are on average twice as likely to be severely deprived of essential goods and services as their urban peers. They are also almost twice as likely to suffer severe nutritional deprivation and three times as likely to never attend school. Of course, not all urban children enjoy the same living conditions. For instance, children who live in squatter settlements may fare even worse than their rural counterparts.

Many of the children in extreme poverty live in countries with fairly high levels of national income. National income is clearly a factor: On average, low-income countries tend to have higher rates of deprivation than middle- income countries. Yet a significant number of children in middle-income countries are still exposed to severe deprivations. For example, while China and Colombia's levels of deprivation are roughly the same, per capita GNI is far higher in the latter. Conversely, although Colombia and Namibia have similar levels of per capita income, their levels of deprivation differ markedly. Namibia's level of deprivation is similar to Togo's, a far poorer country.

Gender Discrimination

Poor access to education, food or healthcare services has particular implications for women and their children. The large disparities in most regions between the numbers of girls and boys who have never attended school are telling evidence of the discrimination that girls and women face. Gender discrimination is widely recognized as a major contributor to children living in poverty. How resources are earned, valued and distributed depend on power relationships between men and women within the household as well as within society.

Safety, Dignity and Protection

Children living in poverty do not only experience material deprivation. Emotional and spiritual impoverishment are also abrogations of their rights. However, these dimensions of child poverty and their interaction with material deprivation and lack of family and community resources are poorly researched and documented, and internationally comparable data related to child protection is still sparse. The Convention on the Rights of the Child makes it clear that it is the duty of governments and parents to provide the protective environment required to ensure that all children experience childhood in safety and dignity. It is equally clear that millions of children worldwide are being denied this protection. These children are just as impoverished as those whose rights to survival, health and education are threatened by a lack of essential goods and services.

Each year, tens of millions of children are the victims of exploitation, violence and abuse. They are abducted from their homes and schools and recruited into armed conflicts. They are trafficked and forced to work in prostitution and sweatshops. They are needlessly deprived of parental care and forced into early marriage. They are subjected to violence and abuse in the home, school and community. The effects of these abuses are farreaching and enduring; they rob children of their childhood, preventing them from achieving anything close to their full potential.

Material Deprivation

Many child protection abuses are linked to deeply entrenched material deprivations. One of the most obvious ways in which material poverty facilitates exploitation and abuse is through child labour. It creates economic need that can force vulnerable children - such as those caught up in armed conflict, or orphaned or made vulnerable by HIV/AIDS - into hazardous labour, often at the expense of their education and recreation. Currently, 180 million children are thought to be engaged in the worst forms of child labour.

Material deprivation makes children more vulnerable to trafficking and commercial sexual exploitation. An estimated 1. 2 million children are trafficked every year;2 million children, the majority of them girls, are sexually exploited in the multibillion-dollar commercial sex industry. While poverty exacerbates child protection abuses, it is equally true that abuse often forces children into material deprivation or exacerbates their existing poverty. Violence and abuse at home can force children onto the streets, where their poverty is likely to become entrenched. Discrimination can be an obstacle to learning at school and can cause children to drop out. Exploitation generates poverty by keeping children out of school, in poor health and subject to further psychological and physical abuse.

Law, and Criminal Justice Systems

Poverty often leads children into contact with the law, and criminal justice systems that are not receptive to the rights of children accused of crimes can perpetuate poverty. When children are accused of crimes such as theft of food or detained for begging, poverty is frequently the underlying cause. And when the response to children accused of crimes is detention, they are separated at an early age from their families and the wider community, and are unlikely to learn the life skills necessary to function effectively in society and to escape poverty in adulthood. Even after their release, they are often stigmatized and may have difficulty reintegrating into the community · conditions that contribute to their further marginalization and poverty later on. In all these cases, the legacy of poverty does not stop with one generation but may affect several generations to come.

Families form the first line of defence for children; the further away children are from their families, the more vulnerable they are. Children separated from their families, both those living or working on the streets and those in institutions, are more likely to be marginalized, abused and live in poverty in adulthood. Those living on the streets are left unprotected against violence and exploitation. They are also at greater risk of contracting HIV. Children in institutional care, while ostensibly protected from the most obvious protection abuses, are segregated from one another according to age and sex and from other people in their communities. This inhibits the development of vital social skills as well as community support and interaction.

The fight against poverty stands a good chance only when children are freed from exploitation, violence and abuse. Unfortunately, there is no quick-fix solution: A child cannot be immunized against abuse. But there is something that can be done. We can begin by ensuring that all children live in a strong protective environment.

Growing up in families whose material conditions are close to the 'norms' in the community is important for children. Research on how children themselves experience and feel about poverty suggests that relative deprivation - when children do not have access to the same opportunities as other children - hurts young people in poor and rich countries alike. Deprivation of goods and services that adults might not always regard as 'essential' can be viewed differently by children, who may feel they are denied the lifestyles and opportunities available to other children.

Relative Deprivation

Relative deprivation in terms of family income and wealth is a factor in absolute deprivations of essential goods and services that children require to survive, grow and develop, and can therefore have grave implications for them. A recent study of 43 developing countries has shown that, on average, children of families in the bottom wealth quintile of the population are more than twice as likely to die before reaching the age of five than children living in families in the top quintile. In Brazil, children whose per capita family income is less than half the minimum wage are three times more likely to die before their fifth birthday, 21 times more likely to be illiterate and 30 times more likely to live in a home without an adequate water supply.

While low family income often interacts with other aspects of poverty - such as limited parental education, and rural or slum environments · to undermine children's rights to survival and access to health care and educational services, studies have shown that it can be a determinant of child health and education achievement independently of these other factors. Large segments of the population in China and India have received only modest benefits from the rapid economic growth of recent years. Similarly, research on child poverty in the Organisation for Economic Cooperation and Development (OECD) countries has shown that the proportion of children living in relative poverty - defined as households where income was less than half of the national median - has risen since the late 1980s.

In 11 of the 15 OECD countries for which comparable data are available, there have been notable increases in child poverty rates over the course of roughly the last decade. At the beginning of the millennium only three countries - Finland, Norway and Sweden - enjoyed a rate of child poverty of less than 5 per cent. And in only four countries - Canada, Norway, the United Kingdom and the United States - has the share of children living in lowincome households seen even a modest reduction over the past decade. With the exception of Norway, these countries still have relatively high levels of relative child poverty, owing to a higher base of comparison in the late 1980s.

The statistical evidence on children living in poverty presents a bleak picture. It confronts us with staggering rates of severe child deprivation that will hinder further progress in reducing child mortality rates and in improving health and nutrition, education and protection. It shows rising rates of relative deprivation that translate to disadvantaged children who gain little or nothing from increased average household incomes and better public services. It demonstrates the extent to which the lack of a protective environment imperils children and places them at risk of exploitation, abuse and violence. These numbers and trends call into question the commitment of national and local governments, the private sector and the international community to act on the Millennium Development Goals and 'A World Fit for Children'. They also call into question the determination of all duty bearers, including parents and communities in addition to the aforementioned parties, to reduce child poverty. All this is even more disturbing as much of the experience and knowledge about how to act on child poverty is already on hand.

Globalization and Economic Growth

Countries that have significantly and sustainably reduced poverty have done so by simultaneously addressing economic and social issues rather than giving exclusive priority to macroeconomic stability or economic growth. There is evidence that even rapid economic growth can be slow to produce positive returns in terms of social development. A key example of this is the under-five mortality rate, whose average annual rate of reduction has slowed sharply in both China and India since 1990 despite robust economic growth in both countries over the same period.

Countries successful in improving access to basic social services for children are ready to spend more - as Costa Rica, Malaysia and Mauritius, for example, have consistently done over the past few decades. While economic growth is clearly required to attain the Millennium Development Goals, a recent World Bank study has found that the two sub-Saharan African countries expected to have the best poverty-reduction performance by 2015 stand out because of their more equitable income distribution rather than their pace of economic growth.

In developing countries, investing in human capital - including education - attracts foreign capital from investors seeking gains from a dynamic and well-educated workforce. Similarly, economic recovery and foreign direct investment have been associated with good education systems and a welltrained workforce in several economies that made the transition from planned systems to market economies during the 1990s. Countries that protect children's rights even in times of crisis will benefit from higher human development levels. A World Bank report showed that Cuba - a country with a high level of human development despite a moderate level of per capita income - cut defence spending sharply in the 1990s while broadly sustaining health and education expenditure.

Recent initiatives by international financial institutions to contain high indebtedness in the least developed countries - principally through the Heavily Indebted Poor Countries Initiative as well as efforts to prevent further high indebtedness - are welcome and necessary. Many developing countries are often already spending more on debt service than on education or health. Several countries spend more than 10 per cent of their gross domestic product on servicing debt, and currently 38 countries qualify for the initiative because they are both extremely poor and heavily indebted.

Meanwhile, the world is currently spending almost 1 trillion dollars on defence annually. This is much more than the estimated annual cost of US$40-70 billion required to meet the Millennium Development Goals by 2015. Many of the world's poorest countries continue to budget far more for military armaments and personnel than for health or education; diverting even a fraction of this expenditure to health or education would provide them with millions of dollars for social investment. It will be interesting to observe in the coming years the economic and social outcomes of countries such as Bolivia, Botswana, Ghana, Kenya and Malaysia, where education commands a far higher proportion of gross national income than military spending.

With the Millennium Development Goals and the Monterrey Consensus driving the international agenda, the world community is now firmly committed to good governance in the broadest sense: promoting human development through transparent public budgets, wide-scale consultations and participatory planning processes. This means rejecting the idea that the world is divided into two blocks of poor and rich countries with asymmetric objectives or responsibilities. It means that those who will implement plans should actually own them, learn from the experiences of other countries and share their own experiences.

Since 1999, national governments in low-income countries have been required to draw up Poverty Reduction Strategy Papers (PRSPs). These must satisfy a set of key criteria in order for countries to qualify for aid or loans from international financial institutions and have been a tool to gain access to debt concessions under the Heavily Indebted Poor Countries Initiative. PRSPs have enshrined poverty reduction as a pre-eminent goal of national and international policy and are increasingly used to promote the Millennium Development Goals.

Poverty Reduction Strategy Papers

The ongoing development of PRSPs - and the growing debate about how to make them more effective, equitable and participatory · represents a significant opportunity. PRSPs rarely make a full transition from a narrowly economic or sectoral perspective to a human rights approach, which would include an emphasis on personal freedom, democracy and social participation alongside fiscal agendas, budget transparency and accountability. Similarly, experience so far shows that the concerns of children, youth and women do not feature strongly and tend to be secondary to the macroeconomic objectives. PRSPs with a strong focus on fulfilling children's rights would address key issues for children and their families, country-specific causes of child poverty and methods to expand opportunities for children.

UNICEF is working with governments and partners to ensure that priorities for children, such as immunization, free education and legislative initiatives to protect the rights of children, are built into PRSPs. However, problems relating to governance, including poor functioning and corruption in public institutions and weak civil society organizations can prevent an enabling environment where child rights, including the right to health and education, can be realized. Efforts to build the capacity of duty bearers in a developing country will therefore need to address constraints of insufficient public resources, governance and quality basic amenities.

The threat to childhood from poverty is multipronged. The response has to be similarly all-embracing, starting with an integrated approach to early childhood that will greatly improve the chances that every child will both survive and thrive. Aggregate public expenditure on support for families and young people correlates closely with the incidence of relative child poverty in OECD countries. Well-developed government-funded institutions can prevent high rates of social exclusion and related risks for children and youth.

The cost of having similarly complex welfare systems is sometimes seen as prohibitive in poorer countries. However, middle-income countries could clearly do more, and international assistance, federal initiatives and innovative local solutions can remove part of the costs for governments in developing countries. The Oportunidades programme, launched in Mexico in 1997, grants cash transfers on the condition that members of a household are certified as attending school and health clinics. The results have been significant and consistent.

Over the last five years the programme has doubled its outreach and it is currently on target to pass the mark of serving 5 million families. In rural areas covered by the scheme, there has been a 57 per cent rise in visits to health clinics and significant reductions in under-five morbidity. School attendance and completion have also been boosted.

A comprehensive child survival programme in Madagascar is helping to reduce under-five mortality. One-third of the country's children under the age of five are moderately or severely underweight. But the root of the problem lies in causes other than a lack of food and includes poor feeding practices, malaria, diarrhoea and other recurrent illnesses. The programme includes activities to vaccinate every child, to ensure that every mother and newborn is protected by insecticide-treated mosquito nets and to provide free oral rehydration packs. Mothers are encouraged to breastfeed their babies: The benefits include fewer illnesses and better nutrition for their infants. They are also counselled on how to improve nutrition and supplement their children's diets with vitamin A, schools are provided with latrines and safe drinking water, and health workers are trained on how to manage the treatment and prevention of childhood illnesses.

Integrated approaches have also proven successful in middle- and high-income market economies - where poverty often manifests itself through educational disadvantage, frequent illness, obesity, teenage motherhood, high unemployment rates for young people, drug abuse and crime. Gender perspectives could improve the efficiency of poverty-reduction schemes Having a gender perspective in public interventions is important in rich and poor countries alike. The OECD countries that have the lowest rates of child poverty as measured by family income both secure generous support for families with children and have high labour market participation rates among women.

Higher employment rates among women have contributed to reducing child poverty in the 1990s in a number of OECD countries. The highly flexible labour market sin the United States and the effective legal protection against gender discrimination in the Nordic countries may not be available to women in other countries. Nonetheless, pursuing labour market and fiscal policies that address economic insecurity among women and diminish persistently high levels of inequality can help reduce poverty. The Oportunidades programme highlighted above, for example, owes much of its success to the fact that in almost every case the cash transfer is paid to a woman. This strengthens her position within the family and increases the likelihood that the money is used to purchase food and other essentials.

Strengthening the Protective Environment

Developing legislation and local initiatives to fortify the protective environment for children will result in both economic development and the fulfilment of child rights. A recent study by the International Programme on the Elimination of Child Labour offers convincing evidence that, over a 20-year period, the economic benefits of eliminating child labour would far exceed the costs. The model envisages urgent action to eliminate the worst forms of child labour, such as bonded labour and the criminal exploitation of children in prostitution. Income-transfer programmes that offer financial benefits to families living in poverty with school-age children would help to defray the costs of transferring their children from work to school.

Participation of Children

Children themselves help us understand what child poverty means. 'Young Lives' is an international research project conducted by the Institute of Development Studies in the United Kingdom that is recording changes in child poverty over 15 years. Through research in Ethiopia, India, Peru and

Viet Nam, the project aims to reveal the links between international and national policies and children's day-to-day lives. The project includes a strong participatory element and has already showcased, for example, children's writings about their experiences of poverty, education and child labour. In Serbia and Montenegro, impoverished by more than a decade of strife, inter-ethnic tension and economic crisis, UNICEF has been working with the government and local non-governmental organizations on a participatory study of child poverty that has made a point of consulting children as well as their parents.

The research eschews the dry traditional techniques of polls and questionnaires and involves children in discussions that are set up like games. While younger children focus on the lack of supplies such as books, toys and playgrounds, older children also mention problems with the way institutions operate. Parents emphasize income poverty more than children, believing it to be the source of all other problems. But the research has shown, above all, that poverty affects the fulfilment of a wide range of basic child rights, from education to health, from play to adequate living standards.

Poverty threatens every right, depriving children of the capacities they require to survive, develop and thrive. Children living in the countries highlighted on this map face some of the worst deprivations of essential goods and services: More than one third of all children are malnourished, lack basic immunizations, or are not enrolled in or attending school. In 13 countries, less than half the population has access to improved drinking water and adequate sanitation facilities. Income-poverty measures are a good indication of where the problem lies. Most countries with high levels of deprivation suffer from low levels of per capita income. But income-poverty measures cannot adequately convey how children actually experience poverty.

India and Senegal have very similar levels of per capita income, for instance, but children in India are more at risk from malnutrition while children in Senegal are more likely to miss out on an education. Eighty-nine per cent of children in Peru receive the DPT3 vaccine, while only 65 per cent of children in the Dominican Republic do - but the per capita income in the former country is less than 4 per cent higher than in the latter. Poverty embodies the multidimensional nature of the threats to childhood: Each deprivation exacerbates the effect of the others, and when two or more coincide, the effects on children can be catastrophic.

Children who must walk long distances to fetch water have less time to attend school - a problem that particularly affects girls. Children who are not immunized or who are malnourished are much more susceptible to the diseases that are spread through poor sanitation. These and other deprivations, such as lack of adequate shelter and access to social services, inhibit children's ability to achieve their full potential. Until every child realizes their right to education, nutrition and health care, childhood will continue to be under threat. Many are already contributing, at all levels and in innovative ways, to ensuring that every child enjoys their right to a childhood. Many more must follow their example.

4

Child Labour

Child labour came under the international spotlight in the 1990s. For the first time since the industrialised world's campaigns on the issue a century earlier, diplomats and economists started discussing why vast numbers of children were working rather than being educated, and what should be done about it. This time, the focus was on developing countries. This new attention to an old issue was largely due to worries raised by people in industrialised countries such as the United Kingdom. Trade unionists, politicians and campaigners for social justice voiced concern that jobs were disappearing rapidly as businesses switched production from the industrialised world to developing countries where labour costs were much lower.

Simultaneously, organisations in developing countries sounded the alarm when they saw children working longer and longer hours - not only producing goods for export, but also providing a cheap and malleable workforce for the local economy. Their worry was echoed by activists in Eastern Europe and the former Soviet Union, who realised that the transition that started in 1989 was provoking an economic crisis which hit children particularly hard. As more attention was given to the work children were performing, so the statistics about the numbers involved became more startling. The estimates of children between 5 and 14 in full-time employment had risen from 100 million at the beginning of the 1990s to 120 million by 1996.

Six years later, when the information available had been scrutinised more carefully, the total was estimated at 211 million, along with a further 141 million young people aged 15 to 17 who were also in employment. At the beginning of the new millennium, 1 in 12 children in the world was reckoned to be involved in work which put their health at risk or caused them serious harm. The late 1990s saw a series of initiatives - by governments and international organisations such as UNICEF, the International Labour Organization (ILO) and the World Bank - to consider the policies needed to address child labour globally, and the priorities for action. Two separate international conferences in 1997, in Amsterdam and Oslo, agreed to a proposal that stopping types of child labour that caused particular harm to children should be a priority - referred to initially as "intolerable" and later as the "worst forms" of child labour.

The term "child labour", coined in Britain during the 19th century, implies that the children involved should not be working. "Youth employment", on the other hand, implies something quite different -that young people need appropriate training and support to enter the labour market and to find jobs when they leave school. Many languages do not have a phrase that implies that children should not be working and use expressions more similar to "child work". The terminology used is important because it implies what should be done in response a "child labourer" should be returned to school; a "youth" or "adolescent" worker should be assisted in getting a job, with more supervision and protection than an adult worker.

Article 32 in UNICEF commits of work that interfere with education and those that cause harm. The Convention spells out a child's right to education, as well as identifying the forms of harm to which children should not be exposed. A second part of the same article describes the measures governments must take to implement this right. They must: (1) Provide for a minimum age or minimum ages for admission to employment; (2) Provide for appropriate regulation of the hours and conditions of employment; (3) Provide for appropriate penalties or other sanctions to ensure the effective enforcement of the present article. Article 28 guarantees every child's right to education and stresses the importance of equal opportunity for all children to have access to education. Make primary education compulsory and available free to all children; Encourage the development of secondary education, including general and vocational education, and to make these available and accessible to all children; Take measures to encourage regular school attendance and to reduce drop-out rates.

Two other provisions in the Convention are also vitally important for working children. Article 3 says government agencies and other institutions taking action concerning a child or children must base their decisions on what is in the children's "best interests". Article 12 emphasises that when a child is capable of forming his or her views, these should be given due attention, in accordance with the child's age and maturity. These general provisions are relevant to organisations such as UNICEF which want to end child exploitation. Every initiative has to ensure it is in children's best interests, and that the views of children, particularly those who are more mature, must be sought and taken into account in deciding what initiatives are suitable.

International Conventions on Child Labour

Two main conventions deal with child labour the Minimum Age Convention and the Worst Forms of Child Labour Convention. Both have been adopted by the International Labour Organization (ILO) - the specialist organisation in the UN dealing with the world of work - and ratified by the UK. The Minimum Age Convention is based on the principle that children should not start work before reaching a minimum age. Between 1919, when it was set up, and the 1970s, the ILO adopted 10 separate conventions specifying the minimum age at which children could start various jobs. In 1973, a general Minimum Age Convention was adopted to apply to every type of employment and every country.

Each country that ratifies this Convention commits itself "to pursue a national policy designed to ensure the effective abolition of child labour and to raise progressively the minimum age for admission to employment or work to a level consistent with the fullest physical and mental development of young persons" (article 1). The Convention says that the minimum age for employment should "not be less than 15 years" but allows developing countries to opt for a minimum age of 14 on a temporary basis. Some countries make 16 their minimum age. The Minimum Age Convention has a special provision allowing children aged 13 and 14 to be employed in "light work". Associated provisions explain that such children are only supposed to work in limited circumstances the government has to specify which types of work are permitted as "light work" and the hours and conditions involved. The Convention also prohibits young people under 18 from being involved in dangerous work without training.

The Convention came into force in 1976 and had been ratified by 135 states by the end of 2004. All these countries have set a minimum age (42 at 14, 59 at 15 and 30 at 16) and have pledged to enforce this. By the mid 1990s, there was evidence that vast numbers of children below the minimum age of 14 were working full-time. Responding to concern about this, the ILO began to draft a new convention. This involved getting international agreement on the circumstances in which children of any age should not be working, as well as identifying the steps for governments to take to eliminate what came to be called the "worst forms" of child labour. The main reasons why children start work instead of attending school, or leave school before completing their primary education.

Trafficking Children

In November 2000, the UN adopted a Protocol to Prevent, Suppress and Punish Trafficking in Persons, Especially Women and Children (the "Palermo Protocol"). The Protocol is linked to the UN Convention against Transnational Organized Crime. In order to move towards ratification of this Protocol, the UK had to criminalise trafficking. This resulted in two pieces of legislation - the Sexual Offences Act 2003 and the Asylum and Immigration Act 2004. The UN also adopted a Protocol Against the Smuggling of Migrants by Land, Sea and Air, making a distinction between migrants who are helped to cross frontiers illegally (that is, smuggled), and others who are trapped in some form of exploitation as a result, usually after being coerced or tricked (trafficked). Child "trafficking" refers to the actions involved in recruiting and moving children under so they can be subjected to what the Protocol calls "exploitation".

Poverty

The main reason why children start work instead of attending school, or leave school before completing their primary education, is that their families are poor and cannot pay the basic costs of food and housing without their child earning something as well. But the reasons why families are poor vary enormously - some are global, some are national and some are historic. Some adult workers are not paid enough to support their families, and sometimes even the wages from both parents' incomes are not sufficient to keep their family housed, clothed and fed. However, it is also common to find families in which one or both parents are not earning anything, maybe because a parent has died or left home, or because adults are unable to get work. Sometimes employers prefer to employ children, finding them more obedient and cheaper than adults.

Even for poor families there are decisions to make about what work children should take on. Parents rarely wish to expose their children to danger, but may see no alternative. All too often, both parents and young people are unaware of the risks involved. The reasons children work can be divided broadly into "supply" and "demand" factors. The very fact that so many different factors are at play is one reason why there is no single solution, no magic recipe for putting an end to the economic exploitation of children.

Family Problems

Families break down for many reasons, leaving the household short of income. Sometimes divorce leaves one parent looking after more children than she or he can afford to feed. Divorce is sometimes brought about by domestic violence, which also directly drives children to leave home when they are still young. The death of either parent precipitates economic disaster for many households. In parts of Africa, this has now become all too common as a result of the HIV/AIDS pandemic. Families also lose their livelihood as a result of natural disasters and human crises that leave people destitute and force children to start earning. The 1994 genocide in Rwanda, in which almost one million people were murdered, left huge numbers of orphans.

Five years later, more than 45, 000 Rwandese households were still headed by children, mostly girls, who bore the responsibility for providing for their brothers and sisters. HIV/AIDS By 2001, the UN estimated that 13 million children around the world under the age of 15 had lost either one or both parents to HIV/AIDS. About half become orphans before they are 10. The result of the premature death of one or both parents is that children take on the responsibility of seeking an income to support themselves and their younger brothers and sisters. In the case of HIV/AIDS, children often take on this role when their one surviving parent becomes seriously ill and is unable to work.

Attitudes to Girls

All around the world, children belonging to particular social groups leave school and start work earlier than other children in the same country. In industrialised countries the obvious differences are based on wealth and social class: children from poor families start work several years before their peers in rich households. In these countries, however, there are likely to be laws, which are enforced, making it compulsory for all children to attend school until a minimum age (16 in the UK). In most parts of the world, gender is also a crucial factor girls are discouraged from staying at school beyond puberty (and are sometimes withdrawn much earlier) and are propelled into adulthood much younger than boys, either into work or an early marriage.

In some countries, school is a threatening place for teenage girls, where they are at risk of sexual harassment from male classmates and teachers, and sidelined by prejudice and poor curricula. Simply because they are girls, many are kept at home or drop out of school. UNICEF estimated that, at the end of 2003, 121 million children of school age were not attending school: well over half (65 million) were girls. Discrimination against minority groups Some children also leave school and start work earlier than others because of their origin or identity. In Latin America, indigenous children start work first. In South Asia, the caste system determines that children from dalit families (who have low status in the caste hierarchy) or adivasi (tribal or indigenous) communities start work first or do not attend school at all.

In southeast Europe, it is children from the Roma minority. In each case, a combination of supply and demand factors are at work the communities concerned feel that the school system was not designed for them and consider it normal for children to abandon school early and start work. Surveys by UNICEF and Save the Children UK in Bosnia and Herzegovina confirm that the vast majority of Roma are unemployed. Although 92 per cent of school-age children attend school on average, in some areas as many as 80 per cent of Roma children do not. Those who are in school often drop out early to seek work. The underlying problem is one of prejudice and discrimination in local social services and the community, rather than a lack of infrastructure or services. Between 1999 and 2001, UNICEF began supporting special educational programmes for Roma children, in cooperation with World Vision.

Employers' Gain

A major proportion of today's working children are employed in a family business or farm. The role of the family as a basic economic unit in many parts of the world still generates a demand for children to start work rather than study. In some cases this does them no harm. The heads of family enterprises regularly comment that school gives their children a less useful training than on-the-job experience. Of course, this approach reduces their child's opportunities later in life.

The relatively low wages paid to children are often a reason why employers prefer them to adult workers. Some children work unpaid, particularly as domestic workers, in conditions that would be denounced as "slavery" if they involved adults. Employers find children more obedient and easier to control. Unlike older workers, they are unlikely to initiate protests or form trade unions. It is also easy for adults to intimidate children. Employers can force child workers into submission when the children are dependent on them for food, lodging and even emotional support. In most parts of the world, it is still considered acceptable for parents to beat their children. Employers take advantage of the public's acceptance of corporal punishment to beat their child workers as a means of controlling them.

Nimble fingers

In the country with the largest number of child labourers in the world, India, adults justify the involvement of children in certain jobs on the grounds that only they have the "nimble fingers" which enable them to give special attention to detail. Some sorts of work, they argue, cannot be performed by adults. This is just one of many myths used to justify the numbers of children working today, myths which offer largely spurious arguments but strike a chord with local public opinion and come to be believed because they are repeated so often.

Inadequate laws

More than 130 countries have signed an international convention saying that children may not work full-time before 14 or 15 years of age. However, in some of the countries concerned, laws on this are confusing or vague and not enforced. There are particular difficulties when laws are inconsistent - for example, one dictating that children must remain in school until they are 12, while another decrees that they may not start work until 14 the inconsistency is almost bound to precipitate children into the labour market before they reach the legal minimum age.

In some countries, there are so many laws affecting the employment of children that parents and employers alike are baffled. Employers can usually point to a loophole to justify a young child working for them. Even when there are laws to regulate health and safety at work, these are rarely enforced in the informal economy where working children are found, routinely exposing them to serious risks.

Another factor is the practical difficulty of establishing a child's actual age in countries where the infrastructure may not be in place for e. g. systematic birth registration. This can disadvantage children in many ways - law enforcers are hampered because they do not have the means to absolutely establish the ages of e. g. teenagers, and, without appropriate documentation, young people may also be denied access to state services such as schools.

Lack of education

Children who receive little or no school education miss out on the knowledge that can create options for them later in life. Without it, they make less contribution as adults and are more exposed to exploitation and abuse. Not attending school is consequently both a cause and effect of child labour. The importance of education for a society's economic and social development is widely acknowledged. However, even countries that have made an explicit undertaking to send every child to school still have to do a great deal to turn this commitment into reality. The shortcomings of existing school systems remain a major factor that "pushes" children on to the labour market when they are too young. Sending children to school does not come without a cost. In many countries, parents still pay a fee for their children to attend primary school, as well as buying books and providing a school uniform. For a poor family these are significant costs, alongside the lack of income for the household while a child is at school.

Monitoring Initiatives

One of the first lessons learnt in the 1990s was an obvious one that it is vital that children do not suffer further harm as a result of initiatives to stop child labour. This means keeping a careful eye on the impact of every initiative. There is no point, for example, in campaigning to stop 13-year-old girls from working in factories if they are sacked and end up worse off as a result. In the mid 1990s, campaigners realised that publicity about children working in developing countries' factories and manufacturing cheap exports was sometimes worsening the situation for those children. This was particularly the case in Bangladesh, where thousands of teenage girls were summarily dismissed when employers thought the US was about to impose a boycott on garments manufactured with the help of children. UNICEF and others

intervened to provide schooling and other alternatives for the dismissed girls.

Listening to the comments children make about the impact of initiatives specifically intended to help them gives a clearer message. In West Africa, researchers talked to teenagers in Mali, where the Government is keen to stop young people from being trafficked to neighbouring countries where they have been subjected to abuse. They found that many teenagers had no prospects of staying at school or earning a living locally, but were finding it harder to go abroad to work as a result of the Government's counter-trafficking measures. Some had even been arrested to stop them leaving. The Government had ordered all young people leaving the country to have special identity papers, but in practice these remained hard to come by and resulted in border officials extorting larger bribes than before from young Malians crossing the border. The review concluded that the initiatives intended to stop the exploitation of children needed to focus more carefully on preventing the harm being experienced by a minority of the young migrants.

In various parts of the world, working children have set up their own organisations that call on policy makers to listen to their views. Some have criticised efforts to abolish child labour and say the priority should be to improve their working conditions. Most support efforts to eliminate particularly abusive forms of exploitation. In the Philippines, SUMAPI, an organisation of 5, 000 child domestic workers, calls for the employment of children to be banned below a minimum age and for tough new laws to regulate the conditions of child domestics who are old enough to work. Creating a "protective environment" UNICEF is supporting a range of projects to end the economic and sexual exploitation of children, as well as other initiatives to promote respect for children's rights. In recent years UNICEF has concentrated on improving the forms of protection available to children who risk exploitation, abuse and violence.

Today, more than 350 million children, aged from 5 to 17, are at work. They can be differentiated on the basis of their age, the effect that working has on their basic rights and, in particular, the extent to which their work causes them harm. More than 140 million of the total are old enough to be working under international standards. Nevertheless, getting on for half of these - 60 million - suffer harm because they are involved in the abuse of the "worst forms" of child labour, from which they should be protected. The remaining 80 million have reasonable jobs, either in industrialised or developing countries.

Out of approximately 211 million working children under 15, more than half (over 120 million) are involved in the "worst forms". So, together with older adolescents, almost 180 million young people below 18 are involved in the "worst forms", approximately 1 in every 12 children in the world today. The vast majority of these, more than 170 million, are engaged in work that is hazardous, posing a health risk and, in some cases, even threatening their lives. Among the working children younger than 15, most are below the minimum age for legal employment. A significant proportion are very young - between 5 and 11 - and many of these are not even paid for their services.

The 19th century images of child labourers as tiny chimney sweeps or tethered to treadmills in Britain's "satanic mills" are very obvious cases of exploitation: incidents of working children who are suffering abuse today may be overlooked since they are not nearly so visible, although they may be equally as extreme. A 10-year-old playing an accordion to tourists in a holiday resort and asking for money may be earning some extra pocket money, but may also be a victim at the beck and call of a modern-day "Fagin".

Stereotypes of what constitutes "work" also influence the types of work that the public thinks of as "child labour". This, in turn, influences the types of jobs that are the subject of laws and regulations, omitting some children's work that we now

know to be harmful. While the stereotypes focus on factories and the formal sector of the economy -conventional men's work - work inside the home is often overlooked, whether it involves children performing household chores for their own family, helping to earn money by supporting a family business, or working in someone else's house as a full-time live-in servant.

More children work on farms than in any other form of work. The ILO's survey in 2000 indicated that 70 per cent of the world's working children were engaged in agriculture, fishing, hunting or forestry. This reflects the dominance of the rural economy in many developing countries. Some only help out on a family farm at peak times when there is a need for manual labour, such as weeding and the harvest. However, agricultural work is not necessarily benign. In the US, farm work accounts for 42. 7 per cent of all fatalities among workers aged 14 to 17. Other hazards in agriculture are mentioned below.

It's not in the factory but on the streets of developing cities where most of today's urban working children can be found. Some actually live on the street, having left or lost their families, while others earn their living there, hawking food, drinks and a whole range of other products, carrying everything from someone's shopping to crippling loads, and running to and fro at their employer's orders. Almost by definition, the informal sector is unregulated whatever labour laws and regulations apply in the formal economy, such as factories and the civil service, are not observed and little attempt is made to enforce them. This applies both to laws governing a minimum age for employment and those covering health and safety at work. The millions of children living and working on the streets around the world come into this category, as do many apprentices sewing and hammering away in small workshops.

Although it was concern about children in developing countries producing cheap exports for the industrialised world that fuelled publicity about child labour in the 1990s, the export economy involves a relatively small proportion of working children under 15. No accurate data is available, but about 5 per cent, some 10 million children, are thought to be involved in producing either agricultural or manufactured products for export. The involvement of children under 15 in the growing and harvesting of agricultural products such as cocoa, coffee, rubber, sisal, tea and tobacco has provoked protests in countries importing these products.

Working as a servant in someone else's house, especially as a live-in servant, has different implications for a child of 8 than for a young woman of 15 or 16. In the Philippines, about 10 per cent of the 300, 000 children reported to work as household helps are between 10 and 14, while most are older. In other parts of the world, recruitment starts before children reach 10. In Haiti there is a long tradition of boys and girls from poor families being sent to live with slightly better off households to work as servants, known as restaveks (from the French phrase meaning "stay with"). It is widely acknowledged that restaveks are treated badly; for example, a special whip is on sale in Haiti for punishing them. Efforts by UNICEF and others have not yet convinced the public in Haiti to abandon this practice and the ill-treatment of children involved.

Some children who work in their own home are simply helping out with household chores. Others are participating in a family business, such as helping to run a shop after school. However, households also take in work on a subcontracted basis, such as stitching pieces of leather to make footballs in Pakistan and India. They and the adult workers in their households are "homeworkers". While children working in their own homes are in an environment that ought to protect them against harm, some are nevertheless exposed to exploitation or hazards.

Children in parts of India work at home rolling tobacco into thin cigarettes, or beedi. They are inevitably exposed to a health hazard from working with tobacco; in addition, many have to work to pay back money which their parents have borrowed. Routinely, laws concerning child employment do not apply to children working at home in a family business. There is consequently a danger that families and employers avoid the terms of the law by claiming that children are working for their own family when this is not the case.

Some children decide for themselves to leave home to seek work, while others are sent away by parents who hope they will "better themselves" elsewhere. Children under 15 who live and work away from their families are exposed to the greatest risk of abuse. They no longer have a relative to check up on how they are and are not mature enough to look after themselves. Indeed, younger children are totally dependent on their employer to look after them and cannot even run away or protest at ill-treatment. Some children may leave home with a trafficker - recruited or deceived by someone who intends to use them for commercial sexual exploitation or put them into a situation close to slavery, or they may come under the control of such a person after leaving home. The ILO estimated that in 2000, some 1. 2 million exploited children had been trafficked.

The ILO's Worst Forms of Child Labour Convention distinguishes "unconditional worst forms", which automatically constitute an abuse wherever they occur, from hazardous work, which it is up to each country to identify for itself. Many unconditional worst forms are close to slavery and are not recognised by the public as genuine "work" - particularly when children earn money by having sex with adults. According to ILO data, approximately eight million children are believed to work in these especially horrific circumstances - forced into bonded labour or other forms of slavery, into prostitution or pornography, or into participation in armed conflict or other illicit activities.

Out of these eight million, the largest group, almost six million, are subjected to forced or "bonded" labour. Children become victims of bonded labour (also known as debt bondage) when they or adult relatives accept a loan and agree that the child should work to pay it back. However, the repayments are not on the basis of a fair exchange: in bonded labour, the value of the work far exceeds that of the original loan. Children sometimes work for years to pay off relatively small sums. For example, in 2001 four child migrants were rescued off a ship supposed to be taking them from West to Central Africa on arrival they were scheduled to work for eight years to pay off the costs of their trip, just 1, 000 kilometres across the sea. South Asia is the area where the largest numbers of children are reported to be "bonded", and certain industries, such as the handknotted carpet industry in north India and Pakistan, have become infamous because of the presence of so many bonded children.

Recruitment of Children

International legal standards ban the recruitment of young people into the armed forces until they are 16 and prohibit under-18s from being conscripted, as well as prohibiting their recruitment by militias or insurgent groups. Nevertheless, each time a new war has broken out in sub-Saharan Africa in the past two decades, there have been reports of boys as young as 11 sent into combat and of girls used both as combatants and in support roles. Wars on other continents have also involved young recruits, with armed opposition groups in Colombia, the Philippines and Sri Lanka all enrolling children, as well as groups closer to home, in Northern Ireland.

Although some youngsters are demobilised before reaching 18, they generally remain deeply marked by their military experience and find it difficult to re-adapt to ordinary life. Furthermore, many people in their communities are terrified that former child soldiers will go on resorting to violence. At the beginning of this decade, an estimated 300, 000 children had been recruited into various armed groups. The total seemed to have fallen by 2004, but the problem remains serious.

Sexual Exploitation

Teenage girls account for the vast majority of the children who earn money in prostitution, but boys are involved as well. Both boys and girls are used to produce child pornography. The number of children involved was estimated at 1. 8 million in 2000. Young children who have not even reached puberty suffer from the interest of paedophiles, while the demand for commercial sex with girls who have only just passed puberty has increased as a result of the HIV/AIDS epidemic. Men in various parts of the world deliberately seek sex with girls of 15 or younger on the assumption that they are less likely to have contracted HIV/AIDS than older women. Some people who are HIV-positive even believe that sex with children, and particularly virgins, will remove their own infection. The role of tourists from richer countries who pay for sex with local children has come under the limelight, but probably accounts for only a small proportion of the problem.

International congresses, attended by representatives of governments and other organisations, were organised in Sweden and Japan in 1996 and 2001 to develop a common agenda to combat this form of exploitation. A great deal has been learnt about the techniques for preventing commercial sexual exploitation, as well as how to protect the children involved and enable them to rebuild their lives afterwards, but the dimensions of the problem are still huge. Children are used in a range of other illegal activities around the world. When this was categorised as a "worst form" of child labour in 1999, the focus was on young people involved in the drug trade. Cases of this sort have been reported in the UK and other parts of Europe, but two other types of illicit activity involve larger numbers of children. In one of these cases in particular, there has been relatively little reaction from the authorities.

Children from both Eastern Europe and other parts of the world have been brought to EU countries in recent years to take part in house break-ins and other crimes. In France, children from part of northwest Romania were taken to Paris.

In 2000, Romanian children accounted for almost one in six of the juvenile offenders appearing in Paris courts. Large numbers of children have also been brought into EU countries to beg, as a profitable way for the adults controlling them to earn an income. In 2003, Albanian children begging in Greece were estimated to be earning 30 to 50 euros a day (£20 to £35). Many of the children involved should have been attending primary school. The authorities allowed them to wander around tourist areas late in the evening, offering flowers for sale or playing music to persuade people to give them money.

Throughout the world, child beggars are deployed outside places of religious worship - churches, mosques and temples - to take advantage of the charity of worshippers, who have no idea how the children concerned use their money and whether they have to hand it over to an adult who is exploiting them.

Danger Works

All sorts of work exposes young people to danger and jeopardises their health (or even their lives). These dangers are sometimes obvious children handling gunpowder in a South Indian city, in a place which specialises in making fireworks and matches; and children working in quarries, where splinters of rock fly around. The fact that children are working in such conditions confirms both their desperation for an income and the attitude of some employers who see children as a disposable, as well as a cheap, workforce. In Kenya, during a recent UNICEF investigation, children working on farms described the hazards they faced. The main ones mentioned included cuts and wounds from pruned coffee and tea bushes, long working hours, lifting heavy loads, exposure to farm chemicals, lack of drinking water and toilets, and excessive noise.

Most of the children worked without the bare minimum of protective clothing, such as gumboots, gloves, raincoats and overalls. Several children had broken a limb after falling from fruit trees. Many were bitten or stung by spiders and insects as they worked in the bushes. The absence of even the most basic medical care caused simple wounds to become infected. Eye and ear infections were common, as were skin allergies from exposure to pesticides and other chemicals - the fields they worked in were regularly sprayed with pesticides.

Children are more vulnerable to the toxic effects of pesticides than adults: in 2003, the US Environmental Protection Agency estimated that children aged between 3 and 15 may experience at least three times the cancer threat the same chemicals pose to adults. However, Kenya's child plantation workers inevitably resumed work much sooner after spraying than was safe. More than 1 in 10 of the young farm workers, boys as well as girls, described being sexually abused by men on the plantations, particularly in the early evening, while awaiting transport to return to their homes. Elsewhere in Africa, children have described accidents while fishing on lakes in Ghana and Uganda, falling into the water and contracting waterborne diseases such as schistosomiasis.

The dangers inherent in other types of work are less obvious. This fact, as well as a child's relatively underdeveloped sense of danger, is a reason why children should not be involved in hazardous work and why inspectors are needed to check the risks that all young workers face. In some European countries, it is predominantly minority groups, such as Roma and recent immigrants, whose children start work while still below the minimum legal age for employment. However, some industries involve more child workers than others. In Portugal, some 47, 000 school-age children were reported to be working instead of attending school, many of them making shoes. The Portuguese government has made efforts for more than a decade to end this practice.

Until recently, many school-age children in other parts of southern Europe skipped school to work in family businesses. However, in these and other EU countries, different categories of children are now subjected to economic and sexual exploitation - those brought into the EU especially for this purpose from other parts of the world. They include children from Albania begging in Greece, children brought from Romania to France, Italy and elsewhere to take part in criminal activities, Eastern European teenage girls forced into prostitution, and children imported especially from West Africa to work as live-in domestic workers in France, the UK and elsewhere.

EU Directive on the Protection of Young People at Work In 1994, the Council of the European Union issued a Council Directive on the Protection of Young People at Work to reduce the discrepancies on youth employment in its member countries. This sets minimum standards for all EU states for both children (those still required by law to attend school), and adolescents and young people who are under 18 but above the minimum legal age for employment. It specifies that children aged 14 and 15 may undertake "light work" and that 13-year-olds may work for a limited number of hours each week, to be set by national legislation. Some exceptions are allowed for children involved in cultural, artistic, sporting or advertising activities.

Certain types of hazardous work are prohibited for all young people below 18, such as work which is "beyond their physical or psychological capacity", involves their exposure to toxins and substances that might affect their health, and involves a risk of accidents, which young people might not recognise or try to avoid. The UK was slower than other EU countries to modify its laws in the light of this Directive. New regulations came into force in August 1998 with minor amendments concerning 16- and 17-year-olds in April 2003. Northern Ireland has slightly different rules, allowing 16- and 17-year-olds involved in sea fishing to start work at 4 am and to continue until midnight. More recently, the EU has also been trying to standardise legislation on human trafficking, including children.

In the case of the UK nationals reported here, "child" or "young person" refers to those of compulsory school age, 16 or under, in accordance with child employment legislation. When talking about young people in prostitution, the definition has been widened to include young people up to the age of 18, in accordance with the Sexual Offences Act 2003. When referring to foreign national children, "child" or "young person" refers to those up to 18, as this is the child/adult cut-off point in asylum legislation. The UN Convention on the Rights of the Child, which underpins all of UNICEF's work - and which makes it explicit that children should be protected from sexual abuse - applies to everyone under the age of 18.

According to the Children's and Young Persons Act 1933, still the prime piece of legislation on child employment, all working young people of school age should be licensed by their local education authority. However, like 79 per cent of her employed peers, Stella does not have a permit to wait tables. The hours that children can work are also set by law. Jobs cannot start before 7am or finish later than 7pm. Outside the entertainment industry, 13 is the youngest that children can work in most cases. During the school week, they cannot work for longer than 12 hours and they should only work for a maximum of two hours on a Sunday. But many young people work earlier, later and longer than this. Here found that 5 per cent of young people work for more than 12 hours during the school week. More than one in five children questioned said they worked for more than two hours on a Sunday. A 15-year-old waitress from Morayshire worked until 10pm during the school week and until 11pm at the weekends.

A 1998 report on child employment in North Tyneside found that 25 per cent of working children were under 13. Almost a quarter of respondents started work before they were 12, or even younger. In England and Wales, permits for children to work are issued by local authority child employment officers, who also have to ensure that children are not taken on without this registration. However, there are only around 25 full-time child employment officers for the whole country. In Cheshire, for example, there are more than 15, 000 school children aged 13 and over, but just three child employment officers who work two days a week each. Child employment is a very low priority for many local authorities.

Education welfare officers, who are assigned to schools to ensure that all legal obligations relating to a child's education are met, can flag up concerns if a child is frequently absent. But they too tend to be overworked and under-resourced. It is unlikely that such a wide-scale breach of adult employment - or any other - law would be tolerated. Yet there have been just 38 prosecutions for the improper employment of children since records began in 2000. One reason for this is that most child employment officers refuse to take evidence from the young person - to avoid them facing the potentially traumatic experience of being forced to appear in court - so in most cases there is insufficient evidence for court proceedings.

There are several likely reasons for this general ignorance, which effectively puts children outside the law. The first is that regulations on child employment are manifold and confusing: although the 1933 Act is the principal relevant statute, there are a plethora of other European directives, national laws and local by-laws that dictate how and when children should work. Often these laws vary from one county to the next in Staffordshire, a child can work behind the counter in a butcher's shop, while in neighbouring Cheshire they can't. Some local authorities ban children from working on milk rounds, while others sanction it. In Croydon, children may deliver milk, but only on Saturdays and Sundays. Worse, more than 9 out of 10 local authority by-laws on school-age working conflict with national legislation. Just 13 councils have by-laws that are completely in step with the national law. A third of English councils allow children as young as 10 to work - something that the 1933 Act explicitly prohibits.

It is also extremely difficult to find information on what is and isn't legal. Officially it is the Department of Health that regulates child employment, but it is not easy to find details on its website of what is permissible and what is not. Just 17 of 149 local authorities in England publish child employment information on their websites. Some local education authorities did not have the rules in written form at all. Even council employees do not understand the regulations; concerned parents who call their council for information are often referred to several different members of staff before someone realises they need to speak to the child employment officer.

There is no minimum wage many experts fear that when the minimum wage for 16-year-olds is introduced, employers will just take on younger people, for less money. The average pay for working children is £4 an hour, one child reported he was paid just 50p an hour. A boy from Llanrwst, Wales, earned an average of just 77p an hour when he spent a summer working for a garage. "Children are a workforce with no bargaining power, " said one child employment expert.

UNICEF strongly believes that one key way to prevent this kind of exploitation is to ensure that children are informed of their rights in the first place, as set out in the UN Convention on the Rights of the Child, rather than feeling that they are at the mercy of unscrupulous adults. With an awareness of their rights, and the resultant recognition that they have a choice in the matter, young people should feel more empowered to avoid, or extricate themselves from, exploitative situations. Even though baby-sitting is not considered a form of employment, it is still work and keeps many of the young people going to bed before 7 am or 3am, even during a school week.

Health and Safety

The employment of 13-year-olds also creates health and safety issues. All employers of school-age workers are supposed to carry out an additional risk assessment, which takes account of the age and inexperience of the child employee. Very few do. A survey of child employment in riding stables, for example, found that one in three of the sample had accidents at work. Children as young as 13 are allowed to drive a tractor on private land. According to health and safety experts, hundreds of children are hurt on farms every year, although accidents are likely to be unreported by the order of 60-70 per cent. In 2003, for example, a 15-year-old boy needed surgery after falling from the back of a farm vehicle being used to track foxes. He had started work at 5:30am and had probably fallen asleep.

Entertainment Work

Children working in the entertainment industry are regulated by yet another set of laws, predominantly the 1968 Child Performance legislation. "This law is interpreted in different ways by different people, so the whole thing needs to be rethought, " said another child employment officer. "There are far more serious dangers of children being abused in these situations as they are often working away from home. Many teachers think that working is a positive experience for their students.

Farms and Factories

In the same way that they exploit adult migrant workers, who often do not speak English and are vulnerable because of their immigration status, gangmasters in the agricultural sector and in factories also exploit foreign national children. Gangmasters take on casual labourers and contract them out to farmers and factory owners. Although they have been able to operate without regulation, under the Gangmasters Licensing Act 2004 they now have to be registered. While some are good employers, others exploit their workers, who tend to come from the least empowered sectors of society: migrant workers and lows killed women. Adults are taken on to work long hours for low pay in poor conditions, and are charged unreasonable amounts for their accommodation, work clothes and transport.

Criminal Activities

While there is little evidence that children are brought into the country explicitly to be exploited for criminal activity, there is evidence that they are exploited criminally once they are here. This can range from enabling an adult to falsely claim child benefits or a housing upgrade to active involvement in criminal activity, such as cigarette or drug smuggling. Customs and Excise do not divulge figures of child drug mules, but police at airports say they occasionally suspect children and give them the appropriate hand scan - which shows if drugs have been touched - or urine test.

In many countries, particularly in West Africa and South and Southeast Asia, sending a girl child or, less usually, a boy to live and work in someone else's house is perceived as not only acceptable but desirable. These children often help out in the house while they also attend school, something that they might not have done had they stayed at home. Parents believe that the higher social status and comparative wealth of the new household will prove to be of benefit to their child. Other parents send their children away out of economic necessity. In any case, family structures in these countries are often looser than in Britain. A family friend is known as, and treated like, an aunty or uncle. Bringing up someone else's child is not unusual. But traffickers have transformed this tradition into a negative practice.

It is extremely difficult to quantify this problem in the UK. By its very nature, domestic slavery remains clandestine. In many of the cases reported, the victims said they were locked in the house and so had very little contact with the outside world - even neighbours may not realise that children are being held. One expert reports that the trafficking of African children to the UK for domestic work is guarded by secrecy, emotional blackmail and the desire of the child to remain in the UK. The child may be aware that their parents have made huge sacrifices to get them into this country in the hope of a better life.

Some people who use children to do their cleaning or their child care may not even accept that they are doing anything wrong, because where they come from it is not unusual for young people to do such work. A neighbour who challenged a woman who brought her eight-year-old girl niece from Nigeria to work in her house in London was told that the girl "was not doing anything that she wouldn't be expected to do back home". There are some available figures on the problem. In London, 14 cases of trafficking for domestic servitude were identified in 2003. The children involved were from Uganda, the Democratic Republic of Congo, Liberia, Nigeria, Somalia, Burundi, Ghana and Eritrea.

Some social services departments, such as Sheffield, now routinely visit children who are privately fostered to ensure that no exploitation is taking place, but most do not. This means that almost anyone can turn up at Birmingham or Luton airport, for example, and claim a child, without any checks carried out on their suitability as foster parents/carers. While figures are not reliable, an estimated 15, 000-20, 000 children are in private foster care in the UK, the majority of them from West Africa. The 2004 Children's Bill will tighten the regulations, but still relies on the foster parent to register with social services - a measure highly unlikely to stop child domestic labour.

Actions of UNICEF

UNICEF is active throughout the world in the fight to protect children from harm, both during emergencies and at other times. Children affected by violence, abuse and exploitation are one of UNICEF's five priorities for 2004 - along with immunisation and related health measures, education (particularly for girls), early childhood development and children affected by HIV/AIDS. UNICEF is also pressing governments to increase their spending on children. Creating a "protective environment" In recent years UNICEF's work has especially emphasised all-round improvements for children - changes that have long-term effects, in contrast to small-scale projects which benefit only a few. This approach means trying to influence the general environment within which children grow up. UNICEF aims to create a "protective environment" for children, ensuring a safety net for all children at risk, with interconnected strands working together to protect children from violence, exploitation and abuse.

One way of improving the protective environment is to persuade governments to improve their laws or to enforce existing ones. In Bolivia, UNICEF promoted a new Code of Boys, Girls and Adolescents that became law in October 1999. Similarly, it used its influence in Viet Nam, where the Government passed a law preventing child prostitution and providing assistance to girls under 18 who have been victims of commercial sexual exploitation.

Providing Education

UNICEF wants to make it easier for children everywhere to go to school and to prevent them dropping out before they finish their basic education. Much of UNICEF's work aims to encourage girls in particular to attend and stay on at school, in the knowledge that this will bring long-term benefits - educated girls tend to marry later, have fewer unwanted pregnancies, and their children have lower mortality rates because of better health practices. Education is also one of the best ways of helping children who have started working full time when young, as well as a way of reducing the number of children who do so. Some projects supported by UNICEF aim to get working children into full-time education, while others provide classes that children can attend while they go on working, referred to as "non-formal education". Although some people may prefer to see children attending school full-time and not having to work at all, in the short- and medium-term this is not feasible for more than a handful of children - providing part-time education for many seems a fairer approach.

The Bal Adhikar Pariyojana (Child Rights Initiative) is a community-based project. It started in 1998 and by mid-2004 extended to 800 villages with a population of about 1. 6 million, a third of whom were under 15. As a result of campaigns by the project and the Government's Department of Basic Education, by September 2003, 80, 649 children who were not attending school (47 per cent of them girls) had been brought back to school. To reach other children, 200 "alternative learning centres" were set up. These provided non-formal education as a first step to reintegrating children into the regular school system. More than 13, 000 children have progressed via these alternative learning centres into ordinary schools. The project is not restricted to promoting education; it also provides small loans on reasonable terms to mothers to enable them to start ventures to earn an income, pay off exorbitant loans and finance their children's schooling. It has the wider objective of creating "child-friendly villages", with a general environment that protects children against economic exploitation and abuse.

In Lesotho, herding livestock is viewed as a tradition that prepares young boys for manhood, and about 20 per cent of boys spend their childhood doing this without ever going to school. Traditionally, boys begin herding at the age of three or four, accompanying their elder brothers, cousins or other boys employed by the family, and they qualify as full-time "herd boys" by the age of seven. "To be employed as a herd boy is beneficial and makes a boy able to endure hardships, " explained one woman. "A boy who goes to school will not find employment. "In an effort to improve the lives and prospects of herd boys, UNICEF and the Government of Lesotho undertook what initially appeared to be an insurmountable challenge: changing traditional attitudes and customs by providing learning opportunities for thousands of herd boys. Now, alongside Lesotho's familiar cattle-posts, the new "learning posts" dot the mountainous landscape.

These learning posts have changed the lives of herd boys in even the most remote parts of the country. After a long day tending his herd, 13-year-old Teboho Lesoana comes to the learning post in the mountain village of Liqobong. In a one-room schoolhouse, Teboho and a group of other herd boys learn by candlelight. The conditions may not be ideal, but they are learning to read, write and do basic arithmetic. This is an important first step. With 245 million working children currently suffering some kind of abuse, UNICEF aims to give priority to those who are most vulnerable or suffering most. This means focusing on children involved in particularly harmful forms of child labour and giving special attention to child workers whose situation has been aggravated by HIV/AIDS or warfare.

Stop Children Suffer

The various causes of child labour outlined here need to be tackled at different levels

— Immediate causes (a parent dies and the family desperately needs extra income).

— Underlying causes (public opinion thinks the most appropriate work for girls is in the house, or that it is acceptable for poor children to work instead of attending school).

— Structural or root causes operating at the level of an entire economy or society. An immediate cause can be addressed by action in the short term, such as providing grants to needy families, while addressing root causes means bringing about major changes in the economic order at national or international level.

No single action, however well intentioned, stops child labour or puts an end to the harm which children suffer. Instead, we need a coordinated set of actions.

— Putting the right laws and policies into place (and ensuring the public knows about them and the government has the political will to implement them).

— Addressing the root causes of child labour.

— Preventing children from leaving school and entering the labour market prematurely.

— A range of activities to protect children who are already at work, in some cases to support them and in others to withdraw them from work that is causing them harm.

Implementing a coordinated set of actions in this manner is very much in line with UNICEF's more recent emphasis on all-round improvements for children by influencing the general environment in which children grow up. We have already learnt a great deal about the impact of different measures, and this has improved the effectiveness of many projects to stop child labour. However, numerous organisations are involved, each tackling different aspects of the problem, and they sometimes adopt different approaches. UNICEF believes that providing practical support to child workers and preventing the worst abuses is more realistic than attempting an immediate ban on the recruitment of under-15-year-olds into any job at all.

Government Armies

In countries where large numbers of children have been recruited into government armies and opposition armed groups, UNICEF plays a leading role in organising their demobilisation and return to ordinary life. In Central Africa, conflicts have affected so many children and so many countries that UNICEF has been organising the demobilisation of tens of thousands of child soldiers in Angola, Burundi and the Democratic Republic of Congo, as well as in some other countries. In the Democratic Republic of Congo, UNICEF made direct contact with the leaders of opposition armed groups, first to persuade them not to recruit children and later, following peace agreements, to take part in discussions about demobilisation.

In Sri Lanka, UNICEF has been involved for many years in trying to convince the armed opposition Tamil Tigers not to enrol children. The assistance provided to children who are demobilised from military units consists of far more than simply sending them home. It includes providing teenagers with basic education and life skills training, which they missed out on in military service, and giving older children an opportunity to learn a skill they can use to earn a living. Some child soldiers are accused of having killed neighbours or relatives, so there have to be negotiations with their families and with community leaders before they can return home. UNICEF works internationally and nationally to combat the commercial sexual exploitation of children. It focuses its efforts on preventing sexual exploitation from happening in the first place, protecting girls (and boys) who have been exploited, and providing opportunities for them to recover and return home.

UNICEF channels support to local groups such as Avenir de l'Enfant in Senegal. With UNICEF support, Ndhïmë Për Fëmijet (Help the Children), a nongovernment organisation in the south of Albania, works with sexually abused or exploited children, many of whom have been trafficked to Greece. The NGO has helped reintegrate 400 children annually into schools in four Albanian cities. Brothers and sisters of the children also receive counselling and support, bringing the number of children assisted through the programme each year to 2, 500. Children without primary carers Children in sub-Saharan Africa have been hit particularly hard by HIV/AIDS, and over 11 million children in the region have been robbed of one or both parents by AIDS.

When parliamentary elections were held at the end of 2002 in Kenya, one country severely affected, UNICEF took a public stand to persuade the new parliament to take more concerted action to address the issue of children orphaned by HIV/AIDS, estimated at almost 900, 000 in a country of 30 million. Within days of being elected, the new government took action. It declared that primary schooling would be free. The cost to the Government was likely to be almost US$100 million (£53 million). When the new school year started in January 2003, 1. 3 million children sought admission to school for the first time, in addition to the 5. 9 million pupils already enrolled. Schools experienced massive overcrowding, but the impact has been vital for children who have lost parents to AIDS. For them, free education represents a unique chance to attend school rather than having to earn a living.

UNICEF contributed $2. 5 million (£1. 3 million) to the Kenyan initiative, for teaching and learning materials, recreational equipment, training for 5, 000 teachers, and basic water and sanitation facilities. The World Bank has promised $50 million (£27 million) over three years in grants to support the education initiative. The British and Swedish governments have also pledged support. Children working as live-in domestics For more than 10 years, UNICEF in Brazil has sought to place the issue of child labour high on the country's social and political agenda. Child labour has been almost halved - notably on sugarcane, sisal, orange, and tobacco plantations, as well as on dumps and other hazardous locations - but some 3. 8 million children are still believed to be engaged in harmful work. Some of these are "invisible" child labourers, not seen as a problem by the public.

Protect from Trafficking

The tradition in parts of West Africa of sending children away to live, work and be educated in the households of relatives or others, hoping this will give them a helping hand to get on in the world, has been manipulated to ensure a supply of full-time "household helps" or skivvies. In Benin, some of these children work in the country's cities, but many are trafficked abroad to other countries in West and Central Africa. Since 1999, UNICEF has been working with local communities to establish committees in villages to warn parents of the dangers facing children who are sent away, and to alert the police when children go missing. So far, more than 170 committees have been established. Fewer children have left as a result.

In the Philippines, up to five million people arrive by boat each year in the capital, Manila. About half are in search of work and a better future, and many are children. A local organisation, Visayan Forum, provides help and advice to children arriving in Manila's port and has set up a halfway house there, operating 24 hours a day. Children intercepted in Manila port are usually taken to Visayan Forum's halfway house. The organisation helps them overcome their traumatic experiences and start afresh. In the wake of the success of the first halfway house, three others have been established in harbours elsewhere in the Philippines. Visayan Forum also helps children understand the nature of child trafficking and the hazards of child labour.

Alongside efforts to ensure that laws in individual countries are appropriate to catch and punish child traffickers, UNICEF has been enlisted to identify the most appropriate ways of protecting children who have been trafficked. Unfortunately, around the world trafficked children are routinely treated as if they were illegal migrants, are sometimes imprisoned for activities they have been forced into by traffickers (such as begging or prostitution), and are very rarely treated as if they have any rights. In one area where teenage girls have been trafficked in large numbers, Southeast Europe, UNICEF developed a special set of "Guidelines for Protection of the Rights of Children Victims of Trafficking in Southeastern Europe". Governments in the region have committed themselves to taking the steps outlined in these guidelines on 11 different issues.

In addition, UNICEF is working for the ratification and implementation of ILO's Convention No. 182 to immediately end the worst forms of child labour. Once a country ratifies Convention No. 182, time-bound national plans of action are needed that empower all partners and ensure the following basics:

— That governments commit and allocate resources and priority attention to educate children and that leaders introduce legislation and provide adequate enforcement measures to protect children's rights. Because measures that reduce social inequality and shore up basic social services mitigate the impact of poverty on families and reduce the likelihood that children will be ensnared in harmful labour, governments must also plan for and spend on human development by investing in basic social services.

— That serious efforts are made to develop the greatest possible awareness of children's rights and the damage to children caused by child labour. Such heightened public awareness depends on the existence of good and reliable data, disaggregated for gender and geographical patterns. It also requires social partnerships among many different groups, including researchers, government sectors, businesses, trade unions, educators, the media, national and international development workers, community leaders and, of course, parents and children themselves.

— That monitoring and enforcement mechanisms are created, including codes of conduct for corporations and businesses in which they and their subcontractors commit to not employing children.

Around the world, successes are helping stem the tide of child labour and protect children. In Thailand, the minimum legal age of employment was raised and a media and public information campaign helped dramatically increase public awareness about abusive child labour. In Bolivia, UNICEF actively promoted a new Code of Boys, Girls and Adolescents that became law in October 1999. The Government of Viet Nam passed a law preventing child prostitution and rehabilitating affected girls under 18. Advocacy in Rwanda helped secure the country's ratification of ILO's Convention 182.

Child labour laws have been strengthened in many countries, and a number of international corporations have adopted codes of conduct concerning child labour. In July 2000, many corporations joined the United Nations Secretary-General in launching the Global Compact, an initiative in support of responsible business operations, in which they agreed to promote and apply nine principles from the fields of human rights, labour standards and the environment. The International Organization of Employers and national organizations in many Latin American countries and elsewhere have pledged support to combat child labour.

The International Confederation of Free Trade Unions and labour unions in industrialized and developing countries have also provided financial and other support to campaigns to end child labour. The results of cooperation have been singularly effective in several instances, providing examples to be followed and emulated. UNICEF and the ILO together managed to achieve the remarkable 1995 Memorandum of Understanding in Bangladesh. This was a milestone agreement, the first-ever collaboration among an industry and international organizations. Together they resolved the problem of how to remove children from the garment industry without exposing them to even more difficult and exploitative situations.

The result was a comprehensive and phased approach, ensuring that the freed children could attend educational programmes. Beginning in 1997, a similar cooperative effort with the ILO and the NGO Save the Children achieved another important breakthrough - the process of getting children out of the soccer ball-stitching industry and into education programmes in Pakistan. This model has since been applied in other industries and countries.

Affirming Child Rights

There are hundreds of millions of children and young people

around the world who are imprisoned, not in physical jails, but in a state of bondage more permanent than locks or bars alone could create. These are children who labour at tasks that harm their bodies and minds, their spirits and future. Only estimates exist, but at least 250 million children between the ages of 5 and 14 work for a living in developing countries, nearly half of them full time. Many millions more are uncounted and uncountable. They are everywhere but invisible, toiling as domestic servants in homes, labouring behind the walls of workshops, hidden from view in plantations.

If poverty, as Nobel laureate Amartya Sen argues, is to be defined not merely in terms of low income but as a state of deprivation of basic capabilities, nothing illustrates that more forcefully than child labour. A result and also a cause of poverty, child labour is a prison that withers both capabilities and potential. A child labourer is a child denied the liberating benefit of education, one whose health, growth and development are threatened, who risks losing the love, care and protection of family and who cannot enjoy the rest and play that are every child's right.

Those who survive these rigours will most likely grow into men and women who, because of these many deprivations, are unable to improve their own lives or participate fully and productively in their societies. The odds are strong, too, that their own children will be locked into similar patterns of deprivation. Some terms are so discordant, so repugnant to the human and humane ear that they should never have had to be coined 'child soldier', 'child prostitute', 'child labourer'. The rights of children must be realized so that no child ever need endure such fates.

A wave of progress has swept much of the world, raising living standards and empowering many to lead fuller, more secure and dignified lives. But it has left millions behind, including children who labour at the expense of health or education. Child labour is not a new problem, and there is a long history of international efforts to combat it. The International Labour Organization (ILO), for example, in 1919 developed the first Minimum Age Convention that regulated the age at which children could work. Then, in 1973, a more comprehensive Minimum Age Convention, Number 138, was adopted, and it remains the fundamental standard.

Although not new and always a thorny problem, child labour has now become increasingly complex, assuming new forms as global realities and relations have changed. Among the underlying causes, poverty and economic disparities are, of course, critical factors. For much of human history, children have contributed to family welfare in a variety of ways, but intensified urbanization and the breakdown of traditional economic systems have made even basic subsistence more precarious and put children at ever higher risk. The results of a nine-country survey in Latin America, for instance, showed that if teenaged children did not work, poverty rates would increase by 10 to 20 per cent.

Gender is another central factor. Girls are expected to be primarily or exclusively domestic workers in many cultures, so household work at young ages is regarded as natural for them. Such domestic work is also often seen as more valuable than any perceived returns from education, especially when parents calculate how, and for which of their children, they can pay school costs and fees. In addition, many schools are threatening places for girls, where they are at risk of sexual harassment from classmates and teachers and sidelined by prejudice and poor curricula. Solely by virtue of their gender, therefore, many girls are kept from school or drop out, ending up in exploitative labour. Of the more than 110 million children out of school, nearly two thirds are girls.

Commercial sexual exploitation and trafficking in children for prostitution have also burgeoned, with at least 1 million children a year, most of them girls, entrapped in a network stretching from South-East Asia and the former Soviet bloc to Latin America. Then, HIV/AIDS has further heightened the labour crisis for children, particularly in sub-Saharan Africa, where the toll is highest. With more than 10 per cent of children in some countries orphaned and more than 13 million children under the age of 15 orphaned overall, extended families, communities and governments are stretched beyond their capacity to care for them.

As school systems disintegrate under the burden of AIDS, with teachers and administrators succumbing, unrelieved hardship and gruelling toil become the only options for children forced support themselves and their siblings. Similarly, the effects of wars and civil unrest and growing economic dislocation swell the ranks of children in the most hazardous types of labour, many of them from minority, indigenous and other marginalized sectors of societies. The poverty and suffering of such large numbers of children and adults are bound to form a critical mass of social instability with grave destructive potential.

A positive development in this bleak landscape, particularly in the past 10 years, is a better understanding of what child labour is and how it can be remedied. This understanding has been shaped and accelerated by the principles and ideals of human rights. Most important to this fuller understanding of child labour has been the adoption and ratification, by virtually all countries, of the 1989 Convention on the Rights of the Child. This landmark treaty, which is the pillar of UNICEF's work, expresses the intertwined and complementary human rights of all children. With the clarity the Convention bestows, child labour can be seen in its broadest and most damaging sense as a human rights violation on many different levels.

As such, it can be addressed only through a complementary range of measures, from laws and mechanisms to create and enforce minimum working-age regulations to the multiple protections enumerated in article 32 of the Convention on the Rights of the Child. These include the child's right to freedom from "economic exploitation and from performing any work that is likely to be hazardous or to interfere with the child's education, or to be harmful to the child's health or physical, mental, spiritual, moral or social development." And in concert with article 32, virtually every other article of the Convention focuses on issues that are in one way or the other related to the effects of work on children, including education, protection, exploitation, health, nutrition, rest and relaxation, play, social security, economic well-being and the responsibilities of parents.

A human rights approach to child labour, therefore, permits, and indeed requires, responses that are as multifaceted as the affronts children endure and the conditions that give rise to them. It also permits and requires wide partnerships and alliances to make the responses a reality. Such a perspective and approach are also reflected clearly in ILO's Convention No. 182 against the Worst Forms of Child Labour, adopted in June 1999. It defines "worst forms" as including all forms of or practices similar to slavery, the sale and trafficking of children, debt bondage, use or procurement of children for prostitution or pornographic purposes, forced or compulsory recruitment of children for use in armed conflict, using children in illicit activities, such as the production and trafficking of drugs, and work that is likely to harm the health, safety or morals of children.

Central in these efforts is the International Programme on the Elimination of Child Labour (IPEC), an ILO programme inspired by child labour concerns raised at the 1990 World Summit for Children. It now works with governments and other partners in 99 countries to initiate policies, set standards, promote advocacy and manage activities to combat child labour. Child labour is one of the core issues and priorities for review at the UN Special Session on Children in September 2001. Heads of State and Government and an array of individuals and organizations committed to protecting children's rights and improving their lives will meet to review and reflect on progress made-and opportunities lost-for children over the past decade since the World Summit for Children.

The Special Session is part of an emerging unified front, a Global Movement for Children, that is coalescing around the many violations of rights and disparities children face, and generating heightened vision and determination to end these infringements and change the world with children. Many organizations and individuals are already working on the multiple violations of children's rights inherent in child labour. As these partnerships are joined and reinforced by others in the growing Global Movement, greater progress, building on the foundation laid over the decades, becomes possible.

Similarly, donor nations can show their commitment by increasing the proportion of their assistance that goes to fund basic social services and by supporting debt forgiveness. This is particularly crucial in the poorest countries, and especially in Africa, where so many factors are converging to threaten children more virulently than ever before. Child labour condemns children to a harrowing present and hopeless future and is a throwback to some of the most shameful aspects of human behaviour. Like slavery, it can and must be consigned to history.

5

Early Marriage

Child marriage is a violation of human rights, compromising the development of girls and often resulting in early pregnancy and social isolation, with little education and poor vocational training reinforcing the gendered nature of poverty. The right to 'free and full' consent to a marriage is recognized in the Universal Declaration of Human Rights - with the recognition that consent cannot be 'free and full' when one of the parties involved is not sufficiently mature to make an informed decision about a life partner.

The Convention on the Elimination of all Forms of Discrimination against Women mentions the right to protection from child marriage in article 16, which states: "The betrothal and the marriage of a child shall have no legal effect, and all necessary action, including legislation, shall be taken to specify a minimum age for marriage..." While marriage is not considered directly in the Convention on the Rights of the Child, child marriage is linked to other rights - such as the right to express their views freely, the right to protection from all forms of abuse, and the right to be protected from harmful traditional practices - and is frequently addressed by the Committee on the Rights of the Child.

Forum against the Sexual Exploitation of Children as a type of commercial sexual exploitation of children. Young married girls are a unique, though often invisible, group. Required to perform heavy amounts of domestic work, under pressure to demonstrate fertility, and responsible for raising children while still children themselves, married girls and child mothers face constrained decision-making and reduced life choices. Boys are also affected by child marriage but the issue impacts girls in far larger numbers and with more intensity.

When a couple lives together as if married - raises the same human rights concerns as marriage. Where a girl lives with a man and takes on the role of caregiver for him, the assumption is often that she has become an adult woman, even if she has not yet reached the age of 18. Additional concerns due to the informality of the relationship - for example, inheritance, citizenship and social recognition - might make girls in informal unions vulnerable in different ways than those who are in formally recognized marriages. Therefore, the following study considers girls in both formal marriage and in cohabitation to determine relationships between early unions (within or outside of marriage) and socio-economic and demographic variables, characteristics of the union, as well as knowledge and access related to reproductive and sexual health.

The literature suggests that many factors interact to place a child at risk of marriage. Poverty, protection of girls, family honour and the provision of stability during unstable social periods are suggested by Innocenti as significant factors in determining a girl's risk of becoming married while still a child. Jenson and Thornton found little overall change in the average age at marriage for age cohorts born between 1950 and 1970 in most regions, as well as little change in the incidence of child marriage.

Focusing primarily on Benin, Colombia, India and Turkey, Jenson and Thornton noted strong correlations between a woman's age at marriage and the level of education she achieves, the age at which she gives birth to her first child and the age of her husband. Women who married at younger ages were more likely to believe that it is sometimes acceptable for a husband to beat his wife and were more likely to experience domestic violence themselves. The age gap between partners is thought to contribute to these abusive power dynamics and to increase the risk of untimely widowhood,although Westoff notes that older husbands may be better providers for the household. Closely related to the issue of child marriage is the age at which girls become sexually active.

The relationship between age at marriage and age at first sexual intercourse is examined here with an eye to fertility trends; however, it is important to note that trends indicate that, while in some countries marriage may be increasingly delayed, sexual activity is not, leading to a greater incidence of pregnancy outside of union. Women who are married before the age of 18 tend to have more children than those who marry later in life. According to Bhattacharya, 97 per cent of women surveyed in India in 1992- 1993 did not use any contraception before their first child was born. However, the Population Council and UNICEF found that, in Pakistan, a substantial number of young married women indicated an interest in the use of contraception in the future.

Pregnancy-related deaths are known to be a leading cause of mortality for both married and unmarried girls between the ages of 15 and 19, particularly among the youngest of this cohort. Protection from HIV/AIDS is another reason for child marriage. Parents seek to marry off their girls to protect their health and their honour, and men often seek younger women as wives as a means to avoid infection. In some contexts, however, the evidence does not support this hypothesis and practice.

Bhattacharya found that in India, 75 per cent of people living with HIV/AIDS are married. In fact, the demand to reproduce and the stigma associated with safe-sex practices lead to very low condom use among married couples worldwide, and heterosexual married women who report monogamous sexual relationships with their husbands are increasingly becoming a high-risk group for HIV/AIDS. In 2003, UNICEF and partners agreed to focus on five indicators related to child marriage:

— Percentage of women first in union by age 18 by age group
— Percentage of girls 15-19 years of age currently in union
— Spousal age difference
— Percentage of women currently in a polygynous union by age groups
— Percentage of ever-married women who were directly involved in the choice of their first husband or partner.

The context and indicators related to child marriage and cohabitation can be approached through the examination of several age groups. One approach is to consider all women in a society. Another would be to observe the situation of girls aged 15-19 to determine the number of girls currently in union and the characteristics associated with that age group. However, the possibility of gauging how many of those girls will be married or in union by their 18th birthday is more complex because many have not yet reached the age of 18. Looking at the 20-24 age group is simpler and allows for the inclusion of all girls who were married or in union by age 18 within the closest time period for which complete data are available.

The number of children who enter into marriage or cohabitation each year varies according to region and across countries. Factors that influence child marriage rates include: the state of the country's civil registration system, which provides proof of age for children; the existence of an adequate legislative framework with an accompanying enforcement mechanism to address cases of child marriage; and the existence of customary or religious laws that condone the practice. Sufficient data were available to generate regional averages for South Asia, Africa and Latin America and the

Caribbean. Among women aged 15-24, 48 per cent were married before the age of 18 in South Asia (9. 7 million girls), 42 per cent in Africa, and 29 per cent in Latin America and the Caribbean.

Propotion of Women's Marriage

At the descriptive level, the proportion of women aged 20-24 married by age 18 tends to be higher in rural areas than in urban areas. There does not appear to be a trend of urban/ rural differences in the proportion of women married by age 18 related to national levels of child marriage; the association varies among countries and across the spectrum of national prevalence. For example, in Chad, where 71 per cent of women aged 20-24 were in union by age 18, living in an urban area was not a highly predictive factor; 65 per cent of urban women aged 20-24 were married by age 18, compared to 74 per cent of rural women.

Similarly, while the national rate of women aged 20-24 being married by age 18 in Namibia (10 per cent) is significantly lower than in Chad, the ratio of urban to rural child marriage levels for this cohort is the same as that seen in Chad (0. 88). High urban/rural differences are seen in Senegal, where 15 per cent of urban women and 53 per cent of rural women were in union by age 18, and in Peru, where 12 per cent of urban women and 35 per cent of rural women aged 20-24 in union by age 18. Urban women were more likely than their rural peers to have been married before age 18 in only Rwanda and Turkmenistan.

Economic pressures are often cited as an explanation for child marriage. The wealth index divides the population into quintiles from the poorest to the richest, allowing for the analysis of the disparity in child marriage rates between the poorest 20 per cent and the wealthiest 20 per cent of society. Cross-country comparisons of disparities are possible by examining the ratio of the percentage of women aged 20-24 who were in union by the age of 18 in the richest 20 per cent to the percentage in the poorest 20 per cent.

In all the countries analysed, child marriage is most common among the poorest 20 per cent of the population. The greatest disparity according to household wealth is observed in Peru, where 19 per cent of women aged 20-24 were married before age 18 - that is, 45 per cent among the poorest 20 per cent compared to 5 per cent among the richest 20 per cent. Conversely, in countries such as Chad and the Central African Republic, with total values of 71 per cent and 57 per cent respectively, less difference is observed between the richest 20 per cent (76 per cent in Chad, 55 per cent in the Central African Republic) and the poorest 20 per cent (66 per cent and 52 per cent, respectively). In the Philippines, the proportion is the same for both quintiles (3 per cent). However, compared to the second, third and fourth quintiles; the prevalence for the richest 20 per cent is considerably lower.

Educational Level

Education is often seen as key to preventing child marriage. In 42 of the countries analysed, women 20-24 years of age who had attended primary school were less likely to be married by age 18 than those who had not. The preventative effect of education was observed most strongly in Senegal, where 20 per cent of women who had attended primary school had been married by the age of 18, compared to 36 per cent of those who had not attended school. The reverse was true in only seven countries. In the Philippines, for example, 37 per cent of women who had attended primary school were married by 18, compared to 33 per cent of women who had not attended school.

Women who attended secondary school were less likely to be married by the age of 18 than those who did not. In the United Republic of Tanzania, for example, women with secondary education were 92 per cent less likely to be married by the age of 18 than women who had attended primary school only. For women who received tertiary levels of education, child marriage rates were often negligible. In only four countries (Cameroon, the Central African Republic, Ethiopia and Guinea) more than 20 per cent of women aged 20-24 who attended higher education were married by age 18. Most notably, in the Central African Republic, 44 per cent of women who attended post-secondary education were married by age 18. In each of these countries, more than 50 per cent of women aged 20-24 were married by age 18.

In many African countries, and in Haiti, Nepal and Yemen, polygynous unions remain a common practice. In Cameroon and Zimbabwe, respectively, 55 per cent and 34 per cent of women in monogamous unions enter into those relationships by age 18, compared to 75 per cent and 56 per cent, respectively, for women in polygynous unions. In five countries, women who enter in union by age 18 are more likely to have entered into a monogamous, rather than polygynous, union. For example, in Ethiopia, 68 per cent of women in monogamous unions entered the union by age 18, while only 54 per cent of women in polygynous relationships entered into those unions by age 18. In Nepal, these rates are 68 per cent and 61 per cent, respectively.

Reducing the risk of early pregnancies and births, as well as the total number of births during a woman's childbearing years, are other benefits cited as reasons to delay marriage until a girl is older. To explore the relationship between child marriage and the number of children a woman has, the proportion of women aged 20-24 who are married by age 18 is considered according to the number of children they have had. It is important to note that within this age group, the number of children each woman has had is only the number to date, and does not represent the potential total number of births over a woman's lifetime. Also, sample sizes become small for women aged 20-24 with more than three children, and childbearing prior to marriage or union is uncommon in most parts of the world. For example, in South Africa, 2 per cent of women with no children, 11 per cent of women with one or two children and 43 per cent of women with three or four children were married by age 18.

Age Difference

Age differences between partners have implications for power dynamics within the household. The analysis found a general pattern according to which women aged 20-24 whose male partners are more than five years older are more likely to have been married before age 18.

Educational Gap

To fully consider the role of education in preventing child marriage, one must also examine the education levels of men and the gap in education between spouses. The differences in education levels between spouses are thought to result in negative consequences related to power imbalance. In Namibia, for example, 27 per cent of couples for whom there is no gap in education levels entered into union before the woman was 18, compared to 45 per cent where the husband received more education. Similarly, in Egypt, 22 per cent of couples with no education gap resulted from child marriage, compared to 38 per cent of couples where the male partner received more education. A significant exception to this trend is Turkmenistan where 20 per cent of couples with no spousal education gap married before the woman was 18, as compared to 12 per cent of couples where the husband received more education.

Closing the education gap between men and women, in addition to increasing the level of education obtained by girls, may be an important intervention to decrease the prevalence of child marriage. This is further confirmed by the fact that smaller proportions of early marriage are observed among couples in which both have similar levels of education. Knowledge of reproductive and sexual health

Knowledge of HIV

In general, women aged 20-24 who know how to prevent HIV infection are less likely to have been married by age 18 than those who do not. For example, in Peru 40 per cent of women aged 20-24 who did not know how to protect themselves from HIV were married by age 18, compared to only 14 per cent of women who did. In South Africa, the values are 20 per cent and 8 per cent, respectively. Exceptions to this trend include Cambodia, the Central African Republic, Chad, Côte d'Ivoire, Ethiopia, India, Rwanda, Turkmenistan and Viet Nam, where 37 per cent of women who know how to prevent HIV were married by age 18, as compared to 10 per cent of women who did not. These exceptions may be due to the targeting of HIVprevention information to married women.

In much of the world, a great deal of pressure is placed on couples to conceive early in their union to ensure the continuity of the family line. As a result, many do not use contraception. By examining the child marriage trends among those who have never used contraception, those who have used only traditional or folkloric methods of debatable efficacy, and those who have used modern contraception, it is possible to assess the knowledge and unmet needs related to young women's access to reliable contraception, and to evaluate their ability to make reproductive choices. The data provide information on the proportion of women aged 20-24 who were married by age 18 and who use various forms of contraception.

In many African countries included in the analysis, women who had never used contraception were more likely to have experienced child marriage than women who had used modern contraception. In Nigeria, 51 per cent of women aged 20-24 who never used contraception were married before they were 18, compared to 22 per cent of women who used modern contraception. Similarly, in Cameroon, 63 per cent of women who never used contraception were married as girls, compared to 36 per cent of those who used modern contraception.

However, in many non-African countries, the opposite trend is true.

In Kyrgyzstan, only 0. 4 per cent of women who never used contraception were married by age 18, compared to 31 per cent of those who used modern contraception, and in Viet Nam the proportions are 2 per cent and 32 per cent, respectively. Comparing women who use modern contraception to those who have never used any form of contraception, however, does not accurately assess a woman's interest in preventing a pregnancy. Some women who do not want to become pregnant at a given time might use traditional or folkloric methods because they lack knowledge of or access to modern contraception. In more than half of the countries included in the study, women who used only traditional contraceptive methods were more likely to be married by age 18 than those who used modern contraception.

In Togo, 37 per cent of women aged 20-24 who used only traditional methods were married by age 18, compared to 21 per cent of women who used modern methods. In Turkmenistan, where the overall prevalence of child marriage is significantly lower than in Togo, 39 per cent of women who used only traditional methods were married by age 18, compared to 23 per cent of women age 20-24 who used modern methods. However, in some countries women aged 20-24 who used modern contraception were more likely to be married by age 18, compared to their peers who had used only traditional methods.

In the Dominican Republic, 58 per cent of women aged 20-24 who used modern methods were married by 18, compared to 19 per cent of women who used only traditional methods; in Namibia, 12 per cent of women using modern methods and 1. 1 per cent of women using traditional contraception were married by age 18. This last finding may be explained by noting that these women may have had access to modern contraception following their marriage. Overall, these findings might be indicative of the different barriers encountered by both unmarried and married women in accessing and using effective contraceptive methods.

Proportion of Girls Marriage

In most countries the proportion of girls aged 15-19 who are married is lower than the proportion of women aged 20-24 who were married by age 18. However, it is important to note that the discrepancies are at least partially due to the fact that many of the girls aged 15-19 have not yet reached their 18th birthday, and are therefore not only still at risk for early marriage but also likely to be married by the age of 18.

As was observed for women aged 20-24 who entered into union by age 18, girls aged 15-19 currently in union are more likely to be found in rural areas than in urban areas. Differences are most prominent in Eritrea, where 10 per cent of urban girls were in union, compared to 45 per cent of those in rural areas. In South Africa, a country with a low overall prevalence of union for this age cohort (3 per cent), a large discrepancy between the proportion of girls in urban areas living in union (1 per cent) compared to their rural counterparts (5 per cent) is observed. No differences are observed in Kazakhstan and Turkmenistan, both of which have relatively low overall prevalence of girls living in union (8 per cent and 5 per cent, respectively). Only in Kenya are urban girls more likely to be in union than their rural counterparts (20 per cent versus 18 per cent, respectively).

Girls 15-19 years old in the poorest 20 per cent of households are more likely to be in union than those in the wealthiest 20 per cent. This trend is seen across countries and regions. In Peru, 24 per cent of the poorest 20 per cent are in union compared to only 1 per cent of the wealthiest 20 per cent. In the Philippines and Namibia, respectively, 22 per cent and 9 per cent of the girls from the lowest quintile are in union compared to 2 per cent and 1 per cent in the highest quintile, respectively. Within the sample of countries analysed, Chad is the only exception: 35 per cent of the poorest 20 per cent of girls were married, compared to 46 per cent of the wealthiest 20 per cent.

Educational Level

In 47 countries, as girls aged 15-19 achieve higher levels of education, they are less likely to be in union. Girls who had attended primary school were less likely to be in union than those who had not. In Zimbabwe, only 4 per cent of girls who had attended primary school were in union, compared to 40 per cent of those who had received no education. Similarly, in Haiti, 15 per cent of girls who attended primary school were in union compared to 43 per cent of their uneducated peers. Only in Indonesia and Viet Nam were girls who had been to primary school more likely to be in union than those who had not. In Niger, the country with the highest overall prevalence of child marriage (60 per cent), the proportion is significantly lower (8 per cent) for those who attended secondary school than those who attended only primary school (40 per cent). Only in the Central African Republic is the proportion of girls aged 15-19 who are in union the same for those who attended either primary or secondary school (34 per cent).

Similarly, Zimbabwe is the only country in which girls who attended secondary school are more likely to be in union than those who received only a primary education (16 per cent and 4 per cent, respectively). In all but three countries (Cameroon, Uganda and Yemen), the proportion of girls aged 15-19 who received higher education and are in union is very low or negligible.

Girls 15 -19 years of age with children were significantly more likely to be in union than girls with no children. In most countries, only a small proportion of girls aged 15 -19 who did not have children were in union, indicating that childbirth tends to occur early in a union. However, in Malawi and Niger, more than 40 per cent of girls aged 15-19 without children were already in union. In the majority of the countries analysed, almost all girls with more than two children were in union. A notable exception is South Africa, where this number is only 35 per cent. Knowledge of reproductive and sexual health

Prvention from HIV

In most countries, girls 15-19 years of age who know how to prevent HIV infection were less likely to be in union than those who did not. Interestingly, in the South Asian countries studied, girls aged 15-19 who know how to prevent HIV infection are more likely to be in union that those who do not, perhaps reflecting the targeting of programmes to unmarried or to married women, depending on the social norms of the particular country.

Due to the pressure to demonstrate fertility and bear children early in a marriage, it is unsurprising that in all but four African countries girls aged 15-19 who use modern contraception are less likely to be in union than those who have never used any form of contraception. In Mozambique, 46 per cent of girls aged 15 -19 who had never used contraception were in union, compared to 31 per cent of those who used modern contraceptive methods. Among all the countries studied, it is more common for this age group that girls who are using contraception are more likely to be in union. These results may be related to the prevalence and stigma of sex outside of marriage or union, the fact that women outside of union do not have access to information or supplies related to contraception, or the fact that the use of contraception is adopted after the early marriage and fertility.

Many women who are attempting to avoid pregnancy use methods other than modern contraception. In 28 countries, girls aged 15-19 who have used modern contraceptive methods are less likely than those who have used only traditional methods to be in union. For example, in Burkina Faso, 81 per cent of girls aged 15-19 who use traditional methods of birth control are in union compared to 28 per cent of those who use modern methods. This pattern may indicate that girls who are married are not able to access or use modern contraception. However, in 13 countries the opposite is true: In Colombia, for example, 18 per cent of girls aged 15 -19 using traditional methods were in union, compared to 39 per cent of those using modern contraception.

In all but six countries, girls in union are more frequently found in rural areas. They are more likely to come from the poorest 40 per cent of society than the wealthier 40 per cent (although not necessarily from the poorest 20 per cent of society in all cases). In 10 countries, however, girls from the wealthiest 20 per cent are more likely to be in union than those from the poorest 20 per cent.

A clear profile is not seen for the distribution of girls who are in union according to education received, perhaps due to differences in access and norms related to education across countries. Most girls who are in union are involved in monogamous relationships. Haiti has the greatest proportion of girls in polygynous unions with 40 per cent of girls in union having co-wives. In general, girls have one or two children, although in 12 countries the majority of girls in union have not yet had any children. More than 4 per cent of girls in union have three or four children in Bolivia (5 per cent), Madagascar (6 per cent) and Mozambique (6 per cent). In all countries analysed, more than 25 per cent of girls who are in union have partners who are 5-9 years older except for Burkina Faso where 65 per cent of girls who are in union have partners more than 15 years older. Additionally, more than 25 per cent of girls in union live with men 15 or more years their senior in Guinea, Mali, Mozambique and Nigeria. A good deal of variation is seen in the gap in education between partners for girls who are married.

In the countries analysed (with the exception of Bangladesh, Comoros, Indonesia and Mozambique), more than 50 per cent of girls aged 15-19 currently in union know how to protect themselves from HIV/AIDS. In most countries, more than 25 per cent of girls aged 15-19 who are in union have never used any form of contraception. Exceptions to this trend are Brazil, Colombia, Gabon and Nicaragua. In Mozambique, 96 per cent of girls in union have never used contraception of any kind. Most notable for programmatic purposes are those countries where a significant portion of girls in union are using folkloric or traditional methods of contraception. For instance, in Bolivia, almost as many girls in union are using only traditional contraception (27 per cent) as are using modern contraceptive methods (25 per cent).

Propation of Women in Polygynous Union

Polygynous unions - relationships in which a man who has more than one wife - remain a practice in many countries, particularly (though not exclusively) in Africa. Polygyny is most frequently observed in Burkina Faso, where 55 per cent of women are in polygynous unions, and less commonly seen in Madagascar (3 per cent) and Nepal (4 per cent).

As the national proportion of women in polygynous unions increases, the proportion of girls married by ages 15 and 18, compared to those who enter union after age 20, tends to move toward parity. In some countries with lower levels of polygynous unions, such as Ethiopia, women are less likely to have entered into such unions before the age of 15 than after their 20th birthday; in other countries, such as Rwanda, they are more likely to have entered into such unions before their 15th birthday than they are once they have reached age 20. In Rwanda, 28 per cent of girls who entered into union by age 15 were in polygynous unions, compared to 13 per cent of women who entered into union after age 20.

In countries with a higher prevalence of polygyny, similar proportions of women had entered into union before the age of 15 or after the age of 20. In Benin, for example, 53 per cent of women who had entered into union by age 15 were in polygynous unions compared to 50 per cent of women who entered into union after the age of 20. A similar trend was observed for girls entering into polygynous unions before the age of 18. In Ethiopia, 13 per cent of women who entered into union by age 18 were in polygynous unions while 16 per cent of women who entered into union after the age of 20 were in such unions; in Rwanda the proportions were 17 per cent and 13 per cent, respectively.

In Burkina Faso the difference in the proportion of women entering polygynous unions before age 15 and after age 20 is reduced: 58 per cent of women who enter into union before the age of 15 are in polygynous unions, compared to 60 per cent of women who enter into union after the age of 20.

Polygynous unions are more common in rural areas than in urban areas in all countries examined, with the exception of Uganda (36 per cent of women in urban areas are in polygynous unions, compared to 32 per cent of women in rural areas). Polygynous unions are more common among women from the poorest 20 per cent of society than among women from the richest 20 per cent of society in all but four countries. Lack of education is another common factor observed across the countries. Women who had received no education were more likely to be in polygynous unions than women who had received a primary education, and in most countries women who received only a primary education were more likely to be in polygynous unions than those who received a secondary education - with the exceptions of Comoros and Uganda.

In Kenya, the proportions were equal: 3 per cent of women who received primary or secondary education were in polygynous unions. In countries with low overall prevalence (such as Nepal), large age gaps between spouses in polygynous unions are more likely than for those in monogamous marriages. In Nepal, 3 per cent of women whose partners are 0-4 years older are found in polygynous unions compared to 9 per cent of women whose partners are 10-14 years older and 20 per cent of women whose partners are 15 or more years older. However, in Guinea, where 53 per cent of women are in polygynous unions, there is less disparity in polygyny rates related to spousal age gap: 40 per cent of women whose partners are 0-4 years older are found in polygynous unions, compared to 47 per cent of women whose partners are 10-14 years older and 67 per cent where the age gap is greater than 15 years.

The greatest proportion of women in polygynous relationships are those in unions where both partners have received no education. A gap in education between partners does not appear to increase the proportion of women in polygynous unions. Women who do not know how to prevent HIV infection are more likely to be in polygynous unions than those who do. In countries with lower rates of polygyny, women who do not know how to prevent HIV are likely to be disproportionately represented in polygynous unions. For example, in Madagascar, 8 per cent of women who do not know how to protect themselves against HIV are in polygynous unions, compared to 2 per cent of those who possess such knowledge. But in countries with higher rates of polygyny, the disparity is lessened:

In Burkina Faso 54 per cent of women who know how to protect themselves and 53 per cent of women who don't are in polygynous unions. Nepal, Nigeria and Uganda are exceptions to the general trend. Women who use folkloric or traditional contraceptive methods are more likely to be in polygynous unions than those who use modern contraceptive methods. For example, in Burkina Faso, 77 per cent of women who use only folkloric methods are in polygynous unions compared to 37 per cent of women who use modern contraception.

Propotion of Girls in Polygynous Union

The preceding analysis considered all women in a given society with respect to the proportion who are in a polygynous union. This section focuses on the situation of girls 15-19 years old who are in polygynous union. The trends in polygyny for girls will be compared to those observed for all women in a country to determine generational trends that may affect the practice of polygyny. In Madagascar and Namibia, a greater proportion of girls aged 15-19 are in polygynous unions compared to the overall proportion of women, indicating that the practice might be increasingly commonplace in those countries.

In all other countries, fewer girls aged 15-19 than all women aged 15-49 are in polygynous unions - perhaps due to a decreased prevalence of polygyny or to the fact that the young age of the cohort implies that either the girls are less likely to be in a union of any kind or that a union that may become polygynous in time has not yet assumed that characteristic. When examining the proportion of women in polygynous unions across age groups, polygyny was observed as an almost exclusively rural phenomenon. For girls aged 15 -19, this trend continued in the majority of countries studied. However, in 10 countries, girls in urban areas were more likely than their rural counterparts to be in polygynous unions, possibly indicating that women from urban areas who enter into polygynous unions do so at an early age.

In the majority of countries, girls from the poorest 20 per cent of the population are more likely to be found in polygynous unions than those from the wealthiest 20 per cent. However, the opposite was found in 11 countries. The proportion of girls in polygynous unions tends to decrease as girls' level of education increases. For example, in Madagascar, 6 per cent of girls with no education were in polygynous unions, compared to 4 per cent of girls with primary education and 2 per cent of girls with secondary education.

The trend holds in countries with higher overall proportions of girls in polygynous unions: In Guinea, 31 per cent of girls with no education were in polygynous unions, while only 29 per cent of those who received primary education and no girls who received secondary education were in such unions. Compared to the proportions of all women in polygynous unions according to educational attainment, however, it is interesting to note that in six countries, girls who received primary education are more likely to be in polygynous unions than girls who received no education.

The greater the difference in age between a girl and her partner, the greater the likelihood that she will be in a polygynous union. For example, in Zimbabwe, 4 per cent of girls whose partners are 0-4 years older, 8 per cent of those with partners 5-9 years older, 15 per cent whose partners are 10-14 years older and 57 per cent of those whose partners are more than 15 years older are in polygynous unions. When examining the education gap between girls and their spouses, it is seen that the polygynous unions most commonly emerge from situations where neither partner has received any education. While in many cases, girls in polygynous unions are more likely to have less education than their partners, (for example, in the Central African Republic), in others, such as Chad, the opposite is seen.

Child Marriage and Violence

According to available literature, women who married younger are more likely to be beaten or threatened, and more likely to believe that a husband might sometimes be justified in beating his wife. Bruce, Lloyd and Leonard report that 40 to 80 per cent of all physical abuse experienced by women is perpetrated by a close family member, usually the husband. Data were available for analysis of the respondents' experiences of violence for nine countries, and for the analysis of attitudes towards domestic violence in five countries. The following analysis considers women of all age groups. Domestic violence is more common among women who had been married as children.

India has the highest levels of domestic violence among women married by 18 with a rate of 67 per cent, compared to

45 per cent of women who had not experienced violence. The trend of increased violence as correlated to child marriage is reinforced when considering the relationship between child marriage and believing that, under specific circumstances, a man may be justified to beat his wife.

Decisison - Making Ability

The ability to make decisions about visiting family and friends is considered indicative of a woman's freedom of movement. In seven of the eight countries where the question was included, women whose partners have the final say over visits were more likely to have experienced child marriage than those who had the final say themselves or where the decision was made jointly. Cambodia was the exception to this finding: 17 per cent of Cambodian women whose partners have the final say over visits to family and friends were married before the age of 18, while 27 per cent and 32 per cent, respectively, of women who made their own decisions or where the decision was made jointly, were girls at the time of their union.

Strategic importance is placed on a woman's participation in making decisions related to her own health. In six of the seven countries where the question was included, women whose partners have the final say over their health were more likely to have experienced child marriage than those who had the final say themselves, or where the decision was made jointly. However, in Turkmenistan, no difference was observed between these two groups of women. Women whose partners made the final decision on large household purchases were more likely to be married as children than those who made the decision themselves in Colombia (34 per cent compared to 25 per cent), Peru (37 per cent compared to 24 per cent) and Zambia (57 per cent compared to 49 per cent). Similarly, in Colombia, Haiti, Kenya and Peru, women whose partners made final decisions on daily purchases and what food should be cooked each day were more likely to have experienced child marriage than women who had the final say.

Surveys in Cambodia and Haiti included the decisionmaking question related to work and contraception. In both countries, women whose partners had the final say on whether or not they were allowed to work were more likely to be married before age 18 (32 per cent and 28 per cent, respectively) than those who had the final say themselves (28 per cent and 25 per cent, respectively). However, in Haiti those respondents who made this decision jointly with their partner were more likely to be married before age 18 than either those who made the decision themselves, or whose partners made the decision for them (32 per cent).

Haitian women who had the final say on contraception were slightly more likely to have been married before age 18 (31 per cent) than those whose partners had the final say (27 per cent). Cambodian women who made decisions on contraception jointly with their partners were more likely to have been married as girls (32 per cent) than either those who decided alone (27 per cent) or whose partners decided (30 per cent). Here again, it is important to note that decisions on contraception are taken a number of years after the early marriage and, in many cases, after a number of children are already born.

Multivariate Analysis

The descriptive analysis provides a picture of child marriage, it does not provide an analysis of the net effects of the variables examined on a girl's risk of being married as a child. To assess the statistical significance across 50 countries, a multivariate analysis, using a logistic regression model, was performed for each country. Ever-married women over age 18 were selected for analysis. The resulting coefficients provide the direction and magnitude of the change in the likelihood that a woman was married before age 18 with a one-unit change in the variable in question. The multivariate analysis confirmed the significance of many of the findings of the descriptive analysis.

As was established, a woman's education level was found to be a highly significant variable for whether she was married as a child.

In 48 countries, women who received some education were significantly less likely to be married as children than those who received no education, indicating the importance of educating girls as a means to prevent child marriage. High levels of fertility are associated with the prevalence of child marriage. Women who had more children were significantly more likely to have been married before age 18 than women with no children. The spousal age gap was found to be highly significant in 44 of the countries examined: women who were more than four years younger than their partners were significantly more likely to be married as children compared to women who were closer in age to their partners, a finding that points to the need to further explore the demand side of the child marriage equation. Also, confirming the findings of the descriptive analysis, in 23 of the 34 countries in which polygyny is practised, women in polygynous unions were significantly more likely to have been married as girls.

In 25 countries women whose spouses received some education were less likely to be married before the age of 18 than women whose partners were uneducated, while in Haiti and Kenya the opposite was observed. However, while the descriptive analysis indicated that women from rural and/or poor families were more likely to be married as children, in over 30 countries the net effects of both household wealth and place of residence were not significant. The differences between the descriptive and multivariate analyses might be explained by the significance of additional factors, such as a woman's education level or the number of children she has had.

Knowledge of HIV-prevention methods was significant in 17 countries; however, the direction of the effect was mixed: In nine countries women who knew how to prevent HIV were more likely to have been married as children, while in eight countries the opposite was true. Mixed results were also observed when considering contraceptive use: In 14 countries, women who had used contraceptive methods, either traditional or modern, were significantly less likely to have been married before age 18 than those who had never used contraception; the opposite was true in seven countries. Interestingly, in India, mixed effects were observed, with women who had used modern contraceptives being more likely, and women who had used traditional methods being less likely, to have been married as girls than those who had never used contraceptive methods.

Age cohort was found to be a highly significant variable in determining the risk that a woman was married as a child. However, the direction of the coefficient was not consistent with a hopeful hypothesis that child marriage is becoming less common among younger women, and confirmed the descriptive analyses of many countries in which child marriage did not decrease for younger generations. In all 50 countries, women from the older cohorts were less likely to have been married as children than women from the youngest cohort. However, the direction of the coefficient reversed when the number of children variable was removed from the model - indicating that age and number of children are closely related variables with respect to their predictive value in the context of child marriage. The findings confirm that younger women tend to have greater risks of early marriage, an effect that becomes visible once fertility level is included in the analysis as a control variable.

Religion and ethnicity were also found to be significant in some of the countries for which data were available. In 13 and 16 of these countries, respectively, being a member of the majority religious or ethnic group made a woman less likely to have been married before age 18 than a woman from a minority religious or ethnic background, although in nine and six countries, respectively, the opposite was true. In four countries, the significance of being a member of a religious or ethnic minority had different effects for different minority groups. For example, in Mozambique, Emakua girls are more likely than Cisena girls to be married before age 18, while Xitsonga and Xitswa girls are less so. For those countries in which race or ethnicity is found to be significant, the targeting of child marriage prevention efforts might be refined to focus on girls from communities most at risk of marrying their girls as children, be they majority or minority groups.

The experience of physical domestic violence was found to be a significant variable when added to the model. Confirming the descriptive analysis, women who have experienced domestic violence were more likely to have been married before age 18 than women who have not experienced domestic violence. Similarly, in three of the six countries (Cambodia, India and Kenya), women who believe that there may be some circumstances in which it is acceptable for a man to beat his wife were significantly more likely to have been married before age 18 than those who believe that there is never justification. In the other three countries, this relationship is not significant.

A woman's participation in decision-making was found to be insignificant, with the exception of India, where women in households in which decisions were often made by other family members were more likely to have been married as girls than those who make household decisions. The logistic analysis of each country provides information that can be useful in determining the most effective and efficient interventions to decrease the prevalence of child marriage. For example, in the descriptive analysis, it was observed that 25 per cent of women aged 20-24 in Cambodia were married before age 18, and that as a woman's level of education increased, she was less likely to have been married as a child.

However, the multivariate analysis revealed that education was only a significant protective variable at the secondary level with respect to its net effects. This indicates that primary education alone may be insufficient to protect girls from child marriage in that country once other variables, such as the number of children a woman has and the age gap between partners, are also considered. In Guatemala, the multivariate analysis found that women who had used modern contraception were 28 times more likely to have been married as children than those who had never used contraception, indicating that contraceptive methods might be more accessible to those who are in union than those who are not.

6

Sexual Exploitation of Children

Commercial sexual exploitation of children is "a fundamental violation of children's rights". It comprises sexual abuse by the adult and remuneration in cash or kind to the child or a third person or persons. The child is treated as a sexual object and as a commercial object. The commercial sexual exploitation of children constitutes a form of coercion and violence against children, and amounts to forced labour and a contemporary form of slavery. ""Sexual exploitation takes three primary forms prostitution, child pornography, and trafficking for sexual purposes. Other forms include child sex tourism and early marriage.

Nobody really knows how many children are victims of commercial sexual exploitation, but a British Columbia report on prostitution and sexual exploitation of youth states "provincial and municipal governments are becoming increasingly alarmed at the current high levels of sexual exploitation of children and youth. "The organization End Child Prostitution, Child Pornography and Trafficking of Children (ECPAT) International confirms this, stating, "The child sex trade is growing in Canada and especially in cities like Toronto, Vancouver, and Montreal. A report by the Canadian Council on social development claims that 'Canada has become a world trade destination for people seeking children through the sex trade. ' The increase in child prostitution is connected to the rising number of homeless Canadian children who live on the streets.

There are a number of predisposing factors related to society, families, and individuals that contribute to children being recruited into the sex trade. Some of the predisposing societal factors are:

— The feminization of poverty and gender inequality.

— High youth unemployment.

— Racism and discrimination aimed at aboriginal youth.

— Economic or social marginalization.

— Consumerism.

— Organized crime networks.

— Computer use and related technological advances. Some of the predisposing family factors are:Intergenerational mental illness; domestic violence; drug and alcohol abuse; sexual, emotional, and physical abuse.

— Attachment disorders.

— Poor parenting.

— Inadequate supervision, affection, and attention.

— Single-parent family status. Some of the predisposing individual factors are:

— Early life traumas caused by emotional, sexual, or physical abuse, or by neglect and deprivation. Homelessness as a result of running away.

— Learning disabilities and neurological disorders such as fetal alcohol effects. Lack of schooling.

— Being gay, lesbian, bisexual, or transgendered.

When children run away from home and end up living on the streets they often become involved in the sex trade to survive. Most children who run away from home have no money or resources and are therefore vulnerable to victimization and exploitation. Yates and colleagues reported youth involved in the sex trade were five times more likely to identify themselves as GLBT (Gay, Lesbian, Bisexual, or Transgendered). The abuse suffered by many GLBT youth at home and school frequently causes them to feel isolated and alienated, which in turn leads to running away behaviors. Children involved in the sex trade experience a high incidence of violence, usually perpetrated against them by johns and pimps. There are significant risks to the physical and mental health of sexually exploited children, including depression, eating disorders, post-traumatic stress, anxiety disorders, dissociation, homicide, and suicide.

There is also a high incidence of substance abuse among exploited children. Exploited children commonly acquire STDs such as HIV, hepatitis B or C, syphilis, chlamydia, and gonorrhea. Approximately 50% to 80% of the child sex trade in BC is carried on in massage parlors, karaoke bars, and "trick pads"; only 20% to 50% of the trade is visible aboveground with children being openly solicited on the streets. In smaller BC communities, the sexual exploitation of children is even less visible. It occurs in private homes, back alleys, and parks, at public docks and truck stops, and on fishing boats. Pimp-related recruitment of children into the sex trade is frequent. District subcultures have emerged in the urban areas of Burnaby, Surrey, and Vancouver.

Aboriginal, Vietnamese, and Sikh girls are extensively trafficked on well-used circuits. Two such circuits are Vancouver/Calgary/Edmonton/ Seattle/Hawaii, and Vancouver/ Las Vegas/Hong Kong/Japan. Aboriginal children and youth Intergenerational social issues have contributed to high numbers of First Nations children being sexually exploited. The residential school policy of the past created a toxic environment where all forms of abuse were common. Children subjected to these dehumanizing institutions frequently passed on the abuse and negative parenting of their own experience to future generations, thus perpetuating the problems. In Canada, aboriginal youth make up 3% to 5% of the general population. In certain areas of BC, aboriginal youth make up the majority of children working in the sex trade.

Estimates of the number of aboriginal sexually exploited youth in BC range from 14% to 60%, depending on the community consulted. Some aboriginal youth are attracted to cities as an escape from severe family dysfunction. However, the reality of living in a city isolated from loved ones and prey to culture shock, poverty, high unemployment, homelessness, substance abuse, and racism leaves many open to sexual exploitation. Recruitment Recruitment into the sex trade is well organized. Common pick-up places are food fairs in malls, fast-food restaurants, bus stops, train stations, community recreational centres, youth containment centres, youth shelters, youth detox centres, schools, and group homes. A typical recruitment scenario involves an older girl befriending a younger girl in school.

Unpopular girls with low self-esteem are usually targeted. The older girl seduces the younger with friendship, gifts, clothes, and compliments. The targeted child is then introduced to a pimp, who continues the seduction. Through parties and offers of "free" cigarettes, drugs, and alcohol, he usually gets her hooked on drugs. In the beginning, she feels connected and important, excited by and attracted to a lifestyle of easy money and unlimit- ed supplies of nicotine, drugs, and alcohol. She feels a sense of belonging within the street culture. The child is then asked to "help, " perhaps by being a "spotter"- keeping track of the licence plate numbers of the johns or counting the tricks other girls are turning. Once the child is truly hooked, she will be asked to repay the monies invested in her recruitment by selling herself for sex.

Later, as children get trapped in their addictions and become dependent on their drug suppliers (usually their pimps), they live from day to day in constant fear of violence.

To bury the pain inherent in their lives, they can sink into a living hell. In a study of 60 sex trade workers in Vancouver's Downtown Eastside, 75% had experienced violence in the preceding 6 months. Leaving the sex trade is rarely an option. Children being commercially sexually exploited soon lose hope in a future for themselves. Once involved in the sex trade, children are kept isolated from their loved ones by their pimps and by their own sense of internalized shame. Such children can also be shunned by government and community programs because they are seen as a "bad influence" on other kids. Child pornography The new world of technology- digital cameras, camcorders, highspeed Internet access, computers with vast stores of memory-allows pedophiles unfettered access to millions of child porn images.

Graphics software gives users the opportunity to "morph" an almost infinite number of child porn pictures. In Canada, morphed child porn images are not illegal, whereas in the United Kingdom they are. In cyberspace there are also some partially hidden systems almost totally dedicated to child porn. These are called "ISQ" and "MIRC. " They are relatively easy to access from the Internet if you know about them. The most obvious use of child porn is as an aid to sexual arousal and gratification through masturbation. It is also used to make deviant sexual behaviors seem normal and to help seduce children by lowering their inhibitions or by blackmailing them.

There appears to be a clear linkage between child pornography and child sexual abuse. Pedophiles also have private clubs on the Internet. One such was the Wonderland Club. Membership was restricted to persons who paid US$100 a month after submitting 10 000 new child porn images to the club's library of child porn. Paid-up members then had full access to the club's computer library, which contained more than 1 million child porn images. Chat rooms for children have become places where pedophiles masquerading as children lure youth into meeting with them. And if a child has a camera attached to his or her computer, a pedophile can switch the camera on remotely without the child knowing. The pedophile can then see Preventing child sexual exploitation Amultidisciplinary approach is needed to tackle this complex societal problem.

A further prevention strategy could involve teaching children about healthy sexuality. All children and youth, regardless of their sexual orientation, need to grow up in a society where they are loved and respected for who they are, and where the healthy expression of their sexuality is celebrated. From a secondary prevention perspective, we need to educate parents, teachers, and health care providers about identifying warning signs when a child is being lured into the sex trade. Such warning signs include; Having unexplained money, new and expensive clothes, or drug-use objects. Having unexplained business cards and receipts. Going out with a change of clothes.

Health care professionals also need to recognize signs of sexual addiction within our society. We need to develop resources to treat sex addicts, similar to the resources we have to treat alcohol and drug addicts. Researchers estimate that sexual addiction affects 8% of males and 3% of females in our society. Many children are sexually exploited by sex addicts. One researcher suggests that girls who have been sexually abused when young can develop a victim-based identity tied primarily to their sexuality. Their "victim identity" conditions them to subordinate roles later on. Programs designed to improve the selfesteem of victimized women are important in preventing sexual exploitation. However, once substance abuse has become established, then secondary and tertiary prevention programs become necessary, with a need for drug and alcohol awareness programs and youth-orientated detox centres.

Child Prostitution

Child prostitution, like other forms of child sexual abuse, is not only a cause of death and high morbidity in millions of children, but also a gross violation of their rights and dignity. Both boys and girls can be prostituted and, according to the report, some of the children are as young as 10 years old. Most of these children are exploited by local men, although some are also prostituted by pedophiles and foreign tourists. In their report, the investigators estimate the number of children exploited by prostitution is highest in India with estimates between 400, 000 and 575, 000; Brazil is second with estimates between 100, 000 and 500, 000; the US is third with 300, 000 children; and in fourth place is Thailand and China with 200, 000 children each.

With regard to illnesses, worldwide, millions of children are infected with sexually transmitted diseases, have abortions, attempt suicide and are raped each year. In parts of southeast Asia, 50% to 90% of children rescued from brothels are infected with HIV. A coordinated international campaign is needed to prevent child prostitution, provide services to children who are prostituted until they can be removed from prostitution, and implement effective recovery and reintegration programs. For such a campaign to be successful, it will require global coordination, implementation at national, regional and community levels, and the leadership of many health professionals.

South East Asia, particularly Thailand and the Philippines, is the key to any discussion of the commercial sexual exploitation of children because it was the situation in this area in the past two decades that raised public awareness of the commercial sexual exploitation of children and mobilised public opinion against 'child sex tourists'. The discourse derived from these two countries has set the parameters and tone of the debate. The issues debated with respect to Thailand and the Philippines have become key to the global discussion of child prostitution to the extent that it is impossible to talk about commercial sexual exploitation without reference to them. Thailand and the Philippines have provided much of the mythology and iconography of the commercial sexual exploitation of children so that it is important to look at these two countries in detail in order to understand the origins and the boundaries of the issue.

The role of non-governmental organisations (NGOs), in particular End Child Prostitution in Asian Tourism (ECPAT), in raising awareness cannot be underestimated. It is they who first brought the issue to public attention, set the agenda and have continued to dominate the debate. Although the countries for which they mainly campaign are Thailand and the Philippines, they are also concerned with Sri Lanka, Taiwan and Korea. Their work is widely disseminated through both the Western media and national English language press. These NGOs also publish articles widely in the popular press and ECPAT is responsible for two influential books, The Child and the Tourist and The Rape of the Innocent, popular paperbacks designed to appeal to a non-specialist audience. Drawing on ECPAT's success, other groups now campaign against child prostitution but ECPAT remains a central information source. It is rare to find an article on child sexual exploitation in a Western newspaper that does not make reference to ECPAT.

A typical example would be a case study of a very young girl forced or tricked into a brothel where she is obliged to service 20 customers a night for very low remuneration. In the story she will be rescued by a welfare agency and sent back to her village, only to discover that she has contracted HIV and will shortly die. It will be stated or implied that it is demand from Western men that causes her to become a prostitute. Aspects of degradation and abuse are repeatedly emphasised, as is the youth of the girl. The language used is often emotive. In the current campaigning literature, both within South East Asia and in the West, the image of child commercial sexual exploitation is of small children being sought out and exploited by Western tourists.

Much press coverage now is concerned with finding and punishing these men. Yet around the slums of the port of

Klong Toey in Bangkok, men who cannot not afford a 'real' (meaning fully grown) woman will find a young girl a reasonable substitute because she is cheaper and easier to control. While this is an aspect of child prostitution that many campaigning groups in Asia would prefer to ignore, it is likely that the majority of young prostitutes are not found in the bars of Bangkok or Manila but in the brothels in the rural areas or the back streets of cities. In many local brothels in Thailand and the Philippines, younger women are said to be prized for their innocence and freshness, while girls even younger are prized for their cheapness. Even among the better-off Thai men, there is a marked preference for younger girls.

A 1994 survey conducted among students, office workers, and residents of a slum area, to assess the impact of HIV on children found that the most desirable age for prostitutes is under 18: 'Many males felt that child prostitutes between 15 and 18 were more desirable than adults, but that it was wrong to sleep with younger ones (under 14)'. In other parts of South East Asia, although the discourse is not as influential on the world stage, the issue is also often constructed on the basis of the idea of the foreign male exploiter. There is less information on Vietnam, Cambodia and China but these three countries share the language of 'social evil', which is behaviour or ideas that are contrary to and damaging for national culture. Child prostitution, like AIDS, is described as a problem imported from other cultures, not always the West, or considered in terms of trafficking so that Vietnamese girls, for example, are forced across the border to Cambodia or China without any acknowledgement of indigenous prostitution.

China however, adds another component to the picture. Chinese girls are said to be the victims of traffickers, especially young girls from the Yunan region but Chinese men, rather than foreigners, are often blamed for the problem. It is also repeatedly claimed that Chinese men will pay to have penetrative sex with a virgin because this is believed to be a cure for AIDS. This is a common assertion in the literature worldwide, even though there is no ethnographic evidence to prove it. In Vietnam and Cambodia in particular, anti-Chinese feeling leads to the repetition of this notion. In addition to the accounts of NGOs and journalists, a relatively small amount of information is produced by anthropologists and sociologists who have worked on limited research projects.

The resulting articles and books are concerned with the cultural background, particularly religion and societal norms that can be predisposing factors in encouraging or discouraging children to become prostitutes. In this respect a major issue is the apparent religious sanction given to prostitution by Buddhist values, which stress models of duty and sacrifice for children especially for girls. One argument is that by supporting her family through prostitution a girl gains merit rather than bringing shame on herself and her family, a justification that is frequently manipulated in some areas of the literature. However, these texts are usually published in the academic Western press, with a relatively small circulation among other academics.

One problem in the NGO literature is that the academic literature seems to be largely ignored or unknown. In addition, within the mainstream, campaigning literature, certain categories become blurred. Thus it is a feature of the reporting that:

— child prostitutes are often by implication only girls;

— pre-pubertal and post-pubertal children are often included in the numbers given for child prostitutes along with young women over the age of 18 years;

— numbers given for Western tourist clients are confused with numbers of Western tourists as a whole, with no account given of local clients;

— within the undifferentiated category of child prostitute, the origins of child prostitutes are hidden, obscuring aspects of origin, such as ethnic or socio-economic factors.

A second major geographical focus is South Asia -- India, Nepal, Sri Lanka and, to a lesser extent, Bangladesh and Pakistan. This has three components, the girl child, religious prostitution and trafficking for sexual purposes. The idea of the girl child arose largely through Indian attempts to assign a special space in social philosophy and policy to girls. 1990 was named The Year of the Girl Child by the South Asian Association for Regional Cooperation (SAARC) and the UNICEF India Office. Two main themes of the year were prevention of child marriages and rehabilitation of child prostitutes. One Indian woman's comment on the material published in the Year of the Girl Child shows the reproductive nature of the information purveyed in the resulting 'spurt of publications':

> Many of the papers are clones of earlier ones. The self perpetuations occur through citations being made circular, until a body of knowledge is assumed to have been created. The sum and substance of much of this writing concern the low status of the girl, her limited opportunities for education and the gender bias in the home. The television screen has also sensitized people to the plight of the girl child as a drudge.

This was not the intention of 'girl child' campaigners such as Sheela Barse, who makes it clear that she is opposed to the 'feminist method of carving out the female persons' group out of the human race and examining it in isolation, on the presumption that females are always wronged'. Barse states that it is more important to establish that girlhood cannot be the entire province either of womanhood in the women's rights movement, or of childhood in the children's rights movement.

Nevertheless, the notion of the 'girl child' has been reified, as if there is something essential about all female children regardless of wealth or ethnicity, something that makes them more vulnerable than boys in general. This focuses on vulnerability to sexual violation, early marriage, unplanned teenage pregnancy and is a new manifestation of the old control over women's sexuality and fertility. It masquerades as concern for their vulnerability but actually implies that females cannot control their own sexuality, which should consequently be under male control. This is reflected in three approaches to development aid programming for girls

Education and Child Survival

The emphasis on the employment of girls as prostitutes, which is a minor exploiter of girls compared to agriculture, domestic service and manufacture; The immense silence about the specificity of certain kinds of exploitation that are exclusive to boys. In India and in Nepal the 'girl child' discourse focuses on religious prostitution (of which devadasi is the best known form) and trafficking in children, while in Bangladesh, the rape of pre-pubertal girls hired as domestic servants is an important theme. In Pakistan, Baluchistan and the North West Frontier provinces of India, much of the literature on the girl child is legal. A further concern is the fate of the daughters of prostitutes who on account of social opprobrium are said to be forced into prostitution.

Religious prostitution is practised in various parts of India and Nepal. Devadasi cults are found in Southern India and also practised in other parts of the country such as Uttar Pradesh and Orissa. They derive customary sanction from oppressive upper-caste temple traditions. Pre-pubertal girls, aged between five and nine years, from poor, low-caste homes, are dedicated by an initiation rite to the deity in the local temple during full moon.

After a girl is married to the deity by the tali rite, she is branded with a hot iron on both shoulders and her breast. She is then employed by the temple priest. Sometimes, even before menarche, she is auctioned for her virginity; the deflowering ceremony known as udilumbuvadu becomes the privilege of the highest bidder. The market value of a girl falls after she attains puberty, when she is said to have no recourse other than prostitution.

In Nepal, particularly the western parts, religious prostitution known as badini and jhuma is also practised. Although little is known about these practices, they do not seem to vary significantly from devadasi. However, the main sexual exploitation issue in Nepal is the traffic with India, the open border between the two countries making it difficult to monitor. It is also stated that, because of corruption, official assistance is given to the sale and the trafficking of young girl. In most accounts Bombay is given as the main destination. The international trade routes most frequently mentioned are from Nepal and Bangladesh to India, and from India and Pakistan to the Middle-Eastern countries.

In sharp contrast to the emphasis on the 'girl child' in the rest of South Asia, in Sri Lanka the discourse revolves around boys and sex tourism. ECPAT and other advocacy organisations have influenced the discourse here, claiming that male western paedophiles are targeting Sri Lanka because of the availability of boys. For instance, it is argued that, despite the civil war, the number of tourists who visited Sri Lanka increased from 102, 000 in 1989 to 169, 000 in 1996, although of course this does not necessarily mean that all tourists are male, let alone sex tourists. According to the literature, the South West coast, Negombo and Hikkawuda are the main destination points.

They are close to the beach and some hotels assist paedophiles in procuring boys mostly aged between six and 15 years, although most boy prostitutes in Sri Lanka appear tend to work independently of either brothels or pimps. Although there is evidence of sex tourism in Sri Lanka, the picture is not clear because of the tendency to reproduce information. One case in point is the frequent reference to the role of Spartacus guides, which provide male homosexual tourists with up to date information about the availability of sexual contacts in most countries, and were notorious in the 1980s, particularly with respect to both Sri Lanka and the Philippines, for giving locations where boy prostitutes could be encountered.

Despite the fact that the magazine no longer explicitly refers to children, and the then publisher of Spartacus has died, the magazine's role in the sex tourism business is constantly reiterated in popular literature on the commercial sexual exploitation of Sri Lankan boys as if no changes had occurred. A third major geographical region with a characteristic discourse that influences global debates might be designated the Anglophone West and consists the United States, Canada, Australia and Western Europe. From the late nineteenth to early twentieth century there was considerable public concern about the 'White Slave Trade'. Many aspects of this earlier discourse are clearly visible in current debates.

Nevertheless, modern concern about what is always referred to in the academic literature as 'juvenile' rather than 'child' prostitution resurfaced in the late 1960s alongside the issue of runaway children. Journalists were quick to use labels like baby-pros or, with respect to pornography, 'kiddie porn'. Then, the concern was for children who joined the 'hippie' culture of America's big cities, in particular San Francisco and New York. Britain and Canada, where many of the same social problems as America were reported, but a few years later, experienced similar concerns in the early to mid 1970s. The earliest indications of a juvenile prostitution 'problem' can be found in the mass media, but academics were also involved from the very beginning.

In addition, since the late 1960s there have been a number of moral panics about child abuse in North America and Western Europe. Thus interest in juvenile prostitution has come in waves, eclipsed at times, by concerns about 'battered children' or more recently 'satanic' or 'ritual' abuse. Thus, there have been few long term studies of juvenile prostitutes, but rather a flurry of papers and articles at times when interest in the issue is high. Currently, concern is focused on young male prostitutes, because they are seen as vectors for the spread of HIV and research into their lives is conducted along bio-medical models that are concerned with certain areas of behaviour and particular attitudes.

Both academics and journalists have remained interested in the issue of delinquency and deviancy psychology, which it is assumed many young prostitutes share but, again, this is linked to bio-medical models with particular perspectives and limited range. Western journalists have a major role in disseminating information about the commercial sexual exploitation of children. Articles on young male prostitutes, often referred to as 'rent boys' in the English language press, as well as young female prostitutes, remain an occasional feature of many newspapers and women's magazines and are presented as campaigning or investigative journalism, while revealing prurient details designed to shock and sensationalise. Popular books written on the issue of child prostitution and pornography are mostly written by journalists with a stated mission to reveal the truth.

In the USA, the source of a good deal of the literature is part of the university sector that specialises in 'objective' non-judgmental studies of AIDS awareness and/or delinquent psychology. In the USA much emphasis is placed on the 'runaway' phenomenon, first noted in the 1960s and now closely tied to the prostitution discourse. The current prostitution problem continues to be seen as having its roots in the alternative culture movements of the late 1960s, with a special emphasis on the hippie communities in San Francisco. It is claimed that many children ran way to join these communes but, on leaving them, found themselves unable to make any money other than through prostitution.

In Canada, the emphasis has been on AIDS prevention and protecting children for their own good and that of society. It is notable that the Canadian literature concentrates on Canadians of European descent. Native Canadians are seldom mentioned, despite the fact that they tend to show higher-than-average rates of what are regarded as predisposing factors such as coming from broken homes with a history of drug or alcohol use, or having been placed in state institutional care. Yet in the rest of the literature, the multiple problems that lead children into prostitution are emphasised.

In the United Kingdom, the stress is on boy prostitutes. 'Rent boys' have become a staple of the British media and even the more serious academic studies, have tended to concentrate more on boys than on girls, despite the smaller numbers of boy prostitutes. The West Midland Police, which covers Birmingham where there is a major red light district, commissioned a report on young male prostitutes and came up with a report based on a sample group of less than 20. While the police have concentrated on boy prostitutes, the advocacy groups discuss young children of both sexes, highlighting the problems they experience when they leave institutional care and the lack of support they are given.

A further contributory factor stressed in Western literature is the role of broken homes. Many of the juveniles surveyed have suffered sexual and physical abuse within the family and many are runaways from abusive situations. In Britain, the emphasis is placed more on children who have been in state institutional care rather than those from abusive families, yet the literature remains framed within the discourse on dysfunctional families. Throughout almost all the books and articles on the subject in the West, runs the theme that these children are outside society, and that reasons have to be found for their deviancy. Their life histories are presented in terms of theories of deviancy. There is a notable absence of views of the children themselves or, when literature does include their opinions, this is often countered by an authorial voice giving reasons why they are wrong.

The particular emphasis on boy prostitutes is related to a concern with the mental health of sexually exploited children in general. In the case of boys, there is considerable discussion about whether these boys are homosexual or 'really' heterosexuals whose commercial sexual activities are focused on financial gain. One concern frequently expressed is that heterosexual boys with homosexual clients may become gay by being prostitutes, resulting in a good deal of discussion about exactly what boys will let there partners do to them and whether they take an 'active' or 'passive' role in sexual activities. A parallel debate is entirely absent in the literature on female prostitution. Nor is there any information about young men who have female clients. The only similar discussion in literature on female prostitution is whether or not girl prostitutes can become good mothers. The underlying implication is that, whether they are boys or girls, juvenile prostitutes will not have learned appropriate gender roles.

Literature on the poor psychological health of young sex workers also seems to take for granted they suffer from low self-esteem, suicidal tendencies and the inability to form relationships, generally without exploring scientifically the causal relationships involved. The assumption is that low self-esteem results from prostitution, rather than that some juveniles become prostitutes because their self-esteem is low. One dissenting voice can be heard in the published words of a woman sex worker. Many texts stress degrading aspects of child prostitution, including being forced into being prostitutes, raped by pimps, terrorised by gang members and becoming dependent on drugs.

There is constant reference to the apparently inevitable links between prostitution and heroin use. Yet there is little information about the long-term effects in adulthood because there is no systematic research on the results of prostitution in childhood, simply the impression from reiterated assumptions that juvenile prostitutes end up either dead or living worthless and useless lives. Some accounts of the lives of boy prostitutes suggest that the average length of time as a prostitute is between two and seven years but longitudinal studies seem not to be carried out.

A further concern for those writing about young girl prostitutes is the part played by males who live off their earnings, with far more attention paid to this than to the role of female adult exploiters. Pimps are almost always portrayed as vicious and evil psychopaths, and the fact that many girls speak fondly of their 'protectors' is explained as codependency. Even though not all prostitutes work for pimps and some men living with prostitutes are part time prostitutes themselves, the overwhelming impression given of pimps is that they are older, manipulative men. The assumption that all girl prostitutes must be controlled in this way is, of course, a reflection of overall societal assumptions about the vulnerability of women and the need to police their sexuality.

These three discourses, from South East and South Asia and the West represent the majority of studies on the commercial sexual exploitation of children. In each case the discourse on children and prostitution is constructed within structures of ideas about society, childhood, gender and sexuality. In South East Asia the literature on children and prostitution tends to dominate current discussion of childhood. There is no developed literature on children and the social phenomenon of childhood, but a long tradition of constructing gender and sexuality on the basis of an image of passive, childlike women as well as defining cultural norms in opposition to external or foreign evils.

The current debates about female children in South Asia, subsumed in the incorrect, essentialist notion of the 'girl child' have been providing a trenchant feminist critique of the unequal status of women in society. This stresses the more vulnerable aspects of female sexuality and thus not only emphasises the oppressive aspects of tradition, through concentrating on the image of girl children as temple prostitutes, but also pivots on the notion of women and girls as objects, as in trafficking. Western discourses on the commercial sexual exploitation of children, on the other hand, are more individualistic and thus concentrate on the deviant behaviour and mental health of individual cases, as well as a concern with the causal relationship between deviant, abusive families and prostitution, showing overall societal concerns only in with respect to the proper assimilation of gender roles.

The literature on child sexual exploitation in Africa and in Latin America is far less developed and cohesive. In both areas, the literature on childhood has different emphases. In so far as they exist at all, child studies in Africa, focus on child health and construct the idea of children as victims, without any particular focus on commercial sexual exploitation of children. Indeed, it is often claimed that this term cannot be applied in most African contexts because the distinction between sexual abuse, sexual exploitation and commercial sexual exploitation can not be clearly drawn, not only in analytical terms within studies, but also within cultural understandings.

Africa's diversity makes the definition of childhood in itself a research issue. The African social science community, includes very few specialists on children's issues outside traditional concerns with health, education and psychology. The main themes in academic research on children in Africa carried out by Western researchers have traditionally been socialisation and initiation or puberty rites. African social science researchers with an interest in child studies now tend to focus on the broad area of child abuse, although, as will be argued below the definition has a particularly African texture.

A further major interest in all circles, in research largely dominated by Western researchers, is HIV/AIDS. In the African context this concerns children rather more than it does in other regions of the world, partly because the pattern of infection has long been recognised to be heterosexual, thus affecting children through vertical transmission; partly because of the existence of a relatively large number of 'AIDS orphans', principally in East Africa. A number of mostly Western psychologists have also been studying children affected by armed conflict, concentrating on aspects of traumatisation and victimisation

The considerable upheavals due to wars, conflicts, natural and man-made disasters, together with mounting impoverishment among African populations, increasingly affect African children. Yet very few socio economic studies of these effects have taken place. Research on children appears to be fragmented and there are few outlets for publication of research on children's issues. Two recent annotated bibliographies of studies of African children and childhood provide no references to published work on sexual abuse, much less on commercial sexual exploitation of children.

The sexual exploitation of children is part of an overall emphasis on children as victims, fitting within the concerns of a relatively-well developed discourse on child abuse and neglect. This latter is largely the outcome of the activities of ANPPCAN, the African member of the International Society for the Prevention of Child Abuse and Neglect. Child abuse is Child labour, Children in prison, Handicapped children, Battering of children, Children under psychological stress, Abandoned children, Children in war situations.

Sexual abuse and/or exploitation are mentioned under child labour, prisons, psychological stress and abandonment in this list. The problems this presents for arriving at even an operational definition for sexual exploitation are clear. This is possibly why, in another ANPPCAN publication, a study of child agricultural labourers (male) and prostitutes (female) makes it clear that by 'prostitute' is meant any unmarried girl who has sexual intercourse. The field of sexual abuse in Africa cannot be separated from the literature of largely-Northern, feminist campaigners against female excision and infibulation. This is likewise implicated in the anthropological literature on initiation.

The study of child sexual exploitation in Africa cannot be separated conceptually from constructions of sexuality and sexual morality. It is notable that the literature shows a particularly marked distinction not only between the behaviours expected of boys and girls, but also the expressed attitudes towards sexual morality of both groups. A further focus of study in this area is the migration nexus, together with the contrasts drawn between rural morality and town morality, and between generations. This is also situated within the overall massive population movements within the continent in the face of natural disaster, war and impoverishment.

Although there is a considerable body of literature on children in Latin America it is dominated by the discourse on so called 'street children'. It is worth noting that the Latin American model of street children has tended to dominate work in this area in all developing countries, largely because the ideas have been disseminated by Western aid agencies. Children who live on the street often engage in sexual relationships, with each other and in the course of prostitution, which may be occasional or virtually full time for both boys and girls. Thus the literature on the commercial sexual exploitation of children often seems to be merged with that on street children. The street children discourse in Brazil and Colombia in particular is characterised by ambivalence.

Street children are worthy of pity if young, and feared if older adolescents. In either case they are often stigmatised and the literature, frequently dominated by writers from outside the region, is often lurid and lacking in any kind of academic rigour. The HIV/AIDS complex has largely overwhelmed the literature on sexuality since the late 1980s, together with a specific interest in street girls in Brazil, due partly to the influence of two charismatic female project directors. The literature on this issue is on the one hand largely tied to project publicity and on the other to medical discourses. More recently, psychologists in several Latin American countries have shown an interest in studying child sexual abuse, which now constitutes a proper field of study and is resulting in some interesting publications.

Prostitution itself is enmeshed in a series of ideas about men and women. These include the idea that men's sexual appetites are uncontrollable and have to be satisfied by women who enjoy sex rather than by 'good women' (mothers, daughters, wives) who do not enjoy sex. This is related to ideas of honour and family. A man's honour is tied up in the chastity or purity of the females in his family, wives, sisters and daughters. In its most macho form, masculinity entails protecting the honour of the women in your own family while proving your virility by manifestations of virility. This means that female prostitutes perform an important role with respect to families. Both journalism and research tend to reproduce the same historical accounts that justify the existence of prostitution as a necessary social evil that protects the purity of mothers, daughters and wives and thus ensures the continuing existence of the family.

However, it should be noted that this role is exclusive to female prostitutes, many of whom, according to most accounts, begin this work around the age of 15 years. As the majority of street children are boys, the prostitution in which they are engaged belongs within an entirely different complex of social ideas, which does not seem to have been researched in depth. The overwhelming majority of studies of children and prostitution in Latin America is concerned with female children. There are two resounding absences within the literature on the commercial sexual exploitation of children on the world scene Eastern Europe and Arab/Islamic countries. However these absences occur for different reasons. Such literature as does exist in Islamic societies is dominated by legal considerations, which is to a certain extent replacing a culture of denial.

Whereas in the past the tendency was to comment that child abuse and exploitation is forbidden by the Koran and therefore does not take place, there now seems to be evidence of considerable reflection on children's issues in general and exploitation and abuse in particular. This remains within religious paradigms, but is adding considerably to understanding of the attitudes of Islam to both children and sexuality. In so far as any link might be said to exist between the literature on child sexual exploitation in Arab countries and Eastern Europe and the former Soviet Union is the dominance of lurid journalism on the topic of trafficking in girls and women. There is an established link in sex trafficking between Arabs and South Asian countries such as India and Bangladesh. One estimate suggests that 200, 000 girls from Bangladesh were taken against their will to work in Arab brothels.

With the sudden economic and social changes of 1989 families in all the former socialist countries of Eastern Europe and the former Soviet Union have been faced with the collapse of welfare systems and the burden of child support has largely shifted to families, many of which are undergoing severe hardship. Children have been particularly badly affected and accounts by journalists suggest that there has been a sharp increase in child sex exploitation. The evidence is extremely patchy and usually sensational, telling for example of the longest in the world situated between Berlin and Prague called the 'Highway of Cheap Love' managed by the 'Chechen Boys, where 'kids are sold like a kilo of bread'.

Nature of Evidence

The single most important factor uniting the literature on the commercial sexual exploitation of children is the way in which information is managed. In general terms, the available global discourse on this theme is characterised by a poor understanding and use of quantitative information, lack of attention to research techniques, the reproduction of myths and unsubstantiated facts, as well as the use of assumptions and campaigning imperatives in place of established bodies of theory. If, as is frequently stated, children indeed deserve the best we (adults) have to give, they are not receiving their just deserts in a field in which they are particularly vulnerable. Or, as has been said with respect to the discourse on street children and its effects, it is not acceptable that international organisations, policy makers, social institutions and individuals who feel entitled to intervene in the lives of children with problems, do so on the basis of obviously unclear and arbitrary knowledge about the reality of these children's lives.

They are based on sound reasoning, the role they should play is that of baseline hypotheses, to be proved or disproved so that the true scale of a problem can be understood and children protected using programmes grounded in a real understanding of their situation. In the case of child sexual exploitation, however, guestimates have become fact, partly because they have become inscribed in rhetorical discourses aimed to raise awareness. The objective appears to be to heighten public and policy interest in the issue by stressing the scale of the problem. Yet this is neither ethically acceptable nor logical.

In the first place, as stated as far back as 1983 by the United Nations Special Rapporteur on the Suppression of the Traffic in Persons and the Exploitation of the Prostitution of Others, 'The important point is not the scale of the problem but its degree of seriousness as a violation of the fundamental rights of the human person'. In the second place, the normal practice within the literature of providing a raw number, such as 'There are 1 million sexually abused children in Asia', does not actually provide an idea of scale. To do this would require some knowledge of source, time, relative location and proportion. A correct statement of scale would be something like 'According to estimates made by A on the basis of B type of calculation, in 1996 there are 1 million sexually abused children in Asia.

This is C% more than the calculation made on the same basis in 1994, D% more than estimated by the same method in Africa in the same year, and represents E% of the total population of Asian children in this age group. ' Scale can only be understood in these terms. Moreover it is a poor excuse for adult society to claim that, after nearly two decades and with information technology that can provide minute details of weather, money markets and economic cycles for every country in the world, to claim that guestimates are the only data available. Some relevant data do exist and more could be collected.

The current situation on the quantification of the commercial sexual exploitation of children is characterised not only by widely differing figures but also by very different definitions. Data on children are frequently hidden within and confused with data on adults. One problem is caused by the different age groupings used. In many studies the juvenile population is defined as under 21, rather than 18, years. Combined with the vague bases for guestimation, this makes it difficult to judge the scale of commercial sexual exploitation of children even within a single national context. In the case of the USA, for example, one study provides an extraordinarily broad estimate of between 100, 000 and 300, 000 of young prostitutes on the basis of a sample of people aged 14 to 34, with a mean age of 22 years.

The Sexual Exploitation of Children in Developing Countries (1989), which claims that there are one million sexually exploited children in Asia, although other texts take this to mean one million prostitutes. It is normal for the highest figures to be given. They are always 'increasing', usually at an 'alarming' rate, reaching 'epidemic' proportions. Yet no reason is given for this except for the 'fact' that customers are turning to ever younger prostitutes because they believe them to be AIDS free. There is no evidence either way for this claim, but it has been endlessly repeated until it has become a 'fact'. This reproduction of inauthentic or innacurate information is a characteristic of the literature on the commercial sexual exploitation of children.

Even before the AIDS pandemic, the literature on child prostitution from all parts of the world repeated, without evidence, that child prostitutes were sought after because they were believed to be free of sexually transmitted diseases (STDs), including the apparently worldwide belief that penetrative sex with a virgin is a cure. Other commonly repeated myths include female customers injecting boys' penises in order to produce or maintain erections. Many of these myths are employed in order to demonise the clients of child prostitutes, as if the violation of children's rights involved were not sufficient condemnation. At other times myths are used as distancing devices as part of the construction of the client as outside the society in question, a foreigner, or a tourist.

Sex Tourism

Just as ECPAT dominates the overall discourse, so the single idea of sex tourism, with which ECPAT is associated, captures media and other attention. ECPAT began as a sub division of ECTWT apparently perceiving child prostitution as an inevitable consequence of tourism. One of the leading anti-tourism campaigners once wrote "too much tourism is the rape of culture, the environment, women and children". The success of the campaigns now apparent in the growing interest in sex tourism in other parts of the world, but is particularly acute in Asia, where it often takes on an expressly anti-Japanese tone. ECPAT's original statement of intent makes this clear.

Although the language of women's rights and children's rights is sometimes used, child prostitutes are seen as a symptom of the wider problem of foreign influence, as in the use of the term 'social evils' in countries such as Vietnam. Although legislation to combat social evils came into force in Vietnam in February 1996, even the Ministry of Social Affairs, which is responsible for implementation, does not have an official definition of the term, which is used as a blanket phrase to mean all that is contrary and harmful to Vietnamese culture, yet associated with gambling, theft and prostitution, none of which are exclusive to non-Vietnamese. As in other 'sex tourism' countries, this mechanism parallels the distancing mechanism in the West that places the emphasis on 'stranger danger', so that sexual abuse within the family is played down in favour of fear of child rape by unknown, asocial men.

If people do think of the possibility of sexual assaults on children they see them as a risk from casual encounters in the street. The belief in the natural relationship between parent and child is the basis for the firm conviction that if danger threatens any child, it can only come from 'outside' the family. When the damage inflicted is sexual, the offending person must be an unknown, a shadowy and frightening stranger, not anyone with whom one has daily contact, let alone someone who is part of the familiar circle of family and friends. Newspapers report the rarer and more dramatic cases of children who disappear and in doing so reinforce the general idea that strangers carry a risk to children involving acts of the greatest perversion, serious damage and even death.

Languages

One factor in the reproduction of inadequate information in the literature of commercial sexual exploitation of children is the style of language used. Language is the means by which ideas are reproduced. Language is never neutral. If a structure of ideas is repetitive, so the words and phrases that it gives rise to will bear the same repetitive characteristics. Literature on the commercial sexual exploitation of children is characterised by assertiveness. Uncertain verb forms such as the conditional or the subjunctive mood are seldom used. Thus writers seldom say that something 'might be the case' or 'it is reported that... '., preferring to present their case in the positive indicative, 'is', 'was, 'were'. Thus sentences often begin 'There is evidence... ', or 'It is claimed.. ' or 'It has been found... ' although the nature and source of such evidence, findings and claims are not presented.

A further immediacy is given to texts by the use of what is called 'the ethnographic present' which is the device of writing about past events in the present tense. A pastiche might be 'Caroline stands outside the nightclub waiting for a client. She is shivering with the cold and hopes that the next man will not be violent like the man who blacked her eye yesterday. She is twelve years old, but she has the eyes of a much older woman. ' This often obscures the fact that the case study was gathered long ago by someone else and that

Caroline, if she ever existed, for it is common for writers to invent a composite or typical person, probably is a much older woman by the time the reader encounters her in the text. Further linguistic devices are implicated in the repetitions and confusions of quantitative data.

Journalists tend to take even greater liberties with language, stressing the emotive aspect of the juvenile's situation and appealing to the readers' sense of outrage. The tone of journalists' coverage of sexual exploitation is often deliberately subjective and emotional. Repetitive use of shocking detail are justified in the public interest. Journalistic scoops are also important. There have been many children 'bought' for a night by journalists in various parts of the world to demonstrate the ease with which children can be bought or sold. Background details may be given but little analysis is presented. There is usually an emphasis in journalists' information on the personal circumstances of each child, without recourse to any wider sociological information.

Information Technologies

New information technologies, such as the Internet, enable pimps and predators to recruit victims or advertise the victims to sex offenders. Children are stalked by perpetrators in chat rooms. Once the perpetrator establishes contact and trust, the perpetrator arranges to meet the child and sexually abuse them, and sometimes, later sell them to other perpetrators. In one case, a girl from Georgia was lured to Greece by a man she met online. There are indications that he planned to use her in the production of child pornography. New information technologies are already used in many aspects of the sexual exploitation and prostitution of children.

Production of Pornography

Girls and boy are trafficked for use in the making of pornography. Over the past few years, several large international child pornography operations have been broken up. The largest, initiated by the U. S. Postal Inspection Service, has resulted in 4, 500 searches and dozens of arrests internationally. The market for child pornography in the U. S. causes the trafficking of children in other parts of the world. For example, Russia has inadequate laws controlling the production and distribution of child pornography. Consequently, Russia has become a premier site for abusing and exploiting children in the making of pornography. There is evidence that orphans and homeless children are abused and exploited and children are trafficked from the rural regions to the larger cities for the making of child pornography.

Operational Definitions

Although it is often claimed that measuring the commercial sexual exploitation is impossible, we would argue that this is an effect of the lack of conceptualisation in the discourse as a whole. Up to this point in time, the main purpose of information gathering on this topic has been advocacy and awareness raising. In view of the fact that 133 nations were represented at the Congress Against the Commercial Sexual Exploitation of Children, each making a declaration that acknowledged the existece of a problem in their country, it can be argued that the advocates have met with considerable success. Now is the moment for a new, more accurate form of data collection, that will provide information of sufficient accuracy to develop programmes of prevention, protection, elimination and rehabilitation.

But perspectives on children and childhood are the very basis of culture, because children are always in the process of developing into adults, which means they call into question, by their very existence, what it is to be a human being in terms of any social group. This also reflects on other fundamental aspects of social life, such as sexuality. Thus the exploration of cultural meanings must be the basis of any research, advocacy or monitoring of the commercial sexual exploitation of children. The abuse, exploitation or commercial use of children's sexuality is a fundamental of their dignity as human beings. The Convention on the Rights of the Child refers to dignity seven times and it has been claimed that it is 'a concept that permeates the document'.

Nevertheless, it is not defined. A former Special Rapporteur to the United Nations on Sale and Traffic points out that 'in the first article of the Universal Declaration of Human Rights, the word 'dignity' comes before 'rights'. This means that human dignity is the foundation and justification of all the rights defined later in the Declaration'. With respect to pornography he suggests that images published should 'take account of all aspects of the fundamental principle of respect for human dignity and which safeguards in particular the dignity of women and the innocence of children'. This raises the question of whether the dignity of children might perhaps be different from that of adults, and rest in their innocence.

Most anthropological writings agree that cultural notions of honour and shame both critically influence, and are informed by, the constructions of sexuality and sexual morality. They often act as the fundamental axis of evaluation. Moreover, such notions are conceptually inseparable from understanding child sex exploitation. Whatever the extent of its significance in each culture, the honour/shame nexus regulates both inter-sex and intra-sex relations and is tied to power. Honour/shame, purity/innocence are mediating concepts by which people and situations are to be judged; and they also provide the terms of reference for determining the acceptable levels of behaviour in other aspects of society. Clearly, traditional beliefs influence notions of honour, shame and purity in most cultures. Further, there is an important correlation between purity and aspects of physical development, such as puberty. This furthers an understanding of puberty in epistemological terms.

There is nothing specifically sexual about the concept of 'purity' and yet it is consistently used to refer to sexuality and is inextricably linked with the concept of chastity. To be pure, especially when talking about either women or children, often means to be sexually untouched but it has further connotations also in that it also means sexually ignorant and passive. Both women and children are supposed to be sexually pure but it takes different forms for both of them and often has very contradictory meanings. Where morality is derived from Christian tradition, the emphasis on purity is very strong and in these contexts, to be a 'good' woman means being a chaste or pure one. The emphasis on virginity for women is strong as are the generally negative connotations of sexuality.

In Thailand, the same division is apparent. Pure women are mothers, impure women are prostitutes. A mother is not supposed to enjoy sex, or to initiate it or to experiment. Men go to prostitutes because they are expected to be the exact opposite of this, sex with them is for enjoyment, not reproduction. Pure women, in these instances, are women who have sexual knowledge that is kept tightly within the socially sanctioned bonds of marriage. They are not sexually untouched but they are sexually restrained and remain sexually ignorant of any man other than their husbands.

However, there are contrary currents to this as well in that while women are urged to be sexually faithful, they are often mistrusted and viewed as highly sexual beings whose purity or honour must be kept by their men folk. Their sexuality is so strong and uncontrollable that it has to be constantly watched and guarded, first by fathers and brothers and then by husbands. This also links into the view that women cannot be trusted sexually and that their power is so irresistible that men must be protected form it. Whether or not this takes the form of certain types of Islamic society, whereby a woman must remain covered so she is not a threat to men and does not tempt them, or even in certain situations in the West, where a woman is said to 'lead a man on' because of what she wears, women are seen as highly sexualized, dangerous beings who use their sexuality, knowingly or not, for male destruction.

In many ways, the sexuality of girls is viewed with the same ambivalence as that of women. On the one hand, girls are expected to be innocent and virginal, having no experience or knowledge of sex yet they are also thought to be sexually knowing. In the West, girl children of around puberty are treated with considerable ambivalence. Some are presented as still children, innocent and therefore to be kept ignorant and there is often tremendous fuss over issues such as teaching 12 year olds about sex education. However, there is also the view of girls as natural seductresses - the Lolitas or sexy school girls who know exactly how to entrap and seduce older men. The current 'super models' capture this uncertainty well, they are getting younger and younger and more and more child like yet they are also presented as sexual.

There is still considerable opposition to Freud's notion that children are naturally sexual and that civilisation represses them but it is fairly clear, even to those who dislike Freud and consider many of his propositions seriously flawed, that children are capable of sexual feelings and that sexual purity in children in the sense that it is something they know nothing about, is a myth. Again, this leads on to further debates about the nature of sexuality and the arguments about what children understand about their sexual feelings and whether they label them as sexual but the notion of the sexual child is still one many people are very unhappy with. There is considerable emphasis in this society on stopping children displaying any sexual behaviour in public; girls are sanctioned for sitting improperly so that they may display their underwear and both boys and girls are told off if they touch their genitals publicly.

Another link between women and girl's sexuality is that of passivity. Both are considered to be passive, waiting for a man to 'discover', develop and deflower them. It is still expected that girls will be taught about sex by an older man. Purity in this case is strongly linked to being passive and waiting. The only instance in which as woman can be active is if she is fighting to preserve her purity. Under Islamic law, for example, a woman who kills while trying to prevent herself being raped is treated leniently while if she is raped the penalties on her are harsh and she is punished for impurity.

The biggest difference however between the sexual purity expected of women and girls however, is the emphasis on sexual ignorance as opposed to sexual restriction. Girls are supposed to be ignorant of sex, untouched and virginal. The distinction between adults and children is their supposed lack of sexual knowledge and it is this that gives them their innocence. Innocence for children also means ignorance and knowledge of their bodies or its functions is considered bad. Whether or not this is the same as purity is debatable. There has undoubtedly been a onflation of purity, innocence and virginity but this is problematic.

Despite attempts to separate any discussions of women's and children's sexuality, the history of both has meant that they have consistently been placed in the same category. As women have become sexually liberated, children have taken the place of women as the innocent in need of protection. It is hard to generalise about purity and innocence because of the huge cross cultural variations and the need for detailed studies of individual societies' purification beliefs.

Children yet it is rarely discussed or defined. It is taken as a given of childhood in the same way as a term like innocence is and is so fundamental, especially to Western societies, that it is rarely questioned. Children's purity and their innocence are directly tied to their ignorance and powerlessness and all are seen as essential components of childhood. It is an area where there is little research or debate yet from the point of view of measuring and monitoring the sexual exploitation of children it is important to arrive at acceptable definitions.

7

Orphaned Children

HIV/AIDS is having a devastating impact on the world's youngest and most vulnerable citizens. More than 20 million people around the world have died from this disease. An estimated 40 million are living with HIV today, including almost 3 million children under age 15. One of the most telling and troubling consequences of the epidemic's growing reach is the number of children it has orphaned or seriously impacted. Today more than 13 million children currently under age 15 have lost one or both parents to AIDS, most of them in sub-Saharan Africa. By 2010, this number is expected to jump to more than 25 million.

HIV/AIDS deprives children of the right to live in a family environment, which is crucial for the development of a positive self-identity and self-esteem. The disease increases the likelihood that children will be institutionalized, live on the street or be subjected to child labour. The death of caregivers, coupled with the stigma attached to HIV/AIDS, can put children at risk of discrimination, further isolating them from others at a time when they are most vulnerable and need as much care and support as possible.

Children orphaned and made vulnerable by HIV/AIDS are often exposed to violence, abuse and exploitation. There are also false assumptions applied to this group, including that they are themselves infected. When caregivers become sick or die, a child's right to an education is often jeopardized as they are pulled out of the classroom and into the adult role of caring and providing for their families. Families are affected long before a parent dies, since from the time adults first fall ill they may not be able to work.

A study in eastern Zimbabwe concluded that there were significant losses of income and capital associated with terminal illness. Further pressure is exerted on these often meagre incomes by increased health-care costs and, eventually, by funeral costs. In the same study, these amounted to around half of the average per capita income. Because of these financial pressures, many children whose families are affected by HIV/AIDS, especially girls, are forced to drop out of school in order to work or care for their families, and they face an increased risk of engaging in hazardous labour and of being otherwise exploited.

Children working to support their families do so at the expense not only of their education but also of rest, play and recreation. They lose out on the opportunity to participate in their community, religion, cultural activities and sports. The loss of these rights means that, in effect, many children orphaned or made vulnerable by HIV/AIDS miss out on their childhood.

In sub-Saharan Africa, most children who have lost one or both parents have been cared for within the extended family, an intricate and resilient system that has traditionally been quick to respond and still takes responsibility for around 90 per cent of orphans in the region. But the tidal wave of loss that the HIV/AIDS pandemic has occasioned has severely stretched this safety net, particularly in the most-affected countries: Botswana, Lesotho, Swaziland and Zimbabwe. Households that have taken in orphans - whether these children are relatives or not - are likely to become poorer as a result because the household income will have to sustain more dependents.

In Uganda, households with orphans had 77 per cent of the per capita income of those without. Despite the undeniable stress placed on the extended family network, it is important to emphasize that retaining some sort of family life is extremely important for children who have lost one or both parents to HIV/AIDS. If preserving the family is the best option for orphaned children, then the family's capacity to care for and protect these children must urgently be strengthened. Women take on the greater burden of care When HIV/AIDS affects a family, women - particularly elderly women, as well as girls and young women - take on by far the greater burden of care. The strain is beginning to show. Two thirds of caregivers in households surveyed in a recent study in South Africa were female, with almost a quarter of them over the age of 60. Female-headed households generally assume more of the care for orphans than those headed by males, often compounding their own poverty.

Too often children or adolescents are forced to assume the burden of caring for sick parents or for their younger siblings. The proportion of households officially headed by children is still small - less than 1 per cent in most countries - but this vastly underestimates the scale of the problem. Though a household in which the lone parent is sick may still formally be headed by that parent, in practice the burden of care and responsibility may have already passed to the children. Similarly, even where children have been taken in by grandparents or other relatives, they may be required to work in order to help sustain the family.

In many cases, assuming this burden of care results in children dropping out of school. Forgoing their education does not just limit the chances that they will be able to create a better future for themselves and their families, it also means they will not receive important, often life-saving information on how to avoid HIV infection or access treatment for HIV/AIDS.

The loss of a parent pervades every aspect of a child's life: their emotional well-being, physical security, mental development and overall health. Food consumption in an AIDS-affected household can drop by as much as 40 per cent, leaving children at higher risk of malnutrition and stunting. In Cambodia, a recent joint study by the Khmer HIV/AIDS NGO Alliance and Family Health International found that about one in five children in AIDS-affected families had been forced to start working in the previous six months to support their family. One in three had to provide care for family members and take on major household tasks. Others were forced to drop out of school, or were sent away from home. These experiences exposed children to high levels of stigma and psychosocial stress, with girls found to be more vulnerable than boys.

Protective Environment

With the death of a parent, children lose part of their safety net. Without the protection of the family environment, they risk missing out on school, engaging in child labour or suffering abuse, violence, exploitation, stigmatization and discrimination. Assessments by the International Labour Organization have found that orphaned children are much more likely than nonorphans to be working in commercial agriculture, as street vendors, in domestic service and commercial sex. Of those children working as prostitutes in Zambia, 47 per cent were found to be double orphans, while a further 24 per cent were single orphans. Around 38 per cent of the children working in the mines in the United Republic of Tanzania - whose ages ranged between 7 and 17 years old - were orphans.

In Ethiopia, more than three quarters of the child domestic labourers interviewed in Addis Ababa were orphaned, 80 per cent of them had no right to leave their jobs and many worked more than 11 hours a day, 7 days a week, with no opportunity to play, watch television or listen to the radio. More than half of the orphans in sub- Saharan Africa, Asia and Latin America and the Caribbean are adolescents. Children in this age group are more vulnerable to HIV infection, not least because psychosocial and economic distress can lead to risky sexual behaviour and substance abuse. As a result, they need comprehensive sexual health education and services to reduce the risk of infection, as well as relationships with caring adults through schools and faith-based or community organizations.

For all of these children, the psychosocial impact can be as grave as the physical. Even in societies where HIV/AIDS is commonplace, children in households affected by the disease or who are living with HIV/AIDS themselves may still be stigmatized. They may end up being mistreated or disregarded by their foster household, or may have to endure separation from their siblings as well as the loss of their parents.

The issues surrounding children orphaned or made vulnerable by HIV/AIDS have been highlighted at two Special Sessions of the UN General Assembly: one on HIV/AIDS in June 2001 and the other on Children in May 2002. The United Nations and its partner organizations have endorsed a framework of action to provide guidance to donor nations and the governments of affected countries on how to respond to the urgent needs of children affected by HIV/AIDS. Specific goals to be achieved by 2005 include developing national strategies to deal with orphans and other vulnerable children, ensuring non-discrimination, mobilizing resources, and building international cooperation. Clearly the highest priority of all is to limit the spread of HIV/AIDS and therefore reduce the number of children being deprived of their parents.

Despite the grim advance of the disease worldwide, there are significant national successes in turning back the tide of the pandemic that can serve as models. Forthright national leadership, widespread public awareness and intensive prevention efforts, for instance, have made Uganda the preeminent example of sustained achievement, while comprehensive action in Thailand averted some 5 million HIV infections during the 1990s. Keeping adults alive is critical. To this end, the World Health Organization, UNAIDS, UNICEF and other partners are supporting the '3 by 5 Initiative', which aims to ensure that 3 million people have access to antiretroviral treatment by the end of 2005.

Antiretrovirals are also key to programmes to prevent mother-to-child transmission of HIV/AIDS (PMTCT): Providing antiretroviral prophylaxis to pregnant women and to babies at birth can reduce the risk of transmission by half. UNICEF is currently supporting such programmes in 70 countries, five of which now have national coverage — Belarus, Botswana, Georgia, Kyrgyzstan and Ukraine. Brazil has successfully implemented antiretroviral treatment for children and adolescents as an integral part of its national treatment policy. In addition, UNICEF is working with the Mailman School of Public Health at Columbia University, New York, and others to roll out 'PMTCT Plus', an initiative to not only prevent infection in newborns but also treat mothers and families living with HIV.

Any reduction in HIV prevalence can take as much as a decade to translate into lower AIDS-related death rates among parents because of the long time lag between infection and death. Consequently, orphan numbers will continue to rise even in countries where inroads are being made against HIV infection. In Uganda, for instance, HIV prevalence peaked in the late 1980s at 14 per cent and by 2001 had shrunk to 5 per cent, yet the number of children orphaned by HIV/AIDS continued to rise until they accounted for 14. 6 per cent of all children in 2001.

This in mind, respecting the rights of children orphaned or made vulnerable by HIV/AIDS must remain an international priority for at least the next two decades. Recognizing the urgent need to address the growing number of children orphaned or made vulnerable by HIV/AIDS and meet the goals committed to by the international community, in March 2004 the UNAIDS committee of co-sponsoring organizations formulated a comprehensive strategy for action on the following five fronts:

— Strengthen the capacity of families to protect and care for children by prolonging the lives of parents and providing them with economic, psychosocial and other support.

— Mobilize and support community-based responses to provide both immediate and long-term support to vulnerable households.

— Ensure access for orphans and other vulnerable children to essential services, including education, health care and birth registration.

— Ensure that governments protect the most vulnerable children through improved policy and legislation and by channelling resources to communities.

— Raise awareness at all levels through advocacy and social mobilization to create a supportive environment for all children affected by HIV/AIDS.

The extended family is, and should remain, the key source of support for children orphaned by HIV/AIDS. When deprived of the opportunity to grow up in a supportive family environment, children receive less stimulation, individual attention and love and are ill prepared for life and healthy social interaction. Children who grow up outside families, whether living on the street or in institutions, often face discrimination and may feel unloved or excluded. In the worst cases, children who lose contact with their families can suffer physical or psychological abuse. Among the approaches that can be adopted to strengthen the ability of families and communities to care for orphaned children are:

— Fostering the economic well-being of households caring for orphans, for example by ensuring they are reached by social safety nets as well as poverty-reduction initiatives, including seed funding for small businesses and methods to improve farming efficiency.

— Offering children and their caregivers psychosocial counselling and support. Improving caregivers' childcare skills, especially in the area of early childhood development, and making communitybased childcare available.

— Helping parents prepare their own wills and identify future careers for their children. Enabling parents to live longer, better and in greater dignity.

— Enhancing young people's life skills, including knowledge of how to avoid HIV infection.

The United Nations Secretary-General's Task Force on Women, Girls and HIV/AIDS in Southern Africa recognized in its 2004 report the particular burden placed upon older female caregivers. It recommends that governments and their development partners provide social grants or other financial support to these women whenever possible. To this end, Swaziland submitted a proposal to the Global Fund to Fight AIDS, Tuberculosis and Malaria to provide stipends to women caring for orphans and vulnerable children. Additionally, securing assets and property rights for women and girls is key to addressing the economic hardship they face because of HIV/AIDS.

Community Responses

When extended families cannot take responsibility for orphaned children, the next option should ideally be the local community. Fostering and adoption are alternatives that allow a child to remain in a family setting, and the greatest continuity and security is provided if such options are available within the child's own village or district. Foster families, whether spontaneously formed or formally arranged, need and deserve to be supported in their role by the wider community as well as through government services. Community-based responses need to be mobilized and reinforced to ensure that the local community becomes a source of strength and support to orphaned children. Among the strategies that can help are:

— Sensitizing local leaders - including religious authorities, teachers and other prominent citizens - to the impact of HIV/AIDS on vulnerable children, mobilizing their support and encouraging them to counter the risks of abuse and exploitation.

— Fostering dialogue on HIV/AIDS within communities in order to dispel myths, combat ignorance and maximize the chances that people will respond to affected children's needs with compassion. Children and adolescents can play a key role, exploring opportunities for discussion and community education in schools, religious gatherings and youth clubs.

— Organizing cooperative support for affected households. This can involve home visits, community day-care programmes or childcare to give caregivers some respite. The support can also be material, for example, assisting vulnerable households through pooled funds.

— Ensuring that community responses are appropriate to children's ages and stages of development.

Orphans and other vulnerable children often have the least access to essential services, yet they are among those with the greatest need. Ensuring that they gain access to those services requires commitment and action at all levels, from the community right up to national governments. Among the key areas are:

— *Schooling*: Schools can offer children a safe environment, with built-in support, supervision and socialization. The best way to maximize the enrolment and attendance of orphans and other vulnerable children is to abolish school fees. In addition, removing the requirement to buy a uniform, introducing school-feeding programmes and ensuring access to life skills education to reduce the risks of HIV infection can also have a major impact.

— *Psychosocial support*: Losing a parent is a traumatic experience, and children need immediate support as they deal with the host of new difficulties and challenges. In the longer term, their new caregivers may also need such help.

— *Health services*: Children orphaned by HIV/AIDS are likely to be more vulnerable in terms of both health and nutrition. It is therefore paramount to ensure they have access to essential health services in early childhood such as immunization, vitamin A supplementation and growth monitoring. For adolescents, education and health services focused on HIV prevention and sexual and reproductive health are particularly vital. Treatment for HIV-positive youth is also an emerging necessity.

— *Safe water and sanitation*: Extended pipelines and new boreholes can help increase access to safe water. Those living with HIV/AIDS need clean water in order to avoid opportunistic infections such as skin diseases. Caregivers need to be informed about proper hygiene and food handling. Lack of access to safe water, especially in sub-Saharan Africa, means that women and girls have to spend long hours fetching it from wells that are often miles away, adding to their work burden and compromising their safety.

— *Justice systems*: Strong and independent legal systems, with judges who are educated about key child protection issues, are vital in protecting orphans and other vulnerable children from abuse, discrimination and property loss.

— *Birth registration*: All children need to be registered at birth to ensure that their rights are not denied, yet in sub-Saharan Africa in 2000, more than two in three births were not registered. Vulnerable children need official evidence of their identity to ensure they have access to public services and welfare.

Protection from Government

Children are cared for primarily within families, but overall responsibility for ensuring their protection and well-being also resides with the national government. Governments must ensure that their laws are in line with current international standards, and that they allocate the resources and take the initiatives required to maximize children's protection. They are responsible for ensuring that the justice system both protects children and understands their rights. They need to make a coherent link between emergency responses - such as providing swift and effective support to families - and longerterm development plans. People living with HIV/AIDS should be actively involved in developing and implementing policies. Among the main areas to be addressed are discrimination, foster care, inheritance rights, abuse and child labour.

Even after two decades of HIV/AIDS awareness, efforts to deal with the impact of the disease are still hampered by fear, ignorance and denial at all levels. Children orphaned or made vulnerable by the disease continue to pay a heavy price as a result, not only because the deaths of their parents might have been prevented in a more open and informed social climate, but also because of their own stigmatization and abuse. In countries where strong political leadership has fostered openness and wide-ranging responses to the HIV/AIDS pandemic, such as Brazil, Senegal, Thailand and Uganda, there has been notable progress and new impetus in the fight against the disease.

The greatest headway is made when young people are given all the information and encouragement they need to protect themselves and can participate in planning and implementing the programmes that support them. Resources for providing support to orphans and other children made vulnerable by HIV/AIDS have increased in recent years, not least through the establishment of the Global Fund to Fight AIDS, Tuberculosis and Malaria and the start up in 2004 of the

US President's Emergency Plan for AIDS Relief. Nonetheless, funding for programmes for orphans and vulnerable children remains far below the level required to adequately protect and support this group.

An enormous gap remains between what has been done and what still needs to be done to protect the rights and address the needs of orphans and vulnerable children. At the end of 2003, for example, only 17 countries with generalized HIV/AIDS epidemics reported having a national policy for orphans and vulnerable children to guide strategic decisionmaking and resource allocation. Closing the gap is possible, but it will require the combined efforts of all those able to respond - governments, donors, nongovernmental organizations, faith-based organizations, the private sector and the thousands of community groups already struggling on the front line of response.

HIV/AIDS is one of the greatest threats to childhood in the world today. But the lines of response to the plight of orphans and vulnerable children are clear - provided the international community has the political and economic will to pursue them:

— Strengthen the protective environment for children at every level, from the family right through to the level of national and international legislation.

— Dedicate the funds needed to support programmes for orphans and vulnerable children, which currently receive only a small proportion of overall HIV/AIDS funding.

— Scale up projects for orphans and vulnerable children.

— Keep adults alive by increasing access to antiretroviral therapy and raising awareness of HIV/AIDS. Prevent new infections among children by applying and scaling up proven techniques and interventions. Eliminate school fees and other barriers to education.

— Combat poverty and conflict, which interact with HIV/AIDS to magnify the negative impact on childhood. and in innovative ways, to ensuring that every child enjoys their right to a childhood.

The United Nations Convention on the Rights of the Child (UNCRC) was unanimously adopted by the General Assembly of the United Nations on 20 November 1989. The Convention has since been ratified by 191 member states of the United Nations and has entered into force as an international treaty. Only the United States and Somalia have not yet ratified it. This near- universal ratification establishes the UNCRC as the global standard for children's rights. The UNCRC covers the cultural, social, economic, and political rights of children and is guided in interpretation and implementation by four principles; non-discrimination; the best interest of the child; the maximum survival and development of the child; and consideration of children's opinions and views in matters that affect them. The rights defined in the Convention are indivisible and form a comprehensive framework for use in determining children's best interests.

The UNCRC defines children "as every human being below the age of 18 years unless, under the law applicable to the child, majority is obtained earlier." Unfortunately, most epidemiological data collection for HIV uses 14 as the cut-off age for children and labels all people above this age as adults. To avoid discriminating against any portion of the global population of children, all persons under the age of 18 should be counted and referred to as children. This means that until all-inclusive data on children becomes available, references and statistics that count children between the ages of 15 and 18 together with adults should be clearly identified as being inclusive of children.

New orphan estimates (maternal, paternal, and double orphans due to AIDS, in addition to orphans due to other causes) have been developed by UNAIDS, UNICEF, USAID, and the U.S. Bureau of the Census, in a joint effort that uses a shared methodology. These estimates are part of a new wave of statistical information about HIV/AIDS that promises to further clarify the main challenges facing the global partnership fighting the pandemic. They are based on new 2001 estimates on adult HIV prevalence and mortality prepared by the UNAIDS/World Health Organization Working Group on Global HIV/AIDS & STD Surveillance. They reflect a need for a single set of numbers to help plan and implement programs and, subsequently, measure progress on the global goals set at the 2001 U. N. General Assembly Special Session on HIV/AIDS.

These estimates consider all orphans, but differentiate between AIDS and other causes. All orphans have essential needs irrespective of parental death. But in order to plan at the national and regional levels, it is important to determine and track the changing magnitude of orphaning. HIV/AIDS is causing the most significant and worrisome changes. In the past, orphan estimates by United Nations agencies were cumulative. The major trends are briefly outlined below.

— Sub-Saharan Africa has the greatest proportion of children who are orphans. In 2001, 12% of sub-Saharan African children were orphans. This is almost double the proportion of orphans in Asia (6. 5%), and more than double that found in Latin America (5%). Much of this difference is attributable solely to HIV/AIDS. Because of AIDS, the number of orphans in sub-Saharan Africa is increasing dramatically, instead of declining. Orphans number more than 34 million in the region, with 11 million due to AIDS. By 2010, 5. 8% of all children in sub-Saharan Africa will be orphaned by AIDS. In 2010, it is estimated that orphans from all causes will number 42 million, of whom 20 million will have lost one or both parents due to AIDS. Total orphans from all causes are expected to decrease in Latin America and Asia by 2010, with those orphaned by AIDS accounting for an increasing percentage of the total.

— While the proportion of orphans due to AIDS in Asia is much less than in sub-Saharan Africa, the absolute number of orphans in Asia is much larger. In 2001, there were more than 65 million orphans in Asia-almost double Africa's 34 million. The percentage of children orphaned by AIDS was much lower at 2. 8%, or 1. 8 million (in comparison, Africa's 11 million orphans due to AIDS account for 32% of the total). This reflects the much larger populations in Asia, and lower HIV prevalence rates. The populations in many Asian countries are so large, however, that even at a low prevalence, the number of people with HIV/AIDS threatens to surpass the numbers in some of the most severely affected African countries. For example, even though India has an adult HIV prevalence of less than 1%, 3. 8 million adults are estimated to be living with HIV/AIDS. This places India second only to South Africa in absolute number of adult infections. HIV is spreading rapidly in India, and even a relatively small increase in HIV prevalence in India would cause a massive leap in total new orphans due to AIDS.

— HIV/AIDS is rapidly increasing the number of orphans who have lost both parents, particularly in sub-Saharan Africa. The death of one parent at a young age usually does not imply that the other parent will die soon. With AIDS, however, if one parent is infected with HIV, the probability that the spouse is HIV-positive is quite high. This means a child could lose both parents in a relatively short period of time. Without HIV/AIDS, the total number of double orphans would have declined, in line with overall orphan rates, from 1990 to 2010. HIV/AIDS, however, will nearly triple the number of orphans in sub-Saharan Africa who will have lost both parents by 2010.

— Orphans in sub-Saharan Africa are concentrated in certain countries, reflecting broader trends in HIV prevalence and population. In 2001, 12 countries in sub-Saharan Africa accounted for 70% of orphans. As might be expected, the three countries with the largest populations also had the most orphans: Nigeria, Ethiopia, and the Democratic Republic of Congo. By 2010, HIV/AIDS will play an increasingly significant role in orphaning in each of these countries. In Nigeria, the percentage of orphans due to AIDS will increase from 18% of the total to 40% (2. 6 million). In Ethiopia, the jump will be from 26% to more than 43% (2. 2 million), and in the Democratic Republic of Congo, it will increase from 34% to nearly 42% (1. 4 million).

— The number of orphans will continue to rise for at least the next decade. In general it takes about 10 years between HIV infection and death from AIDS. So today's prevalence rates will largely determine the pattern of orphaning for the next decade. Because of the 10-year lag between infection and death, even in a country where HIV prevalence has declined, the numbers of orphans will continue to remain high. For example, HIV prevalence in Uganda peaked in the late 1980s at around 14% and then began to decline dramatically to an estimated 5% in 2001. The number of orphans, however, continued to increase for 10 years after the country's epidemic had peaked, and is only now beginning to decline, from 14. 6% in 2001 to a projected 9. 6% in 2010.

Impacts on Children

The impact of HIV/AIDS on children is complex and multifaceted, with the social costs both high and long term. Overall, AIDS is increasing the number of vulnerable, malnourished, poorly socialized, and uneducated young people, which in turn heightens the prospect of social instability. With scarce resources stretched well beyond their limits, the impact of the pandemic is placing tremendous strains on families, communities, and governments who are attempting to help.

The social and economic impacts of AIDS threaten the well-being and security of millions of children worldwide. As parents and other family members become ill, children take on greater responsibility for income generation, food production, and care of family members. They face decreased access to adequate nutrition, basic health care, housing, and clothing. Fewer families can afford to send their children to school, with young girls at particular risk of being denied an education. In both urban and rural areas, many orphans are struggling to survive on their own in child-headed households. Many others are forced to live on the street.

It is difficult to overstate the trauma and hardship that children affected by HIV/AIDS are forced to endure. They try to help, but can only watch as one parent, then often the other, gradually grows ill and dies. There may be little familial planning for the children's future. A myriad of interrelated factors take their toll grief over the death of a parent, fear about the future, separation from siblings, distress about worsening economic circumstances, and HIV/AIDS-related discrimination and isolation.

In addition, orphans and widows can face loss of inheritance, which impoverishes them further. Extended families take in the overwhelming majority of orphans who lose both parents. But in many cases, orphaned siblings are sent to different households and experience a second profound loss through this separation. Many foster families are poor and have to stretch already inadequate resources to provide for both the orphans and their own children. In addition, some step or foster parents treat orphans harshly. Children impacted by HIV/AIDS are also at serious risk of exploitation, including physical and sexual abuse. Isolated from emotional connections with the family, some engage in risky sexual behaviour. Those forced to live on the streets may turn to prostitution and crime as a means to survive. While most of these children were born free of HIV, they are highly vulnerable to infection.

In the countries hardest hit by HIV/AIDS, care for orphans and children affected by HIV/AIDS lies primarily with their families and communities. But HIV/AIDS is placing huge burdens on the extended family system-the backbone of African societies-while also ravaging entire communities. This can leave many orphans with little support. A recent study in Zimbabwe, for example, found that half of street children are orphans, the majority due to AIDS. The impact of HIV/AIDS on the family structure has not been widely studied, but extensive anecdotal evidence suggests that children are increasingly living in various types of families, including households headed by single parents, grandparents, other relatives, and children themselves.

A situation analysis of children orphaned by AIDS in Cote d'Ivoire showed that extended families find it harder to assign substitute parents to children orphaned by AIDS than to children orphaned by other causes. These alternate forms of families are constantly evolving, and psychosocial distress affects their ability to cope. Within them, HIV/AIDS can lead to loss of employment, loss of productive capacity, high expenditures for treatment of sick family members and care for children absorbed into the household, and loss of family property or savings following a death.

A study of Ugandan households in 2000 showed that foster care exacerbated already entrenched poverty in households. Those dependent on subsistence agriculture faced an urgent need to increase cash income to pay for extra commodities, while those relying more on wage-earning activities reported that their incomes were not enough to cope with the additional mouths to feed. Another problem is that orphan caregivers are often poor women. Children in these households are significantly more disadvantaged than children in two-parent families, largely because women have less access to property and employment. Women also may feel pressure to exchange sex for material items or money, increasing their risk of HIV infection.

The widespread loss of life from HIV/AIDS undermines entire communities. Highly skilled personnel in public management, social services, education, and health care are becoming ill and dying in large numbers due to HIV/AIDS. The pandemic is reducing labour and agricultural productivity, weakening social structures, increasing demand for health and other services, and reducing the capacity to deliver those services. It can also contribute to increased crime and social unrest as despair mounts and individuals run out of options.

Since its inception in 1997, the Children on the Brink series has outlined key strategies for supporting orphans and other children affected by HIV/AIDS. These strategies, which focus on helping families and communities cope with the crisis, have been adopted by local, national, and international groups. They form a framework for interventions to match the massive scale and lengthy duration of this unprecedented crisis. The five strategies outlined below were endorsed by the UNAIDS Committee of Cosponsoring Organizations in November 2001. At the same time, the Committee endorsed 12 principles to guide organizations helping children affected by HIV/AIDS.

Strengthen and support the capacity of families to protect and care for their children: The overwhelming majority of orphans and other children affected by HIV/AIDS are living with immediate or extended family members. The safety and well-being of these children depend largely on the ability of these relatives to protect and care for them. For most of them, there is no viable alternative. Even in countries where institutional care is relatively extensive, orphanages provide only for a very small portion of all vulnerable children. Support for families can take many forms.

Attention must be given to both immediate survival needs and the longer-term issues of improving the ability of households and families to cope, including economic strengthening and psychosocial support. Improving access to basic services such as health care and education is essential. Other critical issues include increasing agricultural productivity, improving access to employment and markets, and providing additional means for income generation. In addition, efforts must be made to help those who are ill live longer through basic care for AIDS-related illnesses. Parents can be encouraged to write wills, make arrangements for their children's care once they are unable to do so, and talk to their children about the future.

Mobilize and strengthen community-based responses: The community is the second safety net for vulnerable children and households. Community groups can help vulnerable children directly or assist AIDS-affected families to provide for children's needs. In addition, organized communities are best able to determine which children and households are the most vulnerable, and to channel local or outside resources to those most in need. Many poor communities have organized themselves to assist the children, but they could be much more effective if outside organizations provide more support. Some community responses are ad hoc, while others have been initiated by NGOs or religious bodies, often with the active support of government ministries. In some countries, stakeholders have established district-level structures to stimulate and support efforts in rural villages and urban neighborhoods.

Strengthen the capacity of children and young people to meet their own needs: HIV/AIDS catches children in a double bind. They must support themselves and their families, often under the pressure of serious poverty, yet many are forced out of school just when they most need to prepare for their own futures. Girls are often the first to drop out, which not only undermines their own health and well-being, but also that of the next generation. Keeping vulnerable children in school is the first line of defense. This provides them a secure environment to learn skills that will help them provide for their own needs as they grow into adulthood. Interventions must address key factors that fuel the dropout rate school expenses, caring for relatives, and compensating for lost income. Overall, it is important to recognize that young people are not the problem, but an essential part of the solution. Support for them as they plan and carry out actions to meet their needs is crucial. This goes beyond addressing the impact of HIV/AIDS to preventing infection in the first place. Where HIV prevention has been most successful, young people have been at the forefront.

Ensure that governments develop appropriate policies, including legal and programmatic frameworks, as well as essential services for the most vulnerable children: Governments have a crucial role in ensuring children, families, and communities are able to cope. They often have signed international agreements and national laws obliging them to take action. Governments facing HIV/AIDS epidemics need to further develop and reinforce laws and policies to protect increasing numbers of vulnerable children. Moreover, they need to implement and enforce these policies through ministries, agencies, and other governmental structures. Governments also have ultimate responsibility to ensure that children who fall through the safety nets of both family and community are protected and have access to essential social services.

The governmental response to children affected by HIV/AIDS must be multisectoral and integrated with basic health, education, and development programs. Strategies for governments to pursue include: developing national action plans to guide programming; reviewing, strengthening, and developing child law and protection services; and strengthening delivery of education, health, and other essential services. These efforts require widespread governmental collaboration with international organizations, donors, NGOs, religious groups, community associations, and the private sector.

Strong and supportive leadership has been shown to be essential in countries that have reduced HIV/AIDS prevalence.

While many countries have moved decisively against the disease in recent years, other have shown a lack of political will to tackle AIDS-related problems. Governments may not have sufficient funds to provide all necessary services, but they do have the capacity and the mandate to bring together stakeholders so each can contribute to a collaborative national effort.

Raise awareness within societies to create an environment that enables support for children affected by HIV/AIDS: Increasing awareness among policymakers, community leaders, organizations, and the public about the impacts of HIV/AIDS on children and families helps generate a broadly shared sense of responsibility for action. Stigma and discrimination around HIV/AIDS remain major challenges. Effective public information and social mobilization can accelerate change so HIV/AIDS evolves from "their" problem to "our" problem. A comprehensive situation analysis, particularly with broad participation from stakeholders, can provide much of the information needed to drive such social mobilization. Active involvement of the media, faith-based groups, and key opinion leaders is particularly important.

Effect of HIV/AIDS on Children's Rights

According to the Joint United Nations Programme on HIV/AIDS (UNAIDS) and the World Health Organization (WHO), children and young adults (ie, persons under 25 years of age) accounted for over one-third of the 33 million people living with HIV in 1998. As well, the majority of all new HIV infections in that year came from this population. Four million children under the age of 15 contracted HIV since the epidemic began, most of whom (about 90 percent) became infected from their mothers during pregnancy, labour, birth, or breast-feeding. In 1998 alone, it is estimated that there were 590,000 new infections among children under the age of 15, and 2.5 million new infections among children and youth in the 15-24 age group. Combined, this translates into 8500 new infections among children and young people every day.

Children who became orphans due to the death of one or both parents from HIV/AIDS are a rapidly growing population in urgent need of attention. By the year 2010, the number of orphaned children is expected to reach 40 million. Current estimates from UNAIDS reveal that by 1997 a total of 8.2 million children under age 15 had lost their mothers since the beginning of the epidemic, and that in 1997 there were 6.2 million children alive who had been orphaned by HIV/AIDS. Ninety percent of these children were in sub-Saharan Africa. The need for homes and guardians for large numbers of orphans is impacting entire communities and regions of the world. A study by the Zambian Ministry of Health indicated that 40 percent of all households have one or more orphans. In Zimbabwe, eight percent of all children under the age of 15 have lost their mothers to AIDS.

Children are affected by HIV/AIDS not only through infection or the loss of a parent. For example, many children experience a premature end to their childhood as they are required to become heads of households, drop out of school, work, raise younger siblings, and care for parents and other family members sick from AIDS. Furthermore, children experience greater poverty as a result of the loss due to AIDS of adult wage earners, farmers, and other skilled and contributing household members. These losses affect all of the children in a household and, where infection rates are high, entire communities. Without adequate care and support, children experience losses in health, nutrition, education, affection, security, and protection. They suffer emotionally from rejection, discrimination, fear, loneliness, and depression.

The realization of the survival and developmental rights of children, as defined in the UNCRC, are affected in obvious ways as family and community resources become strained and overburdened by HIV/AIDS. Accomplishments in child survival that were made over the past two decades are endangered. If the AIDS epidemic is not contained, the mortality rates of infants in some countries could increase by 75 percent, and those of children under five years of age by 100 percent (UNAIDS). In the absence of caring adults to protect them, and as they struggle to survive, children who experience increased poverty, abandonment, rejection or discrimination, or an added burden of responsibility for themselves and other family members, are at increased risk for abuse and exploitation. Children's rights are ignored as family property is taken, siblings are separated, the children suffer physical and sexual abuse, or the children become homeless. Girls marry at very young ages in order to have a home.

Children join the 100 million children estimated to be living and working on the streets of the world (UNAIDS) or the more than one million children annually who are sexually exploited for the first time (1996 World Congress Against Sexual Exploitation of Children). Actions that support the protection of children's rights and the implementation of the UNCRC are synonymous with those that reduce the likelihood of infection with HIV. When their rights to survival, development, protection, and participation are realized, children are less likely to find themselves in situations involving a high risk of HIV infection.

Protecting children from situations where they are known to be at risk of sexual abuse and exploitation, and where intravenous drug use is common, directly reduces their risk of infection. Healthy physical and emotional growth and development, access to information about their rights and about sexual health, and a voice in making decisions that affect them - all among the rights of children - are vital steps that, if begun in childhood, enable people throughout their lives to protect themselves from HIV. Lasting solutions for the next generation must address both protection from HIV and protection of children's rights.

Despite the almost universal ratification of the United Nations Convention on the Rights of the Child, children infected with HIV, those affected by the epidemic, and those living in the shadow of HIV infection continue to suffer serious discrimination, exploitation and abuse in most countries. These violations of the rights of children can be the result of their real or perceived HIV status or that of members of their families. They can also make those children not already infected become more vulnerable to infection. The Convention on the Rights of the Child recognizes a child to be every human being below the age of 18 years.

Children infected, children affected and children vulnerable to HIV infection: Children who are infected with HIV are often discriminated against, for example, through denial or limitations of their rights to education, health and social services, as a result of inadequate or inaccessible health services, treatment, care, education and social programmes. The quality of life for children infected with HIV is often negatively affected by societal and family abandonment and rejection, with some children being forced to live on the streets and support themselves through such means as selling commercial sex.

A dramatic difference exists between rich and poor countries in the length of time a child infected with HIV can survive. Drugs to treat HIV infection and other diseases that occur due to the weakened immune system of the child are often not available in poor countries. In addition, the mistaken belief that any sickness in a presumed or confirmed HIV-infected child is due to HIV infection may result in simple treatment of infectious or other curable diseases being denied by health providers or not sought after by family members.

Children affected by HIV/AIDS often suffer from the effects of the epidemic on their close or extended families and their communities. A devastating impact on children is when their immediate family environment and support system is challenged through the sickness, disability and premature death from AIDS of one or both of their parents. Then, of course, children may be affected because of the reduced ability of infected parents and extended families to sustain their livelihoods and to care for them; they may be removed from their homes, have to leave school to care for their families, or have to work or live on the streets. In addition, the structures and services that exist for their benefit are often strained by the consequences of the HIV/AIDS epidemic. For example, in countries that are severely affected, the loss of health professionals and the magnitude of the burden of HIV/AIDS on health and social systems that are already lacking in resources, can become overwhelming.

In a world with AIDS, there are children who are infected with HIV and those who are affected by the epidemic's intrusion into their families or communities. The epidemic, however, casts its biggest shadow on the hundreds of millions of uninfected children who face a lifetime risk of HIV infection as they grow into adulthood. Vulnerability to HIV infection concerns the extent to which individuals are born, grow, and become sexually active in a world which has added the risk of acquiring HIV infection to their lives. The less individuals are able to make free and informed decisions about their lives the more vulnerable they are to acquiring HIV infection. Governments' responsibility in this regard extends to fulfilling the rights of children such as to information, education and services, as well as paying attention to the circumstances that make them especially vulnerable to sexual exploitation and abuse.

Children have a right to be better informed and better protected in a world with HIV/AIDS. The Convention on the Rights of the Child, adopted by the United Nations in 1989, and ratified by almost every country in the world, specifies the human rights to which all children are entitled. The four guiding principles of the Convention - the best interests of the child, non-discrimination, survival and development, and participation - are the lens through which realization of all rights in it are to be analyzed and evaluated.

The rights contained in the Convention include the right to protection from influences that are harmful to development, the right to participation in family, cultural and social life, the right to education, health and social welfare support, the right to a name and nationality, to freedom of expression, to participation in decisions affecting the child's well-being, and to protection from discrimination on any grounds including sex, disability, race or minority status, as well as protection from sexual and other forms of exploitation. A key underlying advance of the Convention on the Rights of the Child is the legal recognition of the child as a complete individual with an identity distinct from that of parents or legal guardians.

Governments that ratify the Convention are responsible under international human rights law for respecting, protecting and fulfilling all of the rights set forth in the Convention. Governments must report to the Committee on the Rights of the Child within two years after ratification and every five years thereafter on their successes and failures in implementing each of the rights contained in the Convention. The Committee then monitors the degree to which governments are meeting their obligations with particular emphasis on the well-being of children and families. Much work remains to be done by governments, NGOs, and intergovernmental agencies to improve the quality of country-level information contained in these reports, as well as the level of analysis and follow-up occurring during and after the report's consideration by the Committee.

The Convention on the Rights of the Child can be understood to provide a blueprint for reducing the vulnerability of children to HIV and for the design of effective HIV/AIDS prevention, treatment and care strategies consistent with human rights norms. Based on the Convention on the Rights of the Child, the following standards should be established and affirmed for children living in a world with HIV/AIDS.

— Children have a right to survival and development. Therefore, realization of all rights must be protected from the impact of HIV/AIDS.

— Children have a right to information and opportunities to develop life skills. Therefore, children should have access to HIV/AIDS prevention education, information and the means for prevention, including attention to the ability to negotiate safer sex practices.

— Children have a right to a safe and supportive environment free from exploitation and abuse. Therefore, special measures should be taken by governments to prevent and minimize the impact of HIV/AIDS caused by such factors as sexual abuse and trafficking, forced prostitution, sexual exploitation, use of illicit drugs, and harmful traditional practices.

— Children have a right to be protected from discrimination and exploitation, irrespective of their HIV/AIDS status or that of members of their families. No discrimination should be suffered by children on any grounds, including in education, leisure, recreational, sports, and cultural activities because of their HIV/AIDS status. Children have a right to access health and social services on an equitable basis, irrespective of their HIV/AIDS status or that of members of their families. All infected children should be provided with adequate HIV/AIDS treatment and care. Attention must be paid to ensure that orphans receive adequate support services.

— Children have a right to be heard and to have their aspirations and needs reflected in decisions affecting their future.

Strengthening children's rights to enhance HIV prevention and care. Children's rights are human rights - the general protection of human rights includes special attention to children in such areas as sexual exploitation and abuse, and the promotion of their rights among others to information, education, health and social services. This is critical to enhance HIV prevention and care strategies and to reduce the impact of AIDS on children, families and communities. A stronger commitment is needed worldwide to improve policies and increase action that promote and protect the rights of children living in a world with AIDS. While the impact of this loss of life differs across families, communities, and societies, one thing is clear a child's life often falls apart when he or she loses a parent. With infection rates still rising and adults continuing to succumb to the disease, HIV/AIDS will continue to cause large-scale suffering among children for at least the next two decades.

HIV/AIDS has created an orphan crisis. This unprecedented orphan crisis will require radically scaled-up national, regional, and community responses for at least two decades-especially in sub-Saharan Africa, where children have been hardest hit. Orphans due to other causes also demand attention. Increases in the number of orphans due to AIDS should be considered as part of a much larger problem of orphaning due to all causes. In 12 African countries, projections show that orphans will comprise at least 15% of all children under 15 years of age by 2010.

Other children are also vulnerable. The safety, health, and survival of all children in affected countries are increasingly jeopardized due to the effects of AIDS on families and communities. Increasing numbers of children are living with sick or dying parents or in households that have taken in orphans. Moreover, the pandemic is deepening poverty in entire communities, with children usually the first to suffer from the deprivation.

AIDS threatens children's lives. The impacts of AIDS on children are both complex and multifaceted. Children suffer psychosocial distress and increasing material hardship due to AIDS. They may be pressed into service to care for ill and dying parents, be required to drop out of school to help with farm or household work, or experience declining access to food and health services. Many are at risk of exclusion, abuse, discrimination, and stigma.

Communities with a high proportion of orphans require urgent assistance. Responses need to be focused and scaled up in communities with high proportions of orphans and other children affected by HIV/AIDS. Because they are at the center of the crisis, these communities are the most overstretched. Collaboration is key. The estimates on orphans due to AIDS presented here are the result of the first unified effort to provide a consistent set of numbers. This effort demonstrates the importance of strengthened collaboration and provides a springboard for expanded responses. No one can tackle this crisis alone.

A pivotal event was the June 2001 United Nations General Assembly Special Session on HIV/AIDS, where member nations issued a Declaration of Commitment on HIV/AIDS. It calls for new commitments to strong leadership at all levels of society, and specifies benchmarks for prevention, care, support, and treatment of HIV/AIDS. The Declaration established two goals specific to children affected by HIV/AIDS: Member countries will develop national policies and strategies that build and strengthen the ability of government, community, and family to support orphans and children infected with and affected by HIV/AIDS by 2003; and Member countries will implement these policies and strategies by 2005.

Reaching these goals will be difficult, but efforts are under way. For example, delegates from 21 West and Central African countries met for the first time in April 2002 to coordinate and strengthen their action to confront the crisis. And prominent African religious leaders met in Nairobi in June 2002 to commit themselves to concerted efforts on behalf of orphans and children made vulnerable by HIV/AIDS.

The statistics show the historical, current, and projected number of children orphaned by AIDS in each country. To provide a better understanding of the impact of HIV/AIDS on overall orphaning, they also include the total number of children orphaned by all causes. For a better comparison of the prevalence trends across countries and regions, the number of countries studied has expanded from 34 in the 2000 edition of Children on the Brink to 88 in the current version. In the absence of HIV/AIDS, the percentage of children who are currently orphans in the three regions studied would be declining due to improvements in mortality rates for adults in the traditional child-rearing years.

Instead, HIV/AIDS is causing the overall orphan rate to rise. By the end of 2001 in the 88 countries studied, 13. 4 million children currently under 15 years of age had lost a mother, father, or both parents to AIDS. This number is expected to jump to 25 million by 2010. Over the same period, the percentage of children orphaned by AIDS compared to the total number of orphans will also rise sharply, from 12. 4% to 24%. Sub-Saharan Africa bears by far the greatest burden 12% of all children in this region are orphans, compared with 6. 5% in Asia and 5% in Latin America and the Caribbean.

The pandemic is causing increases in both the absolute number of orphans and in the proportion of orphans as a percentage of all children in sub-Saharan Africa. The rate of orphaning due to AIDS in sub-Saharan Africa would be even higher if it were not for reduced fertility in HIVpositive women. For biological reasons, they have fewer children, and they often die before they complete their reproductive years.

8

Children Caught up in Conflict

Children are not responsible for war, yet it robs them of their childhood. As of October 2004, more than 1.2 million Sudanese had been violently uprooted from their homes. Many were killed by armed militias, and those who survived by fleeing towards or across the border with Chad found themselves enveloped in a battle for survival of a different kind - against disease, inadequate shelter and poor nutrition. Camps set up to receive them were overwhelmed by the immensity of the humanitarian crisis. Resources were stretched to breaking point and a massive outbreak of disease constantly threatened, particularly for children weakened by the lack of food, adequate water and sanitation. Elsewhere in southern Sudan a conflict that had raged since 1983 between the government and the Sudanese People's Liberation Movement was close to resolution but the tragedy in Darfur has made progress in that peace process very difficult.

The situation in Sudan is a grim reminder of how the nature and complexity of warfare have changed in recent years. In the 14-year period after the cold war ended, from 1990 to 2003, there were 59 different major armed conflicts in 48 locations - and only four of these involved war between nations. There is now greater recognition that ethnically based conflict has increased - inevitably so, given that wars between nations have been largely replaced by more local, internecine forms of hostility. The threat to civilians from conflict has grown enormously. An estimated 90 per cent of global conflict-related deaths since 1990 have been civilians, and 80 per cent of these have been of women and children.

In some cases, civilians are directly targeted; in others, they are indirect victims of stray bullets or explosive remnants of war. The nature of civil war dictates that fighting takes place where people live, rather than on a battleground. And if the roots of a conflict lie in ethnic hatred or resentment, all members of the 'despised' group become vulnerable, not just the combatants representing them. By no means are all the victims of war killed by bullets or bombs; many suffer from the catastrophic impact of conflict on the health of an entire society. In a typical five-year war, the under-five mortality rate increases by 13 per cent and adult mortality increases even more. Even after a conflict is over, its repercussions undermine child survival. Recent research has shown that during the first five years of peace, the average under-five mortality rate remains 11 per cent higher than its corresponding level before the conflict.

Many developing countries are locked in a vicious cycle in which poverty generates the desperation, fear and struggle for resources that can lead to conflict, which in turn gravely aggravates poverty. Of the world's 20 poorest countries, 16 have suf- fered a major civil war in the past 15 years. Civil war typically triggers a prolonged reversal of economic and social development that often results in poverty continuing from one generation to the next.

Impact of Conflict

Children are always among the first affected by conflict, whether directly or indirectly. Armed conflict alters their lives in many ways, and even if they are not killed or injured, they can be orphaned, abducted, raped or left with deep emotional scars and psychosocial trauma from direct exposure to violence, dislocation, poverty or the loss of loved ones. The destruction wrought by war is likely to mean that children are deprived of key services such as education and health care. A child's education can be disrupted by the absence of teachers, or by an environment in which landmines and other explosive remnants of war jeopardize their safety.

Schools can also become caught up in armed conflict, as was seen in September 2004 during the hostage crisis and subsequent calamitous battle in the Russian town of Beslan, which left more than 150 children and even greater numbers of adults dead. In Aceh, Indonesia, as part of the conflict between government forces and rebel groups, 460 schools were burned to the ground during May 2003 alone. In Nepal, schools are regularly used as centres for propaganda and recruitment by the opposition to the government. Attacks on and abductions of teachers and students are frequent.

Children in Conflict

The exact number of children currently caught up in conflict as combatants is unknown, but it is likely to run into the hundreds of thousands. Children are conscripted, kidnapped or pressured into joining armed groups. Not all of them take part in combat, though the proliferation of lightweight weapons has made it possible for even children under 10 to become effective killers. Children are also forced into sexual slavery and to become labourers, cooks or servants, messengers or spies. Girls are particularly liable to be sexually exploited, whether by one commander or a whole troop. Many will also join boys on the front line.

Armed groups and, in some cases, government forces use children because they often prove easier than adults to condition into fearless killing and unthinking obedience. For all such children, whether they are forcibly recruited, join in order to escape poverty or hunger, or enlist to actively support a cause, the first loss is their childhood. Africa and Asia have the highest numbers of children involved in conflict as combatants. And the trend in using children in conflict is not diminishing: During 2003, there was a surge in the recruitment of children in Côte d'Ivoire, the Democratic Republic of the Congo and Liberia.

In the Democratic Republic of the Congo, in particular, there have been widespread reports of atrocities, rape and beatings involving children. Thousands of children in northern Uganda have been abducted by the rebel group Lord's Resistance Army and forced into combat and servitude. Thousands more flee their homes and villages each night to seek refuge in towns where they can avoid attack or abduction. In Myanmar, there are still large numbers of children in the armed forces, while the number of children used by armed groups and urban militias in Colombia has increased to around 14,000 in recent years.

Internally Displaced Children

A family life constitutes one of a child's fundamental rights. War has no respect for this: it drives people out of their homes as they flee battle zones or direct attack, leaving behind not only their property, but also their family and friends. During the 1990s, around 20 million children were forced by conflict or human rights violations to leave their homes. As they flee conflict, families may become separated. Children left alone are more likely to be sexually abused or recruited into combat. Deprived of a support network, they are also more vulnerable to hunger and disease. Some families manage to remain intact until they have found refuge, but the poor conditions in which many fleeing families find themselves increase children's vulnerability to malnutrition and illness. When families leave their homes, it is usually seen as a temporary situation.

All too often, however, the period of exile runs into years or even decades; in such cases, children may spend their whole childhood in camps. In southern Sudan and elsewhere, entire generations of children have never lived at home. Of the 40 million people worldwide who have been forced to flee their homes, around one third are refugees who have been driven across national borders. The other two thirds are internally displaced, a proportion that has been rising steadily in parallel with the increase in civil strife. It is much harder for the humanitarian community to assist internally displaced persons since national governments often view this as 'interference'. Yet the problems of the internally displaced can be as severe as those of refugees, including alienation from support systems, lack of identity papers and discrimination. Unlike refugees, who benefit from international legal protection, in many cases their legal status and care and protection provided by the internal authorities is weak.

Sexual Violence

Sexual violence is often a consciously deployed weapon of war. It can include rape, mutilation, exploitation and abuse. In the conflicts in Bosnia and Herzegovina, and Croatia in the early 1990s, it was a deliberate policy to rape teenage girls and women and force them to bear children, often referred to as the 'enemy's child'. More recent conflicts in the Democratic Republic of the Congo, Liberia, Sierra Leone and Sudan have all involved the use of sexual violence. Adolescent girls are frequently singled out for their youth and relative defencelessness or because they are perceived to be less likely to be infected with HIV. Reports abound from conflict zones of girls being abducted and forced into sexual slavery by militias or rebel groups.

The rise in sexual violence that often accompanies conflict is not restricted to crimes committed by combatants. The chaos and disruption produced by war undermines the rule of law, leaving children — particularly those who have become separated from their families and communities — much more vulnerable to sexual violence or exploitation. Camps for displaced persons can be perilous places for children, where overcrowding, desperation and the weak application of the rule of law can expose them to sexual abuse. In addition, the poverty, hunger and insecurity generated by conflict can force children into prostitution: In Colombia, for example, girls as young as 12 are reported to have submitted sexually to armed groups in order to ensure their families' safety.

All of these factors tend to increase the likelihood of HIV transmission in conflict zones, while the breakdown of school and health systems inhibits safeguards that could counter these risks. In addition, the hopelessness of life in a war-affected area can foster risky sexual behaviour among young people. A conflict in a region with low rates of HIV prevalence will not in itself produce an explosion in the infection rate. But the breakdown of social order and the sexual violence associated with conflict always increase the spread of HIV. When war erupts in an area already affected by HIV/AIDS, as in Rwanda during the 1990s and in the eastern region of the Democratic Republic of the Congo the effect is catastrophic.

Even after a conflict is over, children are often threatened by what it leaves behind. Explosive remnants of war, including abandoned explosives and weapons, landmines and unexploded ordnance, kill and maim thousands of children each year. Explosive remnants of war can prevent access to fields, wells, clinics or schools for whole communities, causing deprivation long after hostilities have ceased. Families may be condemned to live in temporary settlements because of the continuing presence of mines in their communities. Landmines alone claim between 15,000 and 20,000 new victims each year.

Nearly two thirds of the 65 countries that suffered new mine casualties between 2002 and 2003 had not experienced active conflict in that period. A study by Human Rights Watch found that the use of cluster munitions by coalition forces in populated areas of Iraq was one of the major causes of civilian casualties in 2003. Most victims of explosive remnants of war are men, often farmers. But children are also at risk: they tend to be curious about strange objects, and may be attracted to the colourful designs of some butterfly mines and cluster bombs. In addition, many children are responsible for herding animals and fetching water, which involve traversing large tracts of countryside that may include mined areas; they are also less likely than adults to understand signs marking minefields.

Since the United Nations General Assembly first requested that a comprehensive study on the impact of armed conflict on children be undertaken,the plight of children affected by armed conflict has gained greater visibility, both in the international community and at the national and local levels in many countries. Substantial efforts have been made to meet the challenges that conflict poses for children. The report on the obstacles encountered in protecting children from conflict, published by Graça Machel in 1996,increased the attention given to war-affected children's issues throughout the international community.

As a result, the Secretary-General appointed a Special Representative for Children and Armed Conflict to promote the protection, rights and well-being of children at every phase of conflict, and the UN Security Council has taken an increasingly active interest in receiving annual updates on the issue, incorporating child-specific considerations into its deliberations, and hearing the direct testimonies of affected children. While this increased attention to the problems of children in conflict has generally resulted in important advances to better protect them, many of the problems identified in 1996 are even graver today - and new challenges have emerged to test the world's resolve to protect its children.

Anti-War Agenda

Nine years ago, UNICEF set out a 10-point Anti-War Agenda, launched in The State of the World's Children 1996. Appalled by the plight of children in conflict situations that contradicted "not just every normal human concern for their welfare but also the professed beliefs and legal obligations of those responsible," the organization laid down a series of challenges that insisted on the rights of children.

War Crimes

The establishment of the International Criminal Court as a permanent international tribunal that can bring individuals to justice for genocide, war crimes and crimes against humanity has been a profoundly important step forward in recent years. The 1998 Rome Statute, the basis of the Court's establishment, makes it clear that intentional attacks on a civilian population, attacks on schools and the conscription of children under 15 all constitute war crimes. The ad hoc special courts and tribunals set up to consider particular conflicts - like the tribunal in Arusha, United Republic of Tanzania, considering the genocide in Rwanda - also help eradicate the culture of impunity.

The landmark ruling by the Special Court for Sierra Leone in June 2004 - that the recruitment or use of children under 15 in hostilities is a war crime under customary international law - may result in the first-ever conviction for the conscription of children as armed combatants. The decision came in response to an assertion by one of the accused that he was immune from prosecution on the grounds that conscription of children under age 15 had not been established as a war crime until after the inception of the Special Court's jurisdiction, which dates back to 1996. The challenge now lies in making the historic significance of this decision widely known.

Accountability mechanisms can take many forms, including truth and reconciliation commissions such as those in post-apartheid South Africa, or Sierra Leone, national courts, and traditional dispute resolution procedures, such as the gacaca court system in Rwanda. Accountability contributes to the process of healing and helps children understand that they are not to blame for what has happened to them and their society. It calls attention to violations of children's rights and records atrocities committed against them, both of which are vital to understanding the broader context of what happens to children affected by conflict. Accountability can also help break the cycle of violence, restore confidence in democracy and the rule of law, increase the chances of success during a peace process, and strengthen the legitimacy and authority of a new government.

Most children experience war crimes, crimes against humanity and genocide as victims or witnesses. However, some children are also recruited and made complicit in those crimes, as has been the case in recent years in Liberia, Rwanda, Sierra Leone and other countries. Forcing children to commit atrocities during an armed conflict is itself a war crime: it causes severe psychological harm and violates their rights. Child perpetrators should be considered victims of criminal policies for which adults are primarily responsible. International judicial mechanisms should focus on prosecuting the political and military groups that are responsible for planning and ordering the commission of such egregious crimes.

However, in order to restore respect for the rule of law in post-conflict societies, children who may have participated in serious crimes should undergo an appropriate form of accountability, conducted in a way that respects their rights and takes into consideration their age and maturity. This may involve the child's testifying to a truth and reconciliation commission or taking part in traditional healing and reconciliation processes. According to the Convention on the Rights of the Child, the key objective is to promote the reintegration of child perpetrators into society. Any judicial proceedings for children should be in the context of juvenile and restorative justice to ensure the child's physical, psychological and social recovery. These proceedings should involve judges, lawyers, police and social workers who have benefited from child rights training.

Concern about the impact of sanctions on children and other vulnerable members of the population is increasingly widespread and has resulted in attempts to develop sanctions that are much more carefully targeted to avoid harming these groups. The UN is empowered to impose economic and other sanctions on Member States by Article 41 of its Charter. In the 1990s, the Security Council imposed sanctions on Eritrea, Ethiopia, Haiti, Iraq, Liberia, the Libyan Arab Jamahiriya, Rwanda, Sierra Leone, Somalia, Sudan and the former Yugoslavia - and on the Taliban in Afghanistan and the National Union for the Total Independence of Angola (UNITA) in Angola.

Of these, the most comprehensive sanctions were imposed on Haiti, Iraq and the former Yugoslavia. And in each of these countries the impact of the measures on children, the poor and the elderly caused such grave concern that the ethical validity of sanctions was called into question. The negative effects of sanctions inevitably fall most heavily on the most vulnerable members of the population. Healthy adults can generally endure long periods of deprivation but children have far fewer resources to call upon and may suffer irreparable harm.

The 1991 sanctions imposed on Haiti, for example, had a devastating impact on children. A survey conducted in 1994-1995 found that 7. 8 per cent of children under five suffered from acute malnutrition, compared with 3. 4 per cent in 1990. School enrolment fell from 83 per cent in 1990 to 57 per cent in 1994, and the number of children living on the street doubled over the same period. Evidence like this from Haiti, together with the plight of children in Iraq, persuaded the UN that sanctions must be much more carefully deployed in the future. It has become clear that sanctions imposed under Article 41 of the UN Charter are likely to conflict with the organization's responsibility under Article 55 to promote higher standards of living and improve social progress, health and education.

In 1999, the UN Security Council adopted resolution 1261, which addresses the issue of children caught up in armed conflict. In a clause to one of the resolution's articles, the council pledged to consider the impact on children whenever it adopted sanctions under Article 41. In April 2000, it set up a working group to review UN sanctions policy and recommend ways of making sanctions more targeted. In recent years, sanctions imposed on UNITA in Angola, and on Liberia and Sierra Leone, have been restricted to banning trade in arms and diamonds, as well as travel by senior government officials, and their impact and effectiveness have been carefully assessed.

The UN hopes that these targeted or 'smart' sanctions will restore the international community's confidence in measures that stop short of using military force but exert far greater pressure on errant Member States than mere verbal warnings or exhortations.

Zones of Peace

The aspiration to incorporate the idea of children as 'zones of peace' into international law has not been realized. The notion has, however, continued to prove useful and to save lives in some conflict situations. In Sri Lanka, for example, over half a million children in the conflict-ridden north-east were immunized against polio during a UNICEF-supported Sub-National Immunization Day in October 2003. Since 1995, the Government and the Liberation Tigers of Tamil Eelam have annually observed such 'days of tranquillity': ceasefire days in which children across the country have been immunized. A significant recent development has been the specific mention in UN Security Council mandates to UN peacekeeping missions of the need to protect women and children. It is also increasingly common for such missions - in Afghanistan, the Democratic Republic of the Congo and Sierra Leone, among others - to appoint one or more child protection advisers.

In Angola, Colombia and Sri Lanka, among other conflict-ridden states, the idea of schools as zones of peace - safe havens from the violence plaguing their countries - has been actively promoted. Schools must be places of safety for children in every respect, where they are protected by adults they can trust. This is among the first prerequisites of the global push for universal primary education, one of the Millennium Development Goals. If this sense of safety is lost - as it was, tragically, when children died in an armed engagement at a school in western Nepal in October 2003 - the sanctity of childhood itself is impugned.

Progress and challenges: Today, emergencies are more complex than ever before and their numbers are rising. The expertise of humanitarian workers - and their sensitivity to the needs of the people they are aiding - has unquestionably increased. But while progress has been made in providing relief, the long-term rebuilding process has been endangered by the targeting of aid workers, the underfunding of vital aid projects and the inability of humanitarian workers to reach many areas. The problem in Somalia, for example, as in other nations caught up in civil strife, has been compounded by the underfunding of humanitarian programmes and the deliberate murders of aid workers. This has led to heightened restrictions for humanitarian agencies and, consequently, increased deprivation for those most in need. Worldwide, over 200 UN civilian staff lost their lives to violence between January 1992 and March 2002. Hundreds more have been taken hostage, raped or assaulted.

Humanitarian agencies must continually adapt, responding to emerging or abating crises. In 2000, UNICEF formulated a set of core commitments to govern its initial response in protecting and caring for children and women in conflict and unstable situations. Since then, the organization has continued to develop its policy and practice in relation to the array of challenges that conflict poses for children. These include initiatives to assist unaccompanied and internally displaced children, to provide education in emergencies, and to demobilize and reintegrate children actively involved in armed conflict. The core commitments were revised and expanded in 2004.

Education

Peace education is the process of promoting the knowledge, skills, attitudes and values that will enable children, youth and adults to prevent conflict and violence, both overt and structural; to resolve conflict peacefully; and to create conditions conducive to peace, whether at an interpersonal, intergroup, national or international level. Peace education has a place in all societies · not only in countries undergoing armed conflict or emergencies. Because lasting behaviour change in children and adults only occurs over time, effective peace education is necessarily a long-term process. While often based in schools and other learning environments, peace education should ideally involve the entire community.

One area in which the past decade has seen significant progress is the use of education in emergency situations. In the past, education was not seen as a frontline service during emergencies - its provision was often deferred until the situation had stabilized. This is no longer true: Education is increasingly seen as one of the first essentials in an emergency. Schools can provide physical protection for children, and education can itself inject stability and normalcy into their lives. In Afghanistan, Iraq, Liberia, and in Darfur, Sudan, UNICEF has made it a priority to get children into school - in many cases for the first time in their lives - as well as to provide safe drinking water, nutrition and basic health care.

In collaboration with other UN organizations such as the Office of the UN High Commissioner for Refugees and the World Food Programme, as well as with nongovernmental organizations within the inter-agency Emergency Education Network, UNICEF aims to create a safe environment for children in which they can learn, play and receive psychosocial support, and where mothers can spend private time with infants or receive counselling. In a wider conflict zone the goal is to reopen schools, rebuild infrastructure or launch back-to-school campaigns. The participation of older children and adolescents in times of crisis and conflict is imperative. If they are left without opportunities to envision and contribute to a better future, their youthful optimism is frustrated under the extreme conditions of war. Addressing their rights to participation is therefore not negotiable: it is an imperative.

In 1996, there were 22 major armed conflicts worldwide. In 2003, there were 19 such conflicts, the second-lowest annual number since 1990. Yet it is difficult to claim that there has been significant progress in mediating and resolving conflict. For example, today there are 25 million people in 52 countries who are internally displaced by violence and persecution, broadly the same number as in the mid-1990s.

There have been some notable achievements over the past nine years. The longstanding conflict in Angola, still active in 1996, has finally been laid to rest. Huge efforts have been made to bring resolution to conflicts in Burundi, Liberia and Sierra Leone. Yet for every step forward - the ongoing peace process in Sudan after two decades of war between the Government and the Sudanese People's Liberation Movement, for example - there seems to be a step backward, as a new conflict erupts elsewhere or, in the case of Darfur, in a different area of the same country. Far from seeming safer, the world at the beginning of the 21st century appears more riven by conflict and fear - and its dominant political discourse to be one of war.

UNICEF and its partner agencies are dedicating a large proportion of their resources to addressing the social and economic inequalities that can lead to violence. By emphasizing outreach to vulnerable groups, including girls, rural communities and the poor, these programmes combat marginalization, defuse tensions and promote effective social integration. UNICEF's role in lobbying governments to pursue equitable development policies has expanded over the past decade and is helping to equip communities with the tools they need to resolve issues peaceably. If ever there were children needing their right to protection fulfilled it is those caught up in armed conflict, from those forcibly recruited as soldiers to those who see their homes and communities destroyed. But the world also needs to protect millions of children in the future from the damage to their childhood that conflict inflicts. The only sure way of doing so is for the international community to take more urgent and serious steps towards preventing war and resolving existing conflicts.

If we are to safeguard children from the brutality of armed conflicts, a number of actions must be pursued, and the international community must demonstrate the political and economic will required to implement them.

— Put children first, before and during conflicts.

— End the recruitment of child soldiers.

— Strengthen the protective environment for children at every level, from the family right through to the level of national and international legislation.

— Eradicate the culture of impunity, and strengthen accountability.

— Prevent conflict by addressing the underlying causes of violence and investing more resources in mediation and conflict resolution.

— Make monitoring and reporting on child rights violations in conflict zones a priority, including gathering reliable data on children who are actively involved in armed conflict and other war-affected children.

— Expand demobilization and mineawareness campaigns.

— Restart education for children caught up in armed conflict as soon as possible.

— Enhance humanitarian agencies' capacity to respond to conflicts by developing early warning systems and better preparedness.

— Combat poverty and HIV/AIDS, which interact with conflict to magnify the negative impact on childhood.

9

Children's Rights: Creating a Culture of Human Rights

Children's rights and what the world wants for its children, are articulated most clearly in the Convention on the Rights of the Child. This Convention and its near-universal acceptance by the community of nations and the work of the Committee on the Rights of the Child, have brought into sharp focus for the first time the human rights of children. In the closing years of the millennium, the universality of the response is a clear indicator of a broad-based global commitment to recognition of "the equal and inalienable rights of all members of the human family" as "the foundation of freedom, justice and peace in the world". Children uniquely touch the conscience of the world, and the Convention has placed children effectively centre-stage in the quest for the universal application of human rights.

Special Case for Children

"Mankind owes to the child the best that it has to give..." Recognition by the world community of the priority to be accorded to children goes back to the earliest declarations of human rights. "To look into some aspects of the future, we do not need projections by supercomputers. Much of the next millennium can be seen in how we care for our children today.

Tomorrow's world may be influenced by science and technology, but more than anything, it is already taking shape in the bodies and minds of our children.

Special cases are necessary for;

— children are individuals - they have equal status with adults as members of the human family. They are neither possessions of parents, products of the State, nor people-in-the-making. Governments have a moral responsibility to recognize the human rights of children as individual citizens at all levels of society. Using the Convention's definition of children as every human being below the age of 18, we are considering over 2 billion people constituting in some regions half of the population (52% in Sub-Saharan Africa).

— the healthy development and active participation of children are uniquely crucial to the optimum development of any society. A parallel concern should be to safeguard their future environment.

— children grow towards independence only with the help of adults - parents and families first. But when those adults cannot meet children's needs, society must fill the gap. And children's dependence and their developmental state make them particularly vulnerable - they are more sensitive than adults to the conditions under which they live: poverty, poor housing and environmental pollution are but a few examples.

— children are more affected by the action - or inaction - of government than any other group. Education policies dominate their waking hours, public health policies target their developing bodies and life styles. And almost every area of government policy affects children to some degree, either directly or indirectly.

— children generally have no vote, no part in the political process although many States are at present introducing laws and policies to encourage the involvement of children in decision-making, to listen to children in the family, schools, health services, local communities, even in governments; the process is, however, everywhere still in its infancy. The views of children barely touch the actions of central government.

— there are current changes in many societies which are having a disproportionate impact on children, and generally in a negative sense - changes in the family structure, in employment patterns and the introduction of market forces into the management of public services. The state of children is a very sensitive barometer of the effects of social and economic changes, and those effects are particularly devastating in situations of armed conflict.

— there are the huge costs of failing children. Governments are fully aware from research findings that what happens to children in the early years, within the family and within other forms of care, significantly determines their positive or negative growth and development. This, in turn, determines their cost or contribution to society spread over the rest of their lives.

As a consequence, the economic motive joins the moral and the social in providing cogent reasons for all governments to accord children a high priority and careful attention. These may seem obvious points which derive from common sense. But they need to be convincing particularly with regard to governments if we are to promote child-centred societies.

The world has moved slowly to recognize the human rights of children. It was in 1924 that the League of Nations endorsed the first Declaration of the Rights of the Child which originated with the Save the Children International Union. The Charter of the United Nations speaks of promoting and encouraging respect for human rights and fundamental freedoms "for all", and the Universal Declaration of Human

Rights, adopted by the General Assembly of the recently established United Nations in 1948, stresses that "All human beings are born free and equal in dignity and rights..." The Universal Declaration, while upholding "everyone's" rights, in addition confirmed that motherhood and childhood are entitled to special care and protection, and promoted the family as the natural and fundamental group unit of society.

Also in 1948, the General Assembly adopted its first brief seven point Declaration of the Rights of the Child, building on the 1924 Declaration: "By the present Declaration of the Rights of the Child... men and women of all nations, recognizing that Mankind owes to the child the best that it has to give, declare and accept it as their duty to meet this obligation in all respects..." A proposal was accepted, almost immediately, to draft a more detailed Declaration. Ten years later, the 1959 Declaration of the Rights of the Child was adopted, retaining some of the earlier language and adding detail. In 1961, the two International Covenants, on Civil and Political Rights and on Economic, Social and Cultural Rights, were adopted, completing the International Bill of Human Rights and providing legal as well as moral obligations to respect "everyone's" human rights.

Poland's formal proposal for the Convention on the Rights of the Child came on the eve of the International Year of the Child, and a Working Group was formed in that year - 1979 - by the Commission on Human Rights. Its deliberations and the gradual expansion and amendment of the original Polish text are documented in various publications. The detail of the Convention's 42 substantive articles owes much to the Universal Declaration of Human Rights, the Covenant on Civil and Political Rights and the Covenant on Economic, Cultural and Social Rights - illustrating the indivisible and interdependent nature of human rights.

On 20 November 1989, the General Assembly unanimously adopted the Convention on the Rights of the Child (CRC) which entered into force in September 1990. In the same month, the World Summit for Children was held in New York, encouraging all States to ratify the Convention, with world leaders making a "solemn commitment" to accord a high priority to the rights of children: "The well-being of children requires political action at the highest level. We are determined to take that action". The world community has maintained the pressure, and the 1993 World Conference on Human Rights set the end of 1995 as the target for universal ratification. By the last day of that year, 185 States had ratified the Convention. At the end of 1997, only two countries had still to ratify.

Universal ratification undoubtedly creates a significant global movement for children, leaving universal implementation as the ongoing challenge. The commitment of the world community to the human rights of children is fundamental. Translating the commitment into action to improve the lives of all of the world's two billion children is a task that is incumbent on everyone. While the Convention addresses governments, its standards and principles can only achieve reality when respected by everyone - within the family, in schools and all the other public and private institutions and services provided for children, in neighbourhoods and communities, in courts and at all levels of administration.

The Convention is a powerful instrument for the world's children and affirms that children are the subjects of rights, not simply objects of concern or beneficiaries of services. They are entitled to the action of States, institutions and individuals and for their rights to be fully realised we all need to support the cause of realizing the human rights of children - for the benefit of all.

Families Role in Children's Lives

The Preamble sees the family as the fundamental group of society, the natural environment for the growth and well-being of all its members, particularly children. The Convention places obligations on the State to respect parents' primary responsibility for their children; and to respect parents' rights, duties and responsibilities to provide direction and guidance to their children. There are State obligations to support parents and parenting; to provide care when parents cannot; to prevent separation of children from parents except in very exceptional circumstances and to promote family reunification. The detailed aims for education defined in article 29 include the development of respect for the child's parents.

The Convention seeks respect for children - but not at the expense of others' human rights or responsibilities. The Convention confirms that children, like the rest of us, have a right to express their views and to have them taken seriously - children should be seen and heard. But the Convention does not uphold the child's right to make decisions for him-or herself from an early age. There must be respect for the "evolving capacities" of the child - a common sense concept recognizing that the child's path from total dependence to adulthood is gradual, and the responsibility of everyone of us.

Discrimination against Disadvantaged Children

The principle of non-discrimination is included in all the basic human rights instruments, and it has been carefully defined by the bodies responsible for monitoring their implementation. There is an accepted definition of discrimination - "any distinction, exclusion, restriction or preference... which has the purpose or effect of nullifying or impairing the recognition, enjoyment or exercise, on an equal footing, of human rights and fundamental freedoms in the political, economic, social, cultural or any other field of public life".

The Human Rights Committee, which monitors the implementation ofthe International Covenant on Civil and Political Rights, has emphasised that the "enjoyment of rights and freedoms on an equal footing... does not mean identical treatment in every instance". The principle of equality sometimes requires States Parties "to take affirmative action in order to diminish or eliminate conditions which cause or help to perpetuate discrimination prohibited by the Covenant". The Committee on the Rights of the Child has frequently commented on the need to identify the most vulnerable and disadvantaged children in a State, has expressed concern about their situation and has recommended action to ensure that such children enjoy their rights under the Convention.

While not enforceable through a court, ratification of the CRC gives States clear obligations under international law.

Upon ratification or accession, States take on obligations under international law, and they lay open their treatment of children to international accountability through the reporting process. It is crucial to have the external authority of the Convention to appeal to and to have a transparent reporting process overseen by an independent Committee with the power to challenge and promote action in favour of children. In this challenging task, both Governments and organizations like UNICEF and the growing networks of non-governmental organizations advocating for children, need to take a firm stand on behalf of children and uphold the authority of the Convention.

Role of Goverment

While the task of realizing children's rights is a universal one, the Convention on the Rights of the Child addresses Governments primarily. The commitment of Governments to act in favour and on behalf of children requires much more than signing and ratifying the Convention. The Committee on the Rights of the Child has consistently encouraged States to take special measures and develop special institutions for children. In this regard, the Committee has been most innovative and most influential in creating a higher political priority for children, and promoting a growing sensitivity to how the action and/or inaction of government affects children.

Through its reporting guidelines and its comments on individual States' reports, the Committee has urged Governments to:

— develop a comprehensive national agenda for children, based on the Convention;

— ensure that all legislation is fully compatible with the Convention - incorporating the Convention into domestic law or ensuring that its principles take precedence in cases of conflict;

— make children visible in the process of policy development throughout government by introducing a child impact assessment;

— ensure effective coordination of children's policies across government departments, between the various levels of government, and between government and public as well as private bodies, including NGOs;

— develop permanent mechanisms for coordination, monitoring and evaluation, again using the Convention as the framework.

— ensure sufficient data collection on the state of all children under the jurisdiction of the State;

— allocate available resources to their maximum extent for policies with regard to children and carry out adequate budget analysis to determine the proportion spent on children;

— introduce training activities on the Convention for all those involved in government and working with or for children;

— raise awareness of the human rights of children among adults and children;

— develop independent statutory offices for children to voice children's concerns and take a firm stand on behalf of children's interests - children's ombudspersons or commissioners.

There are no right or wrong structures - as a member of the Committee on the Rights of the Child said during examination of one State's report: "... given the wide range of administrative and legislative systems among the 174 States parties, the Committee was in no position to specify particular solutions. Indeed, a degree of diversity in the mechanisms set up to implement the Convention might lead to a degree of competition, which could be very beneficial. The important point was that the Convention should be the main benchmark and inspiration of action at the provincial and central levels... "

Under the Convention States must undertake "all appropriate legislative, administrative and other measures for the implementation of the rights recognized in the Convention". A commentary in the 1997 edition of the Manual on Human Rights Reporting by the Committee's first Rapporteur, emphasizes that the obligation in article 4 is for action - to take progressive steps towards the realisation of children's rights: "They should therefore not simply remain passive, but rather adopt appropriate measures designed to ensure and protect children's rights. Passivity is not an answer in situations where the State might be tempted to believe that it has already attained a sufficiently developed level of implementation - in fact, the realization of children's rights and, in general, of human rights, is by nature a permanent and endless process of demanding search for betterment, where there is always room for improvement.

Passivity is not an answer either in difficult social and economic national conditions. Under these circumstances the State should undertake all possible steps aiming at improving the existing situation, creating the necessary conditions for the enjoyment of the fundamental rights of children, being guided by the best interests of the child and paying particular attention to the most disadvantaged groups".

The Convention establishes the Committee on the Rights of the Child "for the purpose of examining the progress made by States in achieving the realization of the obligations undertaken in the Convention". Ten experts "of high moral standing and recognized competence in the field covered by the Convention" are nominated and elected by States Parties. Although elected by States representatives, the members of the Committee do not represent their country, Government or any organisation to which they may belong. They serve instead in their personal capacity, their mandate derives from the Convention and they are solely accountable to the children of the world.

The current members of the Committee are from Barbados, Brazil, Burkina Faso, Indonesia, Israel, Italy, Lebanon, Russian Federation, South Africa, and Sweden. They meet in Geneva three times a year - in January, May/June, and September/October. "States Parties" to the Convention must submit an Initial Report within two years of ratification and a Periodic Report every five years thereafter. The Committee assesses the situation in each country and prepares a document - the "Concluding Observations". The Concluding Observations always follow the same format and identify the positive aspects of the process, the factors and difficulties impeding implementation, and the principal areas of concern, and end with the formulation of suggestions and recommendations to be taken into account in the future.

State-by-State Examination

The main task of the Committee on the Rights of the Child is to examine the reports from the 191 States Parties to the Convention. It is a daunting task. By the end of its October 1997 session, the Committee had examined 80 Initial Reports, and the first Periodic Reports had started to arrive in Geneva. The Committee normally spends a day and a half discussing each report with government representatives, completing examination of six State reports at each session.

In preparation for these meetings with States Parties, a Working Group of the Committee meets for a week, holding private sessions at which UNICEF and other international agencies and children's rights NGOs (non-governmental organizations) from the countries whose reports are to be examined provide an analysis of the situation of children and highlight any areas of concern. The Committee prepares a list of questions and issues arising from the reports that the Committee wishes to discuss and sends it to the States Parties in preparation for their examination.

In order to avoid a mammoth backlog in the examination of reports without diluting the necessary rigour of the process, appropriate budgetary decisions should be taken to increase the capacity of the Committee and its supporting secretariat in the Office of the High Commissioner for Human Rights.

Public Scrutiny

The significance of the process of reporting, examination and wide dissemination of reports under the CRC is that for the first time States become internationally and publicly accountable for their treatment of children. In the Committee's Guidelines for Initial Reports, the Convention is divided into eight thematic clusters of articles which, in the words of the Committee, "reflect the Convention's holistic perspective of children's rights: that they are indivisible and inter-related, and that equal importance should be attached to each and every right recognized therein".

The Committee has also organized General Discussion days on themes linked to the Convention, thus promoting further awareness and understanding of the human rights of children in areas such as:

— Children in armed conflict

— Economic exploitation of the child

— The role of the family in the promotion of the rights of the child

— The girl child

— Administration of juvenile justice

— The child and the media

The Committee can request special studies: a recommendation to the General Assembly that a study on the impact on children of armed conflict should be conducted resulted in the GraHa Machel study. It can also highlight a country's need for technical or other assistance with regard to implementing the Convention: in reality, the Convention emphasizes the essential importance of international cooperation for promoting and protecting the human rights of children.

Achievements

Promoting respect for all human rights: The near-universal ratification of the Convention on the Rights of the Child has had a catalytic effect, encouraging ratification of other fundamental human rights instruments. The close relationship of the Committee with the other Treaty Bodies and the development of collaboration among all United Nations agencies ensures a holistic approach to human rights, to the benefit of children and all other members of society.

Developing special institutions, structures and procedures for children in States Parties on all continents: Prior to 1989, very few countries had taken any steps to ensure visibility with regardto therights of the child in Governments' policies. National commissions and inter-ministerial committees for children, national plans of action, agendas and strategies for children, child impact assessment, State of Our Children reports and "Children's Budgets" are currently becoming the rule rather than the exception.

Developing the law for children: The Convention and the reporting process require all States to review their constitutions and their laws from a child's perspective. The result in many cases has been wholesale reform. Some States have developed an entirely new concept, a children's rights statute, as well as special sections in Constitutions. The process roots out traditional concepts of ownership and discrimination and replaces them with concepts of parental and State responsibility and universal principles and standards.

Highlighting and detailing the goals of child survival and development: The systematic and progressive reporting process, and the degree of detail which the Committee on the Rights of the Child insists on States providing, give fresh impetus to reach the fundamental targets for survival and development set by the World Summit for Children and by successive global conferences.

Drawing attention to forgotten and invisible children: The non-discrimination principle, requiring recognition of all rights for all children within each jurisdiction, has forced States to acknowledge, care for and reintegrate the forgotten and marginalised children: children languishing in institutions, children living and/or working on the streets, unaccompanied refugee children, children in hidden forms of exploitative child labour, children bought and sold across frontiers.

Invigorating the power and influence of child advocacy: The special importance accorded in the reporting process under the CRC to the involvement of civil society and the role of NGOs concerned with children's rights has encouraged their growth and given visibility to the importance of their work. The CRC has given their advocacy authority, a focus on rights and a detailed framework. The NGO Group for the Convention has been established, and NGO coalitions are now active in many States and regions. In addition, special independent offices to promote children's rights and interests -children's commissioners and ombudspersons -are being set up with legislation which explicitly gives legitimacy to their action in the framework of the Convention: they are innovative and powerful voices for children.

Children's voices being heard and taken seriously: The Convention calls for children being seen and heard in government, with children's elections and children's parliaments, youth councils and child mayors' meetings, summits and seminars on children. In schools, student councils experience democracy in action; local planning and transport decisions benefit from the views of children. In fact, at every level, politicians, officials and the adult world in general are beginning to recognize the special benefit to societies of seeking and respecting the active participation of children. Also within the family environment, legal frameworks defining the concept of parental responsibility include provisions requiring respect for the child's views.

Violence towards children under challenge as never before: The CRC requires protection from all forms of physical and mental violence. The Committee has rigorously pursued the child's right to physical and personal integrity, condoning no level of violence towards children. It emphasizes, in particular, that corporal punishment and other all-too-common humiliating forms of discipline in the family and in schools and other institutions are not compatible with the Convention. As the Committee has commented:... its provisions were intended to prompt those in authority in each country to find the most effective way in their own societies to break cycles of violence that were often perpetuated from generation to generation under the cover of tradition and customs. Through this innovative challenge to childhood experiences of violence, the Convention and the Committee provide new hope of reducing all the many forms of adult violence that threaten the safety and security of all people.

Forcing States to look at the dark side of children's lives: The CRC and the reporting process have forced States and societies to discard denial and acknowledge the reality of extreme violence and exploitation, abuse and neglect of many millions of children.

Developing justice systems for children that cure rather than cause crime: Together with the detailed United Nations standards on juvenile justice, the Convention's principles are leading States to develop distinctive systems of youth justice, avoiding wherever possible criminalization and deprivation of liberty, focusing on rehabilitation and reintegration, and checking the populist punitive policies that lead to greater criminality and violence.

Reviewing definitions of childhood: The CRC's definition of the child -every human being below the age of 18 years... - together with the Committee's detailed questioning has required States to consider what constitutes childhood. They are required to look systematically, in the context of the Convention in its entirety, at the ages set for protection (for example, from hazardous labour, criminal responsibility, imprisonment and participation in armed conflict), and at any age limits placed on the exercise of particular rights. One of the Committee's particular concerns has focused on discrimination, including the gender disparity of the age for marriage.

Challenges

Progress, however, has been uneven and has perhaps been weakest in basic education, under-five mortality, child malnutrition, maternal mortality and sanitation. The goal of universal access to basic education by the year 2000 is unlikely to be met. An estimated 140 million primary school-age children still do not attend school -about 60 per cent of them are girls. Every year some 12 million children die, mostly from preventable causes. While the global reduction in under-five mortality continues, the majority of children live in countries that will most probably not achieve the goal of reducing it by one-third or to 70/1000 by the year 2000. Similarly, no significant progress has been achieved in reducing maternal mortality and the goal of reducing it by half cannot be met.

In 1995, an estimated 174 million children under five were malnourished in the developing world. The goal is to reduce the rate of child malnutrition by half, to approximately 15 per cent, by the year 2000, but little measurable progress has been made since 1990. Global coverage of adequate sanitation is estimated to have declined from 36 to 34 per cent between 1990 and 1994; in consequence, achievement of the goal of universal access by the year 2000 is unlikely to be met.

Despite the Convention's standards and those in other United Nations instruments, there are unproductive moves towards increasingly punitive systems of juvenile justice in some States. While child exploitation, including sexual exploitation, is more visible, there are few signs of systematic action to end it which are sensitive to the child's needs. And despite the positive response of much of the world community to the pleas to ban anti-personnel mines, armed conflicts continue to shorten and ruin the lives of millions of children.

The challenge remains daunting, but not impossible. Recent experience shows that when political commitment is mobilized, communities empowered and adequate resources allocated, then sustainable progress can be achieved. But this is certainly not the time for aid to falter. Official development assistance (ODA) has declined worldwide by about 17 per cent since1992. Current ODA falls short by about $100 billion a year against the United Nations target of 0.7 per cent of GNP. Current estimates suggest that basic health and basic education together receive little more than one per cent of total bilateral aid.

Other Activities of United Nation

Developing and monitoring the implementation of Standards Relating to the Human Rights of Children

Early Stages

The first paragraph of the Preamble of the Charter of the

United Nations gave special emphasis to the future by proclaiming: " We the peoples of the United Nations determined to save succeeding generations from the scourge of war... have decided to combine our efforts to accomplish these aims..." Three years later, in 1948, the Universal Declaration of Human Rights, the first international proclamation of human rights standards, enunciated the entitlement of "all members of the human family" (Preamble) to enjoy human rights and fundamental freedoms.

The Declaration also refers specifically to children's rights. It states that children are entitled to special care and assistance and that all children, "whether born in or out of wedlock, shall enjoy the same social protection". Further, education is envisaged by the Declaration as the tool for the full development of the human personality. These provisions of the Charter and of the Universal Declaration were developed in the following years in numerous international human rights instruments to reflect more specifically the rights of the child.

The International Covenant on Economic, Social and Cultural Rights clearly affirms that States parties should ensure the widest possible protection and assistance to the family particularly while it is responsible for the care and education of dependent children; undertake special measures on behalf of all children and young persons, without any discrimination for reasons of parentage or other conditions, and all steps necessary for the healthy development of the child.

The International Covenant on Civil and Political Rights states that every child has, without any discrimination as to race, colour, sex, language, religion, national or social origin, property or birth, the right to such measures of protection as are required by his/her status as a minor; the right to a name and to a nationality. Other articles of the Covenant make reference to specific situations such as the protection of children in the case of dissolution of a marriage (art. 23.4) and the separation of juvenile offenders from adults (art. 10). While specific reference to children and their rights is lacking in the Convention on the Elimination of All Forms of Racial Discrimination and the Convention Against Torture, the provisions of both these instruments are clearly relevant to the situation of many children and are applicable to them.

In 1989, the General Assembly unanimously adopted the Convention on the Rights of the Child which entered into force less than one year later. Other documents which focus on specific situations in which children might be involved, have also been elaborated providing the basis for further developments in the promotion and protection of children's rights. These include the Declaration on the Protection of Women and Children in Emergency and Armed Conflict, adopted by the General Assembly in 1974 and the Declaration on Social and Legal Principles relating to the Protection and Welfare of Children, with Special Reference to Foster Placement and

National and International Adoption by the General assembly in 1986

It is important to note that the two International Covenants as well as the specialized human rights treaties, including the Convention on the Rights of the Child, are all legally binding instruments. When a State becomes party to any one of them it undertakes to guarantee all the specified rights to all individuals under its jurisdiction and to provide for effective remedies in the case of violations.

The Committee on the Rights of the Child (CRC) was established in 1991 under article 43 of the Convention on the Rights of the Child, to monitor its implementation. The Office of the High Commissioner for Human Rights (OHCHR) is servicing the Committee on the Rights of the Child by providing technical and substantive support. OHCHR is also playing the role of catalyst between all partners with the view to strengthen the implementation of children's rights at the country level. In this regard, OHCHR develops technical assistance and advisory services programmes in a wide range of countries.

Additionally, the High Commissioner for Human Rights has launched in 1996 a Plan of Action to strengthen the implementation of the Convention on the Rights of the Child. The purpose of this plan, for which support from States parties to the Convention has been solicited, is to provide substantive support to the Committee's work with the States parties' reporting process and assist where necessary in transforming recommendations into reality through the provisions of adequate resources, coordination and follow-up.

The Commission on Human Rights (CHR) and its Sub-Commission on the Prevention of Discrimination and Protection of Minorities also address the issues impacting children. For example, the Working Group on Contemporary Forms of Slavery of the Sub-Commission has elaborated programmes of action on the sale of children, child prostitution and child pornography and for the elimination of the exploitation of child labour and debt bondage. Both programmes were adopted by the CHR in 1992 and 1993, respectively. In 1990, the Commission appointed a Special Rapporteur on the sale of children, child prostitution and child pornography.

The Special Rapporteur has a mandate to collect and analyze comprehensive data and to recommend measures aimed at eliminating the sale of children, child prostitution and child pornography at the international, regional and national levels. A Working Group responsible for elaborating a preliminary draft optional protocol on the sale of children, child prostitution and child pornography is also currently addressing this important issue. It should also be noted that the World Congress Against Commercial Sexual Exploitation of Children, held in Stockholm in 1996, produced an important Declaration and Agenda for Action which has further advanced international efforts to protect all children.

In 1994 the Secretary-General appointed Ms. Graça Machel to prepare a study on the impact of armed conflict on children. As follow-up and pursuant resolutions by the CHR, a working group was also established for elaborating guidelines for a possible optional protocol on the involvement of childrenin armed conflicts whose primary purpose is to raise the minimum age for recruitment into the armed forces.

Brief mention should also be made of the various committees which have been established to oversee implementation of the two International Covenants and Conventions: the Committee on Economic, Social and Cultural Rights, the Human Rights Committee, the Committee on the Elimination of Racial Discrimination, the Committee on the Elimination of Discrimination against Women, the Committee against Torture. The structure and working methods of these treaty bodies are similar to that of CRC as described above. They contribute to improving respect for the rights of the child in their particular areas of competence.

The promotion and protection of the rights of children is also an important aspect of the work of United Nations agencies and programmes. The focus which specialized agencies and other parts of the United Nations place on the issue of children and their rights depends, of course, on their specific mandates and fields of concern. The United Nations Children's Fund (UNICEF), established in 1946, has been at the forefront of the struggle for the rights of children. It is the specialized agency most involved in children's issues within the United Nations system and is present in most parts of the world, both through regional and country offices and its network of national committees.

The United Nations High Commissioner for Refugees (UNHCR) is directly involved in protecting the rights of children. In recognition of the special vulnerabilities of child refugees, UNHCR has developed specific operational guidelines and programmes for children. The International Labour Office (ILO) aims to establish national policy to effectively end child labour and protect children from exploitation; it is also developing a new convention focusing on eliminating the most intolerable forms of child labour. The United Nations Educational, Scientific and Cultural Organization (UNESCO) continues to strive for universal recognition of the child's right to an education which includes human rights, tolerance and respect for others. The World Health Organization (WHO) targets issues concerning children's health and their right to enjoy adequate health standards. These are just a few examples of the important work which the United Nations undertakes on behalf of children.

United Nations Children's Fund (UNICEF)

Founded in 1946 as the UN International Children's Emergency Fund, UNICEF marked its fiftieth anniversary in 1996 by adopting a new Mission: "UNICEF is mandated by the United Nations General Assembly to advocate for the protection of children's rights, to help meet their basic needs and to expand their opportunities to reach their full potential. UNICEF is guided by the Convention on the Rights of the Child and strives to establish children's rights as enduring ethical principles and international standards of behaviour towards children..."

The Convention on the Rights of the Child is the normative and ethical reference for UNICEF's work, in advocacy and awareness campaigns, in its cooperation with Governments, collaboration with other international organisations, especially those within the United Nations system, as well as in its partnerships with NGOs and other actors of civil society. In reality UNICEF is particularly well placed to pursue such an important mandate in view of its country presence in most parts of the world, both through its regional and country offices and the network of national committees in industrialised countries.

UNICEF has been actively involved in the campaign for the universal ratification of the Convention, promotes the effective implementation of its provisions and ensures support to the Committee on the Rights of the Child - including in its monitoring role and in the organisation and follow-up to thematic debates. UNICEF Anti-war Agenda and Steps to Ending Child Labour are meaningful illustrations. Reference should also be made to the support provided by UNICEF to the organisation of visits by members of the Committee to various countries -a unique and innovative initiative which has decisively contributed to a better understanding and observance of the Convention worldwide.

There are compelling strategic reasons for placing children's rights at the heart of the development agenda. Children's rights have been repeatedly recognized as a common field for action in various UN conferences during the last decade. In UNICEF's experience, children can be a powerful unifying force, they can transcend political parties, and even in times of war they can bring days of tranquillity and corridors of peace to enable vaccination campaigns to succeed.

UNICEF believes that the promotion of human rights and fundamental freedoms goes hand in hand with the strengthening of international peace and security. In this regard, UNICEF supports the implementation of the recommendations of the Machel study on children in armed conflict and will continue, during 1998, to support the work of the Special Representative, to see the age for recruitment into the armed forces set at eighteen, to stop children being used as combatants under any circumstances or otherwise involved in hostilities, and to cease the use, stockpile, production and transfer of anti-personnel land mines. In this regard, UNICEF recognises the importance of promoting the consideration of children's rights and of being guided by their best interests in the drafting of statutes for the establishment of an International Criminal Court.

UNICEF will continue to support and promote national strategies designed to eradicate child labour and the exploitation and abuse of children. Moreover, the momentum gained at the Oslo Conference will be seized as a special opportunity to mobilise national action and international cooperation in this regard during 1998. In addition to ongoing programme activities addressing the rights of children and women, some activities planned by UNICEF for 1998 deserve mention:

CRC Programming

— UNICEF will continue to promote the use of the CRC as a programming tool for country programmes

— In the context of the CRC, UNICEF will develop indicators on child rights to monitor progress in their implementation

— A special focus will be given to internal training activities on child rights, within an overall human rights context throughout 1998

Publications, communication and information materials to create awareness of, and promote respect for, human rights, particularly of children and women

UNICEF is working on:

— distribution of a comprehensive Child Rights Handbook on the implementation of the CRC

— the production of a child rights booklet on implementation of the CRC

— State of the World Children's Report 1999 (launched in 1998) will address non-discrimination through detailed discussion of the education of girls

— the Progress of Nations will have a special focus on the anniversary of the Declaration of Human Rights a co-production with UNIFEM - areview of the Beijing

Platform, in the form of a resource guide providing a tool for a more focused assessment of the progress made in implementing the Beijing Platform for Action.

— publication of a report on progress made for girls since Beijing at the national level and envisages a publication on adolescent girls to come out of the Addis consultation - due in March 1998

— releasing globally in February, 100 public service television aminated spots - each addressing an article of the Convention on the Rights of the Child - which have been donated to UNICEF by the major animation studios around the world

— the UNICEF initiative - the International Day of Children's Broadcasting - which will focus, in 1998, on the Convention on the Rights of the Child - with particular emphasis on issues related to gender equality

— promotion of the Convention on the Rights of the Child focussing on the participation of children at the 'Children's Television Summit' to be held in London, March 1998

— the distribution of a video produced in Bangladesh portraying children talking about what child rights mean to them

— production of a documentary on the work of the Committee on the Rights of the Child

— plans to continue the production of a series of education shorts on the articles of the Convention on the Rights of the Child targetting children 8 - 12 years of age

Consultations and Meetings

— UNICEF will participate and focus on gender equality at the CRC/Cedaw meeting, January 1998

— CSW, March 1998 - UNICEF will address girls' human rights, violence against women and the impact of armed conflict

— UNICEF will focus on the rights of children and women at the opening and closing ceremonies of the "Goodwill Games" in mid July, in New York. UNICEF is organising a dinner for and about children to coincide with the Games.

— In view of its past experience and as reflected in the recent Electoral Process in Mexico, UNICEF will continue to promote the Elections for Children model in a number of countries, where children can fully express their views on their fundamental rights through a survey run simultaneously with major national elections.

United Nations High Commissioner for Refugees

Protecting the Rights of Refugee Children and Adolescents

Human rights and refugees are not separate issues. Today's human rights violations create tomorrow's refugee movements. While most current population displacements take place in the context of armed conflicts, the immediate causes of flight are almost invariably to be found in actual or anticipated human rights violations. More than half - currently 52 percent overall - of the world's 22.7 million refugees and other "persons of concern" to UNHCR are children and adolescents under the age of 18. In some refugee situations this figure rises to about 66 percent. These massive displacements are features of the post-Cold War crumbling of failed states, civil strife, ethnic conflict, massive human rights abuses and "total wars" fought from street to street and village to village without regard to human rights standards. In this ethical vacuum, the young are no longer just incidental casualties but, increasingly, specific targets in calculated strategies to eliminate "tomorrow's enemy".

Violations of Rights

Displacement in armed conflict violates almost every right of a child - the right to life, health, survival and development, the right to grow up in a family environment and to be nurtured and protected, the right to an identity and to an effective nationality, the right to education and prospects for the future. Many of today's conflicts last the full length of childhood, so that from birth to adulthood displacement and armed conflict are the only reality known to millions of children and adolescents.

Indeed, no aspect of a child's life is spared from the effects of becoming a refugee. Before and during flight, they are prime victims of multiple physical dangers such as landmines, shelling and snipers. Physically less able than adults to survive illness, malnutrition or deprivation of basic necessities, younger children are the first to die when resources are scarce. In the chaos of conflict, escape and displacement, children are at high risk of becoming separated from their families - a trauma potentially more devastating than even the displacement itself. Separated minors are the most vulnerable of all young refugees.

Girls are especially at risk of sexual violence, exploitation and abuse, not only from those they are fleeing from but also from "helpers" such as refugee camp leaders and peace-keeping troops. Boys are vulnerable to under-age military recruitment because they are available and can be more easily forced, intimidated or persuaded into joining armed forces or groups. Thus they become both the victims and perpetrators of violence and present serious difficulties for demobilisation and reintegration into families and communities. Education, probably already threatened by the circumstances that have forced the population to flee, may halt completely, especially in the case of adolescents and girls. In some countries children born to refugees may be denied birth registration and the asylum state's nationality, and may become stateless. Minors may also experience added difficulties in gaining legal status as refugees.

Convention on the Rights of the Child: for protecting the rights of refugee minors

In conjunction with refugee instruments, the Convention on the Rights of the Child (CRC), the guiding force behind UNHCR's Policy and Guidelines on Refugee Children, is a fundamental part of the legal framework for protecting refugee minors and promoting their best interests. Particularly important to UNHCR's work, the CRC addresses issues such as birth registration, preservation of a child's identity, special protection for separated minors and facilitation of family reunification, protection during armed conflicts and from under-age recruitment, prohibition against torture and limitations on deprivation of liberty, and provision of rehabilitative care.

In addition, there is a specific provision on the special protection needs of refugee children. With its prohibition against discrimination, the CRC thus represents a comprehensive code of rights for all children within a state's jurisdiction (including refugees and asylum seekers), and not just its nationals. In light of its almost universal ratification, it has even wider geographical applicability than the 1951 Convention and 1967 Protocol relating to the Status of Refugees. Even where a host country is a party to refugee instruments, the array of CRC rights may offer higher standards of protection to young refugees. The Committee on the Rights of the Child is an important forum for international scrutiny of states' respect for the human rights of refugee children.

Arising out of an initiative of the Committee on the Rights of the Child, the United Nations Study on the Impact of Armed Conflict on Children ("the Machel Study") has laid the foundations for a major platform for action by UNHCR in protecting the rights of displaced minors. As the Machel Study points out, UNHCR is "often the first to respond to emergencies" and is therefore in a unique position to exercise leadership regarding humanitarian assistance in this area. UNHCR has formulated a wide-ranging strategy to implement recommendations of the Machel Study for the benefit of all minors of concern to the Office, not just those who are war-affected.

Of particular importance is the establishment of performance objectives for protecting the rights of children in all phases of UNHCR operations during refugee emergencies, from contingency planning and emergency responses to care and maintenance stages, through to repatriation and reintegration. Other elements of this strategy include enhancements in staffing, training and budgeting, as well as a recent Evaluation of UNHCR's Efforts on Behalf of Children and Adolescents, which will pave the way for further improvements in the ways the Office protects and assists minors. The High Commissioner has asked field offices to draw up and implement a plan of action to follow-up on this strategy, concentrating on five key areas - under-age military recruitment, sexual exploitation, education, separated minors, and adolescents.

Addressing challenges faced in providing protection and assistance to refugee children and adolescents and enhancing the systematic response to these needs thus continue to be high on UNHCR's agenda. But UNHCR cannot, of course, play its part in isolation. Refugee problems are too large and too complex to be solved by humanitarian organisations alone. Making the Convention on the Rights of the Child a reality for refugee children and adolescents requires the full commitment, active co-operation and collaboration of the whole international community - including countries of origin and of asylum, international organisations and NGOs - as well as refugees themselves. In the words of UNHCR's Guidelines on Refugee Children:

"Although vulnerable, children are also resources with much to offer. They are people in their own right, with suggestions, opinions and the ability to participate in decisions and activities that affect their lives. Efforts on behalf of refugee children fall short if they are perceived only as individuals to be fed, immunized or sheltered, rather than treated as participating members of their community"

UNHCR initiatives for promoting the rights of refugee children and adolescents in 1998 are;

— *Implementation of UNHCR's follow-up strategy to the United Nations Study on the Impact of Armed Conflict on Children*: Each country operation is required to incorporate into its 1998 programmes and budgeting and fund-raising cycles a plan of action showing how the office intends to implement UNHCR's follow-up strategy to the Machel Study.

— *Evaluation*: Initiatives arising from a recent Evaluation of UNHCR's Efforts on Behalf of Children and Adolescents will pave the way for further improvements in the ways UNHCR protects and assists younger refugees.

— *Staffing*: Five new Regional Policy Officers (Children) will be deployed in critical regions, to help field operations with needs assessments and programme innovation and co-ordinate policies and programming on a regional basis.

— *Training*: "Action for the Rights of Children", a joint UNHCR-International Save the Children Alliance project, will provide a comprehensive package of field-based training for UNHCR and implementing partners' staff, combined with pilot projects on critical issues.

— *Refugee Children and Adolescent Trust Fund:* This trust fund: additional to regular programming - will be used to jump-start child rights and youth programmes in various operations, in order to reorient programming strategically for children and adolescents.

— *Protection workshops*: A series of regional and headquarters consultations will explore issues relating to the protection of refugee children and adolescents and enhance implementation of UNHCR's Policy and Guidelines on Refugee Children.

— *Public information*: Activities to commemorate the 50th Anniversary of the Universal Declaration of Human Rights will include a brochure on refugee children and human rights, activities for awareness raising in schools, human rights features on UNHCR's Web site, as well as posters, videos, exhibitions and advertisements.

— *Advocacy and promotion of international standards*: UNHCR will continue to promote the human rights of refugee minors in a broad range of fora - e.g. through close co-operation with the UN Secretary-General's new Special Representative for Children in Armed Conflict and other relevant agencies; keeping the issue of refugee children high on the agenda of the Committee on the Rights of the Child; and support for an Optional Protocol to the Convention on the Rights of the Child to raise the minimum age for military recruitment to 18 years.

— *Human rights and peace education*: Peace education programmes are planned for refugee camps in Kenya in 1998, with further programmes planned for other countries in late 1998-99. Tolerance promotion programmes in Kyrgyzstan and the Crimea will be further developed. A Universal Declaration of Human Rights 50th Anniversary kit of educational materials to promote peace, conflict resolution and human rights will be designed for refugee schools, illustrating the theme that human rights are a product of responsible and socially co-operative behaviour. A guide on "The Human Rights of Children and Women: Awareness Training for Adult Refugees", drawing on previous field experiences, is being launched to help UNHCR field offices and NGOs organise training in this area.

— *Harmful traditional practices*: Harmful traditional practices (such as female genital mutilation, early/forced marriage and early childbirth, and son preference or female foeticide/infanticide/neglect) primarily affect girls. UNHCR is issuing a policy to help field offices and implementing partners in eradicating such practices by sensitizing refugee populations to the violation of human rights and harmful health consequences involved.

— *Adolescents*: A proposed UNHCR initiative in partnership with other UN bodies and NGOs aims to put adolescents on the international community's agenda, through close examination of the range of responses required to address adolescents' specific needs, from early emergency response to later programming in camps, through to return and reintegration phases. This project will include action-oriented research and field investigations, pilot projects and programme implementation and evaluation of best practices.

— *Children and adolescents in complex emergencies*: An international conference, organised by UNHCR in partnership with the Government of Norway, the Norwegian Refugee Council and Redd Barna, is planned for mid-1998.

General Assembly Resolution Relating to the Rights of the Girl Child

The General Assembly,

— Recalling its resolutions 50/42 of 8 December 1995, 50/154 of 21 December 1995, 50/203 of 22 December 1995 and 51/76 of 12 December 1996,

— Also recalling the Beijing Declaration and the Platform for Action of the Fourth World Conference on Women, the Copenhagen Declaration on Social Development and the Programme of Action of the World Summit for Social Development, held at Copenhagen from 6 to 12 March

1995, the Programme of Action of the International Conference on Population and Development, held at Cairo from 5 to 13 September 1994, the Vienna Declaration and Programme of Action of the World Conference on Human Rights, held at Vienna from 14 to 25 June 1993, the Plan of Action for Implementing the World Declaration on the Survival, Protection and Development of Children in the 1990s of the World Summit for Children, held in New York on 29 and 30 September 1990, the World Declaration on Education for All and the Framework for Action to Meet Basic Learning Needs adopted at the World Conference on Education for All, held at Jomtien, Thailand, from 5 to 9 March 1990, and the Declaration and Agenda for Action of the World Congress against Commercial Sexual Exploitation of Children held at Stockholm from 27 to 31 August 1996,

— Deeply concerned that girls, in particular adolescent girls, continue to be silent and invisible victims of violence, abuse and exploitation and that some legal systems do not address adequately the vulnerability of girls in the administration of justice including the need for better protection of child victims and witnesses,

— Recalling that in 1998 the fiftieth anniversary of the Universal Declaration of Human Rights will be observed and the mid-term review of the implementation of the Programme of Action of the International Conference on Population and Development will be carried out and that the Commission on the Status of Women at its forty-second session will review the implementation of the sections of the Platform for Action on the girl child and the human rights of women,

— Welcomes the appointment of the Special Representative of the Secretary-General on children and armed conflict, in accordance with section II of Assembly resolution 51/77 of 12 December 1996,

— Stressing that discrimination and neglect of the girl child can initiate a lifelong downward spiral of deprivation and exclusion from the social mainstream,

— Deeply concerned about discrimination against the girl child and the violation of the rights of the girl child, which often result in less access for girls to education, nutrition, physical and mental health care and to girls enjoying fewer rights, opportunities and benefits of childhood and adolescence than boys and often being subjected to various forms of cultural, social, sexual and economic exploitation and to violence and harmful practices such as incest, early marriage, female infanticide, prenatal sex selection and female genital mutilation,

— Also deeply concerned that in situations of poverty, war and armed conflict, girl children are among the victims most affected and thus their potential for full development is limited,

— Concerned that the girl child has become a victim of the human immunodeficiency virus/acquired immunodeficiency syndrome and sexually transmitted diseases, which affect the quality of her life and leave her open to further discrimination,

— Reaffirming the equal rights of women and men as enshrined, inter alia, in the preamble to the Charter of the United Nations, the Convention on the Elimination of All Forms of Discrimination against Women and the Convention on the Rights of the Child,

1. Stresses the need for full and urgent implementation of the rights of the girl child as guaranteed to her under all human rights instruments, including the Convention on the Rights of the Child and the Convention on the Elimination of All Forms of Discrimination against Women;

2. Urges all States to take all necessary measures and to institute legal reforms to ensure the full and equal enjoyment by the girl child of all human rights and fundamental freedoms and to take effective action against violations of those rights and freedoms;
3. Also urges all States to enact and enforce legislation protecting girls from all forms of violence, including female infanticide and prenatal sex selection, female genital mutilation, incest, sexual abuse, sexual exploitation, child prostitution and child pornography, and to develop age-appropriate safe and confidential programmes and medical, social and psychological support services to assist girls who are subjected to violence;
4. Calls upon all States and international and non-governmental organizations, individually and collectively:

   (a) To set goals and to develop and implement gender-sensitive strategies to address the rights and needs of children, in accordance with the Convention on the Rights of the Child, to take into account the rights and particular needs of the girl child, especially in education, health and nutrition, and to eliminate negative cultural attitudes and practices against the girl child;

   (b) To take measures to ensure the non-discrimination and equal enjoyment of all human rights and fundamental freedoms of the girl child with disabilities;

   (c) To generate social support for the enforcement of laws on the minimum legal age for marriage, in particular by providing educational opportunities for girls;

   (d) To give attention to the rights and needs of adolescent girls, which call for special action for their protection from sexual and economic exploitation and abuse, harmful traditional and cultural practices, teenage pregnancy and vulnerability to sexually transmitted diseases and human immunodeficiency virus/acquired immunodeficiency syndrome and for the development of life skills and self-esteem, reaffirming that the advancement and empowerment of women throughout the life cycle must begin with the girl child at all ages;

(e) To take measures to increase awareness of the potential of the girl child and to promote gender-sensitive socialization of boys and girls from early childhood, aimed at achieving gender equality, development and peace within the family and the community;

(f) To ensure the equal participation of girls and young women on the basis of non-discrimination and as partners with boys and young men in social, economic and political life and in the development of strategies and the implementation of action aimed at achieving gender equality, development and peace;

(g) To strengthen and reorient health education and health services, in particular primary health-care programmes, including sexual and reproductive health, and to design quality health programmes that meet the physical and mental needs of girls and attend to the needs of young expectant and nursing mothers;

5. Urges States to enact and strictly enforce laws to ensure that marriage is entered into only with the free and full consent of the intending spouses, to enact and strictly enforce laws concerning the minimum legal age of consent and the minimum age for marriage and to raise the minimum age for marriage where necessary;

6. Also urges States to eliminate all barriers so as to enable girls, without exception, to develop their full potential and skills through equal access to education and training;

7. Encourages States to consider ways and means to ensure the continuing education of married women, pregnant women and young mothers;

8. Urges States to take special measures for the protection of children, in particular to protect girls from rape and other forms of sexual abuse and gender-based violence in situations of armed conflict, paying special attention to refugee and displaced girls, in line with the recommendations of the expert appointed by the Secretary-General to study the impact of armed conflict on children and to take into account the special needs of the girl child in the delivery of humanitarian assistance;

9. Urges States parties to fulfil the obligations they have undertaken under the Convention on the Rights of the Child and the Convention on the Elimination of All Forms of Discrimination against Women to protect women and girls from all forms of violence, including domestic violence, sexual trafficking and child prostitution;

10. Urges States to implement measures to protect women and girls from all forms of violence, in line with the recommendations of the Special Rapporteur of the Commission on Human Rights on violence against women, its causes and consequences;

11. Requests all States to implement, on an urgent basis, measures to protect children from all forms of sexual exploitation, including measures in line with those outlined in the Declaration and Agenda for Action of the World Congress against Commercial Sexual Exploitation of Children;

12. Calls upon Governments, civil society, including the media, and non-governmental organizations to promote human rights education and the full respect for and enjoyment of the human rights of the girl child, inter alia, through the translation, production and dissemination of

age-appropriate information materials on these rights to all sectors of society, and particularly to children;

13. Calls upon Governments to encourage efforts by civil society, non-governmental organizations including women's organizations, to establish community-based groups or local committees which could assist with the safety and welfare of children;

14. Requests the Secretary-General, as Chairman of the Administrative Committee on Coordination, to ensure that all organizations and bodies of the United Nations system, individually and collectively, in particular the United Nations Children's Fund, the United Nations Educational, Scientific and Cultural Organization, the World Food Programme, the United Nations Population Fund, the United Nations Development Fund for Women, the World Health Organization, the United Nations High Commissioner for Human Rights, the United Nations Development Programme and the United Nations High Commissioner for Refugees, take into account the rights and the particular needs of the girl child, especially in education, health and nutrition, and eliminate negative cultural attitudes and practices against the girl child in the implementation of the outcome of all recent global conferences, in particular the Platform for Action of the Fourth World Conference on Women, and of the system-wide medium-term plan for the advancement of women for the period 1996-2001;

15. Calls upon the Commission on Human Rights, while considering, in accordance with the agreed conclusions 1996/1 of the Economic and Social Council its input to the Commission on the Status of Women on ensuring women's equal enjoyment of their human rights, in particular those relating to economic resources, to pay particular attention to all the human rights of the girl child;

16. Requests all human rights treaty bodies, special procedures and other human rights mechanisms of the Commission on Human Rights and the Subcommission on Prevention of Discrimination and Protection of Minorities to regularly and systematically adopt a gender perspective in the implementation of their mandates and to include in their reports information on and qualitative analysis of violations of human rights of women and girls, and encourages the strengthening of cooperation and coordination in that regard;
17. Calls upon States and international and non-governmental organizations to mobilize all necessary resources, support and efforts to realize the goals, strategic objectives and actions set out in the Platform for Action of the Fourth World Conference on Women;
18. Calls upon all States, all relevant organizations and bodies of the United Nations system and non-governmental organizations to implement commitments to goals and actions relating to the girl child and to report on initiatives and progress to the Commission on the Status of Women at its forty-second session, pursuant to the decision of the Commission to review the progress made in the implementation of the Platform for Action of the Fourth World Conference on Women relating to the girl child in 1998.

General Assembly resolution relating to the Rights of the Child

The General Assembly,

— Recalling its resolutions 51/77 and 51/76 of 12 December 1996, 51/186 of 16 December 1996 and Commission on Human Rights resolution 1997/78,

— Also recalling the Declaration and Plan of Action adopted by the World Summit for Children in 1990, notably its solemn commitment to give high priority to the rights of children, to their survival and to their protection and development, and reaffirming the Vienna Declaration and Programme of Action, which, inter alia, states that national and international mechanisms and programmes for the defence and protection of children, in particular those in especially difficult circumstances, should be strengthened, including through effective measures to combat exploitation and abuse of children such as female infanticide, harmful child labour, sale of children and organs, child prostitution and child pornography as well as other forms of sexual abuse, and which reaffirms that all human rights and fundamental freedoms are universal,

— Underlining the need for mainstreaming a gender perspective into all policies and programmes relating to children,

— Profoundly concerned that the situation of children in many parts of the world remains critical as a result of inadequate social and economic conditions, poverty, natural disasters, armed conflicts, displacement, exploitation, racism and all forms of intolerance, unemployment, rural-to-urban migration, illiteracy, hunger, disability, and drug abuse, and convinced that urgent and effective national and international action is called for,

— Inviting Member States to promote the values of peace, understanding, and dialogue in the education of children, and awareness of the urgent need to combat poverty, malnutrition, and illiteracy worldwide,

— Recognizing that legislation alone is not enough to prevent violations of the rights of the child, that stronger political commitment is needed and that Governments should implement their laws and complement legislative measures with effective action,

— Recommending that within their mandates, all relevant human rights mechanisms and all other relevant organs and mechanisms of the United Nations system and the supervisory bodies of the specialized agencies pay attention to particular situations in which children are in danger and where their rights are violated and that they take into account the work of the Committee on the Rights of the Child,

— Stressing the need to strengthen partnerships between Governments, international organizations and all sectors of civil society, in particular non-governmental organizations, in order to achieve these objectives,

— Reaffirming that the best interests of the child shall be a primary consideration in all actions concerning children,

I. *Implementation of the Convention on the Rights of the Child*

1. Welcomes the unprecedented number of 191 States that have ratified or acceded to the Convention on the Rights of the Child as a universal commitment to the rights of the child;

2. Urges once again all States that have not yet done so to sign and ratify or accede to the Convention as a matter of priority, with a view to reaching the goal of universal adherence established by the World Summit for Children and reiterated by the Vienna Declaration and Programme of Action;

3. Recognizes the important role of the Committee on the Rights of the Child in creating awareness of the principles and provisions of the Convention and in providing recommendations to States parties on its implementation;

4. Invites the Committee on the Rights of the Child to further enhance the constructive dialogue with the States Parties and the transparent and effective functioning of the Committee;

5. Requests the Secretary-General to ensure the provision of appropriate staff and facilities for the effective and expeditious performance of the functions of the Committee on the Rights of the Child, and takes note of the Plan of Action of the United Nations High Commissioner for Human Rights to strengthen the implementation of the Convention on the Rights of the Child;

6. Calls upon States parties to implement fully the Convention, to cooperate closely with the Committee on the Rights of the Child and to comply in a timely manner with their reporting obligations under the Convention, in accordance with the guidelines elaborated by the Committee;

7. Also calls upon States parties to withdraw reservations incompatible with the object and purpose of the Convention and to consider reviewing other reservations;

8. Recalls that the amendment to article 43 (2) of the Convention, which would increase the membership of the Committee on the Rights of the Child from 10 to 18 experts, was adopted by the Conference of States parties on 12 December 1995, that this amendment was approved by the General Assembly on 21 December 1995 in its resolution 50/155, and therefore calls upon States parties to take appropriate measures so that acceptance of the amendment by a two-thirds majority of States parties can be reached as soon as possible in order for the amendment to enter into force;

9. Calls upon States parties to the Convention to ensure that the education of the child shall be carried out in accordance with article 29 of the Convention and that the education be directed, inter alia, to the development of respect for human rights and fundamental freedoms, for the Charter of the United Nations and for different cultures and to the preparation of the child for

responsible life in a free society, in the spirit of understanding, peace, tolerance, gender equality and friendship among peoples, ethnic, national and religious groups and persons of indigenous origin;

10. Also calls upon States parties to the Convention, in accordance with their obligation under article 42 of the Convention, to make the principles and provisions of the Convention widely known to adults and children alike, and also calls upon States parties to encourage training on the rights of the child for those involved in activities concerning children, for example through the programme of advisory services and technical cooperation in the field of human rights;

11. Stresses that the implementation of the Convention contributes to the achievement of the goals of the World Summit for Children as emphasized in the report of the Secretary-General on the progress at mid-decade on implementation of General Assembly resolution 45/217 of 21 December 1990 on the World Summit for Children;

12. Encourages the Committee, in monitoring the implementation of the Convention on the Rights of the Child, to continue to pay attention to the needs of children in especially difficult circumstances;

II. *Children with disabilities*

1. Welcomes the increased attention given by the Committee on the Rights of the Child to the equal enjoyment by children with disabilities of the rights of the child;

2. Calls upon all States to take all necessary measures to ensure the full and equal enjoyment of all human rights and fundamental freedoms by children with disabilities, and to develop and enforce legislation against discrimination against children with disabilities;

3. Also calls upon all States to promote for children with disabilities a full and decent life, in conditions which ensure dignity, promote self-reliance, and facilitate the child's active participation in the community;

4. Emphasizes the right to education as a human right, and calls upon States to make education accessible to children with special educational needs in a manner conducive to the child's achieving the fullest possible social integration and individual development, and to adopt an integrated approach to providing adequate support and appropriate education for such children;

5. Welcomes the decision by the Economic and Social Council to request the Special Rapporteur on Disabilities of the Commission for Social Development to pay special attention to children with disabilities, and the invitation to enhance the cooperation between the Special Rapporteur and the Committee on the Rights of the Child, and also requests the United Nations High Commissioner for Human Rights and the United Nations Children's Fund to work closely with him;

6. Calls upon all States, in complying with their reporting obligations to the Committee under article 44 (1) of the Convention, to include, in accordance with the Committee's guidelines, information on the situation and the needs of children with disabilities, including disaggregated data, and on the measures taken to ensure such children their enjoyment of the rights under the Convention;

III. *Prevention and eradication of the sale of children and of their sexual exploitation, including child prostitution and child pornography*

1. Welcomes the interim report of the Special Rapporteur of the Commission on Human Rights on the sale of children, child prostitution and child pornography, and expresses its support for her work in examining, all over

the world, the question of the sale of children, child prostitution and child pornography;

2. Requests the Secretary-General to provide the Special Rapporteur with all necessary human and financial assistance to make the full discharge of the mandate possible and to enable her to submit an interim report to the General Assembly at its fifty-third session and a report to the Commission on Human Rights at its fifty-fourth session;

3. Supports the work of the open-ended inter-sessional working group of the Commission on Human Rights on the elaboration of a draft optional protocol to the Convention on the Rights of the Child related to the sale of children, child prostitution and child pornography, and expresses the hope that it will make further progress prior to the fifty-fourth session of the Commission with a view to finalizing that work before the tenth anniversary of the Convention on the Rights of the Child;

4. Calls upon all States parties to fulfil their obligation under article 34 of the Convention, and also calls upon all States to support efforts in the context of the United Nations system aimed at adopting effective national, bilateral and multilateral measures for the prevention and eradication of the sale of children and of their sexual exploitation, including child prostitution and child pornography, in particular by criminalizing the sexual exploitation of children;

5. Requests all States to implement on an urgent basis measures to protect children from all forms of sexual exploitation and sexual abuse, including measures in line with those outlined in the Declaration and Agenda for Action of the World Congress against Commercial Sexual Exploitation of Children;

6. Calls upon States to criminalize all forms of sexual exploitation of children, including commercial sexual

exploitation, and to condemn and penalize all those offenders involved, whether local or foreign, while ensuring that children victims of this practice are not penalized;

7. Also calls upon States to review and revise, where appropriate, laws, policies, programmes and practices to eliminate all forms of sexual exploitation of children, including commercial sexual exploitation;

8. Further calls upon States to enforce relevant laws, policies and programmes to protect children from sexual exploitation, in particular by penalizing all those offenders involved, and to strengthen communication and cooperation between law enforcement authorities;

9. Stresses the need to combat the existence of a market that encourages such criminal practices against children;

10. Urges States, in cases of sex tourism, to develop or strengthen and implement laws to criminalize the acts of nationals of the countries of origin when committed against children in the countries of destination, to ensure that a person who exploits a child for sexual abuse purposes in another country is prosecuted by competent national authorities, either in the country of origin or in the country of destination, to strengthen laws and law enforcement, including confiscation and seizure of assets and profits and other sanctions, against those who commit sexual crimes against children in countries of destination, and to share relevant data;

11. Requests States to step up cooperation and concerted action by all relevant law enforcement authorities and institutions with a view to dismantling national, regional and international networks in trafficking in children;

12. Invites States to allocate resources to provide comprehensive programmes designed to heal and to rehabilitate into society child victims of trafficking and

sexual exploitation, including through job training, legal assistance and confidential health care, and to take all appropriate measures to promote their physical and psychological recovery and social reintegration;

IV. *Protection of children affected by armed conflict*

1. Expresses grave concern at the numerous damaging effects of armed conflicts on children, including the use of children as combatants in such situations, and emphasizes the need for the world community to focus increased attention on this serious problem with a view to bringing it to an end;

2. Invites all States to accede to relevant international human rights and humanitarian law instruments, and urges them to implement those instruments to which they are parties;

3. Calls upon all States and other parties to armed conflict to respect international humanitarian law and, in this regard, calls upon States parties to respect fully the provisions of the Geneva Conventions of 12 August 1949 and the additional protocols thereto of 1977, while bearing in mind resolution 2 of the twenty-sixth International Conference of the Red Cross and Red Crescent, and to respect the provisions of the Convention on the Rights of the Child which accord children affected by armed conflict special protection and treatment;

4. Calls upon States and United Nations bodies and organizations to treat children during conflict and in post-conflict situations as a priority concern in human rights, humanitarian and development activities, including in field operations and country programmes, to enhance coordination and cooperation throughout the United Nations system and to ensure effective protection for children affected by armed conflict;

5. Recommends that the humanitarian concerns relating to children affected by armed conflict and their protection

be fully reflected in United Nations field operations, which, inter alia, promote peace, prevent and resolve conflicts, and implement peace agreements;

6. Underlines the importance that measures to ensure respect for the rights of the child, including in the areas of health and nutrition, formal, informal or non-formal education, physical and psychological recovery, and social reintegration, be included within emergency and other humanitarian assistance policies and programmes;

7. Stresses the need for Governments and other parties to armed conflict to take measures, including the establishment, for example, of "days of tranquillity" and "corridors of peace", to ensure humanitarian access, the delivery of humanitarian relief and the provision of services, such as education and health, including immunization of children affected by armed conflict;

8. Supports the work of the working group of the Commission on Human Rights on a draft optional protocol to the Convention on the Rights of the Child related to the involvement of children in armed conflict, and expresses the hope that it will make further progress prior to the fifty-fourth session of the Commission with a view to finalizing this work;

9. Urges States and all other parties to armed conflict to adopt all necessary measures to end the use of children as soldiers and to ensure their demobilization and reintegration into society, including through adequate education and training, in a manner that fosters their self-respect and dignity, and invites the international community to assist in this endeavour;

10. Welcomes increased international efforts in various forums with respect to anti-personnel mines, recognizes the positive effect on children of those efforts, and in this regard takes due note of the conclusion of the Convention on the Prohibition of the Use, Stockpiling, Production and

Transfer of Anti-Personnel Mines and on their Destruction and its implementation by those States that become parties to it, as well as of the amended Mines Protocol of the Convention on Prohibitions or Restrictions on the use of certain conventional weapons which may be deemed to be excessively injurious or have indiscriminate effects;

11. Calls upon all States and relevant United Nations bodies, including the United Nations Voluntary Trust Fund for Assistance in Mine Clearance, to contribute on an ongoing basis to international mine clearance efforts, and urges States to take further action to promote gender- and age-appropriate mine-awareness programmes and child-centred rehabilitation, thereby reducing the number and the plight of child victims;

12. Reaffirms that rape in the conduct of armed con- flict constitutes a war crime and that under certain circumstances it constitutes a crime against humanity and an act of genocide as defined in the Convention on the Prevention and Punishment of the Crime of Genocide, and calls upon all States to take all measures required for the protection of women and children from all acts of gender-based violence, including rape, sexual exploitation and forced pregnancy, to strengthen mechanisms to investigate and punish all those responsible and bring the perpetrators to justice;

13. Urgently requests that appropriate measures be taken by Member States and United Nations agencies, within the scope of their respective mandates, to ensure humanitarian access to children affected by armed conflict, to facilitate the extension of humanitarian assistance, including education, and to ensure the physical and psychological recovery and reintegration into society of child soldiers, victims of landmines and victims of gender-based violence;

14. Recommends that whenever sanctions are imposed their impact on children be assessed and monitored and humanitarian exceptions be child-focused and formulated with clear application guidelines;

15. Recalls the importance of preventive measures such as early warning systems, preventive diplomacy and education for peace to prevent conflicts and their negative impact on the rights of the child, and urges Governments and the international community to promote sustainable human development;

16. Calls upon all States, in accordance with the norms of international humanitarian law, to integrate in their armed forces' training and education programmes, including those for peacekeeping, instruction on responsibilities towards the civilian population, particularly women and children;

17. Welcomes the appointment of Mr. Olara Otunnu as the Special Representative of the Secretary-General for Children in Armed Conflict in accordance with General Assembly resolution 51/77 of 12 December 1996;

18. Invites Governments, specialized agencies, relevant United Nations bodies, notably the Office of the United Nations High Commissioner for Human Rights, the Office of the United Nations High Commissioner for Refugees, the United Nations Children's Fund, and regional, intergovernmental and non-governmental organizations, as well as the Committee on the Rights of the Child, to cooperate with the Special Representative and to contribute to his work, including his annual report;

19. Recommends that the Secretary-General ensure that the necessary support is made available to the Special Representative for the effective performance of his mandate, encourages the United Nations Children's Fund, the Office of the United Nations High Commissioner for Refugees, and the Office of the United

Nations High Commissioner for Human Rights to provide support to the Special Representative, and calls upon States and other institutions to provide voluntary contributions for that purpose;

20. Invites Member States and relevant United Nations bodies and non-governmental organizations to consider how the impact of armed conflict on children can best be integrated into events designed to commemorate the tenth anniversary of the World Summit for Children and the entry into force of the Convention;

V. *Refugee and internally displaced children*

1. Urges Governments to pay particular attention to the situation of refugee and internally displaced children by continuing to design and improve the implementation of policies for their care and well-being with the necessary international cooperation, in particular with the Office of the United Nations High Commissioner for Refugees and the United Nations Children's Fund and international humanitarian organizations;

2. Calls upon States and United Nations bodies, in recognizing the particular vulnerability of refugee and internally displaced children, to protect both their safety and their developmental needs, including health, education, and psycho-social rehabilitation;

3. Expresses its deep concern about the growing number of unaccompanied refugee and internally displaced children, and calls upon all States and United Nations bodies and agencies to ensure the early identification and registration of unaccompanied refugee and internally displaced children, to give priority to programmes for family tracing and reunification, and to continue monitoring the care arrangements for unaccompanied refugee and internally displaced children;

4. Calls upon all States and other parties to armed conflicts to recognize the particular vulnerability of refugee and

internally displaced children to the damaging effects of such conflicts, stresses the special vulnerability of child-headed households, and calls upon Governments and United Nations bodies to give these situations urgent attention, to enhance protection and assistance mechanisms, and to involve women and youth in the design, delivery, and monitoring of measures taken to this effect;

5. Invites the Representative of the Secretary-General on internally displaced persons to take into account the situation of internally displaced children in his preparation of guiding principles which are to form part of a comprehensive framework for the protection of internally displaced persons;

VI. *Elimination of exploitation of child labour*

1. Reaffirms the right of the child to be protected from economic exploitation and from performing any work that is likely to be hazardous to or interfere with the child's education, or to be harmful to the child's health or physical, mental, spiritual, moral or social development;

2. Welcomes the measures taken by Governments to eliminate the exploitation of child labour, while recalling the Programme of Action for the Elimination of the Exploitation of Child Labour, and calls upon relevant United Nations agencies, in particular the United Nations Children's Fund and the International Labour Organization, to continue to support national efforts in this regard;

3. Also welcomes the recent holding of various international conferences on various forms of child labour;

4. Further welcomes the efforts by the Committee on the Rights of the Child in the area of child labour, takes note of its recommendations and encourages the Committee as well as other relevant human rights treaty bodies,

within their respective mandates, to continue to monitor this growing problem when examining reports of States parties;

5. Calls upon all States to translate into concrete action their commitment to the progressive and effective elimination of all forms of exploitative child labour, and urges them, as a matter of priority, to eliminate all extreme forms of child labour, such as forced labour, bonded labour and other forms of slavery;
6. Calls upon all States that have not yet done so to consider ratifying the conventions of the International Labour Organization concerning the abolition of forced labour and the minimum age for employment, including for particularly hazardous work for children, and to implement those conventions;
7. Calls upon all States to support the negotiation, with a view to its early finalization, by the International Labour Organization of a future instrument aimed at eradicating the most intolerable forms of child labour;
8. Also calls upon all States to set specific target dates for eliminating all forms of child labour that are contrary to accepted international standards and for ensuring the full enforcement of relevant existing laws and, where appropriate, enacting legislation necessary to implement their obligations under the Convention on the Rights of the Child and International Labour Organization standards ensuring the protection of working children;
9. Further calls upon all States to recognize the right to education by making primary education compulsory and ensuring that all children have access to free primary education as a key strategy to prevent child labour;
10. Also calls upon all States to systematically assess and examine, in close cooperation with international organizations such as the International Labour

Organization and the United Nations Children's Fund, the magnitude, nature and causes of the exploitation of child labour, and to develop and implement strategies for combating these practices, with a specific emphasis on the situation of girls, their right to education and access to schools on an equal basis with boys, in close cooperation with the United Nations Educational, Scientific and Cultural Organization;

11. Calls upon all States and the United Nations system to strengthen international cooperation, as a means of assisting Governments in preventing or combating violations of the rights of the child, including the exploitation of child labour;

VII. *The plight of children living and/or working on the streets*

1. Expresses grave concern at the large number of children living and/or working on the streets, and at the continued growth in incidents and reports worldwide of such children being affected by serious crime, drug trafficking and abuse, violence and prostitution;

2. Welcomes the continuing efforts of Governments, the United Nations system, and civil society to tackle this multifaceted problem;

3. Calls upon Governments to continue actively to seek comprehensive solutions for the problems of children living and/or working on the streets, including by helping to alleviate the poverty of such children, their families, or guardians, by taking measures to ensure their reintegration into society, and by providing, inter alia, adequate nutrition, shelter, health care and education, taking into account that such children are particularly vulnerable to all forms of violence, abuse, exploitation and neglect;

4. Emphasizes that the provisions of the Convention on the Rights of the Child and other relevant human rights instruments must constitute the standard in efforts to

deal with this problem, and recommends that the Committee on the Rights of the Child and other relevant human rights treaty monitoring bodies continue to give attention to it when examining the reports of States parties;

5. Strongly urges all Governments to guarantee the respect for all human rights and fundamental freedoms, particularly the right to life, and to take urgent measures to prevent the killing of children living and/or working on the streets and to combat torture and violence against them, and to ensure strict compliance with the Convention on the Rights of the Child and other relevant human rights instruments, including the requirement that legal and juridical processes respect the rights of the child;

6. Calls upon the international community to support, through effective international cooperation, the efforts of States to improve the situation of such children and encourages States parties to the Convention on the Rights of the Child, in preparing their reports to the Committee on the Rights of the Child, to take full account of the particular needs and rights of such children and to consider requesting technical advice and assistance for initiatives aimed at improving their situation;

VIII. *Decides*:

(a) To request the Secretary-General to submit a report on the rights of the child to the General Assembly at its fifty-third session, containing information on the status of the Convention on the Rights of the Child and the problems addressed in the present resolution;

(b) To request the Special Representative of the Secretary-General for Children in Armed Conflict to submit to the General Assembly and the Commission on Human Rights an annual report containing relevant information on the situation of children affected by armed conflict, bearing in mind existing mandates and reports of relevant bodies;

(c) To continue its consideration of this question at its fifty-third session under the item entitled "Promotion and protection of the rights of the child".

The Vienna Declaration and Programme of Action-The rights of the child

Part I

21. The World Conference on Human Rights, welcoming the early ratification of the Convention on the Rights of the Child by a large number of States and noting the recognition of the human rights of children in the World Declaration on the Survival, Protection and Development of Children and Plan of Action adopted by the World Summit for Children, urges universal ratification of the Convention by 1995 and its effective implementation by States parties through the adoption of all the necessary legislative, administrative and other measures and the allocation to the maximum extent of the available resources. In all actions concerning children, nondiscrimination and the best interest of the child should be primary considerations and the views of the child given due weight.

National and international mechanisms and programmes should be strengthened for the defence and protection of children, in particular, the girl child, abandoned children, street children, economically and sexually exploited children, including through child pornography, child prostitution or sale of organs, children victims of diseases including acquired immunodeficiency syndrome, refugee and displaced children, children in detention, children in armed conflict, as well as children victims of famine and drought and other emergencies. International cooperation and solidarity should be promoted to support the implementation of the Convention and the rights of the child should be a priority in the United Nations system-wide action on human rights. The World Conference on Human Rights also stresses that the child for the full and harmonious development of his or her personality should grow up in a family environment which accordingly merits broader protection.

Part II B: Equality, dignity and tolerance

4. The rights of the child

45. The World Conference on Human Rights reiterates the principle of "First Call for Children" and, in this respect, underlines the importance of major national and international efforts, especially those of the United Nations Children's Fund, for promoting respect for the rights of the child to survival, protection, development and participation.

46. Measures should be taken to achieve universal ratification of the Convention on the Rights of the Child by 1995 and the universal signing of the World Declaration on the Survival, Protection and Development of Children and Plan of Action adopted by the World Summit for Children, as well as their effective implementation. The World Conference on Human Rights urges States to withdraw reservations to the Convention on the Rights of the Child contrary to the object and purpose of the Convention or otherwise contrary to international treaty law.

47. The World Conference on Human Rights urges all nations to undertake measures to the maximum extent of their available resources, with the support of international cooperation, to achieve the goals in the World Summit Plan of Action. The Conference calls on States to integrate the Convention on the Rights of the

Child into their national action plans. By means of these national action plans and through international efforts, particular priority should be placed on reducing infant and maternal mortality rates, reducing malnutrition and illiteracy rates and providing access to safe drinking water and to basic education. Whenever so called for, national plans of action should be devised to combat devastating emergencies resulting from natural disasters and armed conflicts and the equally grave problem of children in extreme poverty.

48. The World Conference on Human Rights urges all States, with the support of international cooperation, to address the acute problem of children under especially difficult circumstances. Exploitation and abuse of children should be actively combated, including by addressing their root causes. Effective measures are required against female infanticide, harmful child labour, sale of children and organs, child prostitution, child pornography, as well as other forms of sexual abuse.

49. The World Conference on Human Rights supports all measures by the United Nations and its specialized agencies to ensure the effective protection and promotion of human rights of the girl child. The World Conference on Human Rights urges States to repeal existing laws and regulations and remove customs and practices which discriminate against and cause harm to the girl child.

50. The World Conference on Human Rights strongly supports the proposal that the Secretary-General initiate a study into means of improving the protection of children in armed conflicts. Humanitarian norms should be implemented and measures taken in order to protect and facilitate assistance to children in war zones. Measures should include protection for children against indiscriminate use of all weapons of war, especially anti-personnel mines. The need for aftercare and rehabilitation of children traumatized by war must be addressed

urgently. The Conference calls on the Committee on the Rights of the Child to study the question of raising the minimum age of recruitment into armed forces.

51. The World Conference on Human Rights recommends that matters relating to human rights and the situation of children be regularly reviewed and monitored by all relevant organs and mechanisms of the United Nations system and by the supervisory bodies of the specialized agencies in accordance with their mandates.

52. The World Conference on Human Rights recognizes the important role played by nongovernmental organizations in the effective implementation of all human rights instruments and, in particular, the Convention on the Rights of the Child.

53. The World Conference on Human Rights recommends that the Committee on the Rights of the Child, with the assistance of the Centre for Human Rights, be enabled expeditiously and effectively to meet its mandate, especially in view of the unprecedented extent of ratification and subsequent submission of country reports.

10

Convention on the Right of Child

The Convention on the Right of Child was adopted by the General Assembly of United Nations on 20 November 1989. The details of the Convention are given below.

Preamble

The States Parties to the present Convention,

Considering that, in accordance with the principles proclaimed in the Charter of the United Nations, recognition of the inherent dignity and of the equal and inalienable rights of all members of the human family is the foundation of freedom, justice and peace in the world,

Bearing in mind that the peoples of the United Nations, have, in the Charter, reaffirmed their faith in fundamental human rights and in the dignity and worth of the human person, and have determined to promote social progress and better standards of life in larger freedom,

Recognising that the United Nations has, in the Universal Declaration of Human Rights and in the International Covenants on Human Rights, proclaimed and agreed that everyone is entitled to all the rights and freedoms set forth therein, without distinction of any kind, such as race, colour, sex, language religion, political or other opinion, national or social origin, property, birth or other status,

Recalling that, in the Universal Declaration of Human Rights, the United Nations has proclaimed that childhood is entitled to special care and assistance,

Convinced that the family, as the fundamental group of society and the natural environment for the growth and well-being of all its members and particularly children, should be afforded the necessary protection and assistance so that it can fully assume its responsibilities within the community,

Recognising that the child, for the full and harmonious development of his or her personality, should grow up in a family environment, in an atmosphere of happiness, love and understanding,

Considering that the child should be fully prepared to live an individual life in society, and brought up in the spirit of the ideals proclaimed in the Charter of the United Nations, and in particular in the spirit of peace, dignity, tolerance, freedom, equality and solidarity,

Bearing in mind the need to extend particular care to the child has been stated in the Geneva Declaration of the Rights of the Child of 1924 and in the Declaration of the Rights of the Child adopted by the General Assembly on 20 November 1959 and recognised in the Universal Declaration of Human Rights, in the International Covenant on Civil and Political Rights (in particular in articles 23 and 24), in the International Covenant on Economic, Social and Cultural Rights (in particular in Article 10) and in the statutes and relevant instruments of specialised agencies and international organisations concerned with the welfare of children,

Bearing in mind as indicated in the Declaration of the Rights of the Child, "the child, by reason of his physical and mental immaturity, needs special safeguards and care, including appropriate legal protection, before as well as after birth",

Recalling the provisions of the Declaration on Social and Legal Principles relating to Protection and Welfare of Children, with Special Reference to Foster Placement and Adoption Nationally and Internationally; the United Nations Standard Minimum Rules for the Administration of Juvenile Justice (The Beijing Rules); and the Declaration on the Protection of Women and Children in Emergency and Armed Conflict,

Recognising that, in all countries in the world, there are children living in exceptionally difficult conditions, and the such children need special consideration,

Taking due account of the importance of the traditions and cultural values of each people for the protection and harmonious development of the child,

Recognising the importance of international cooperation for improving the living conditions of children in every country, in particular in the developing countries,

Have agreed as follows:

Part I

Article 1

For the purposes of the present Convention, a child means every human being below the age of eighteen years unless under the law applicable to the child, majority is attained earlier.

Article 2

1. States Parties shall respect and ensure the rights set forth in the present Convention to each child within their jurisdiction without discrimination of any kind, irrespective of the child's or his or her parent's or legal guardian's race, colour, sex, language, religion, political or other opinion, national ethnic or social origin, property, disability, birth or other status.

2. States Parties shall take all appropriate measures to ensure that the child is protected against all forms of discrimination or punishment on the basis of the status, activities, expressed opinions, or beliefs of the child's parents, legal guardians, or family members.

Article 3

1. In all actions concerning children, whether undertaken by public or private social welfare institutions, courts of law, administrative authorities or legislative bodies, the best interests of the child shall be a primary consideration.
2. States Parties undertake to ensure the child such protection and care as is necessary for his or her well-being, taking into account the rights and duties of his or her parents, legal guardians, or other individuals legally responsible for him or her, and to this end, shall take all appropriate legislative and administrative measures.
3. States Parties shall ensure that the institutions, services and facilities responsible for the care or protection of children shall conform with the standards established by competent authorities, particularly in the areas of safety, health, in the number and suitability of their staff, as well as competent supervision.

Article 4

States Parties shall undertake all appropriate legislative, administrative, and other measures for the implementation of the rights recognised in the present Convention. With regard to economic, social and cultural rights, States Parties shall undertake such measures to the maximum extent of their available resources and, where needed, within the framework of international cooperation.

Article 5

States Parties shall respect the responsibilities, rights and duties of parents or, where applicable, the members of the extended family or community as provided for by local custom, legal guardians or other persons legally responsible for the child, to provide, in a manner consistent with the evolving capacities of the child, appropriate direction and guidance in the exercise by the child, appropriate direction and guidance in the exercise by the child of the rights recognised in the present Convention.

Article 6

1. States Parties recognise that every child has the inherent right to life.
2. States Parties shall ensure to the maximum extent possible the survival and development of the child.

Article 7

1. The child shall be registered immediately after birth and shall have the right from birth to a name, the right to acquire a nationality and, as far as possible, the right to know and be cared for by his or her parents.
2. States Parties shall ensure the implementation of these rights in accordance with their national law and their obligations under the relevant international instruments in this field, in particular where the child would otherwise be stateless.

Article 8

1. States Parties undertake to respect the right of the child to preserve his or her identity, including nationality, name and family relations as recognised by law without unlawful interference.

2. Where a child is illegally deprived of some or all of the elements of his or her identity, States Parties shall provide appropriate assistance and protection, with a view to re-establishing speedily his or her identity.

Article 9

1. States Parties shall ensure that a child shall not be separated from his or her parents against their will, except when competent authorities subject to judicial review determine, in accordance with applicable law and procedures, that such separation is necessary for the best interests of the child. Such determination may be necessary in a particular case such as one involving abuse or neglect of the child by the parents, or one where the parents are living separately and a decision must be made as to the child's place of residence.
2. In any proceedings pursuant to paragraph 1 of the present Article, all interested parties shall be given an opportunity to participate in the proceeding and make their views known.
3. States Parties shall respect the right of the child who is separated from one or both parents to maintain personal relations and direct contact with both parents on a regular basis, except if it is contrary to the child's best interests.
4. Where such separation results from any action initiated by a States Party, such as the detention, imprisonment, exile, deportation or death (including death arising from any cause while the person is in the custody of the State) of one or both parents or of the child, that State Party shall, upon request, provide the parents, the child or, if appropriate, another member of the family with the essential information concerning the whereabouts of the absent member(s) of the family unless the provision of the information would be detrimental to the well-being

of the child. States Parties shall further ensure that the submission of such a request shall of itself entail no adverse consequences for the person(s) concerned.

Article 10

1. In accordance with the obligation of States Parties under article 9, paragraph 1, applications by a child or his or her parents to enter or leave a State party for the purpose of family reunification shall be dealt with by States Parties in a positive, humane and expeditious manner. States Parties shall further ensure that the submission of such a request shall entail no adverse consequences for the applicants and for the members of their family.

2. A child whose parents reside in different States shall have the right to maintain on a regular basis, save in exceptional circumstances personal relations and direct contacts with both parents. Towards that end and in accordance with the obligation of States Parties under article 9, paragraph 1, States Parties shall respect the right of the child and his or her parents to leave any country, including their own, and to enter their own country. The right to leave any country shall be subject only to such restrictions as are prescribed by law and which are necessary to protect the national security, public order (order public), public health or morals or the rights and freedoms of others and are consistent with the other rights recognised in the present Convention.

Article 11

1. States Parties shall take measures to combat the illicit transfer and non-return of children abroad.

2. To this end, States Parties shall promote the conclusion of bilateral or multilateral agreements or accession to existing agreements.

Article 12

1. States Parties shall assure to the child who is capable of forming his or her own views the right to express those views freely in all matters affecting the child, the views of the child being given due weight in accordance with the age and maturity of the child.

2. For this purpose, the child shall in particular be provided the opportunity to be heard in any judicial and administrative proceedings affecting the child, either directly, or through a representative or an appropriate body, in a manner consistent with the procedural rules of national law.

Article 13

1. The child shall have the right to freedom of expression; this right shall include freedom to seek, receive and impart information and ideas of all kinds, regardless of frontiers, either orally, in writing or in print, in the form of art, or through any other media of the child's choice.

2. The exercise of this right may be subject to certain restrictions, but these shall only be such as are provided by law and are necessary:

   a) For respect of the rights or reputations of others, or

   b) For the protection of national security or of public order (order public), or of public health or morals.

Article 14

1. States Parties shall respect the right of the child to freedom of thought, conscience and religion.

2. States Parties shall respect the rights and duties of the parents and when applicable, legal guardians, to provide direction to the child in the exercise of his or her right in

a manner consistent with the evolving capacities of the child.

3. Freedom to manifest one's religion or beliefs may be subject only to such limitations as are prescribed by law and are necessary to protect public safety, order, health or morals, or the fundamental rights and freedoms of others.

Article 15

1. States Parties recognise the rights of the child to freedom of association and to freedom of peaceful assembly.

2. No restrictions may be placed on the exercise of these rights other than those imposed in conformity with the law and which are necessary in a democratic society in the interests of national security or public safety, public order (order public), the protection of public health or morals or the protection of the rights and freedoms of others.

Article 16

1. No child shall be subjected to arbitrary or unlawful interference with his or her privacy, family, home or correspondence, nor to unlawful attacks on his or her honour and reputation;

2. The child has the right to the protection of the law against such interference or attacks.

Article 17

States Parties recognise the important function performed by the mass media and shall ensure that the child has access to information and material from a diversity of national and international sources, especially those aimed at the promotion of his or her social, spiritual and moral well-being and physical and mental health. To this end, States Parties shall:

a) Encourage the mass media to disseminate information and material of social and cultural benefit to the child and in accordance with the spirit of Article 29;

b) Encourage international co-operation in the production, exchange and dissemination of such information and material from a diversity of cultural, national and international sources;

c) Encourage the production and dissemination of children's books;

d) Encourage the mass media to have particular regard to the linguistic needs of the child who belongs to a minority group or who is indigenous.

e) Encourage the development of appropriate guidelines for the protection of the child from information and material injurious to his or her well-being, bearing in mind the provisions of Articles 13 and 18.

Article 18

1. States Parties shall use their best efforts to ensure recognition of the principles that both parents have common responsibilities for the upbringing and development of the child. Parents or, as the case may be, legal guardians, have the primary responsibility for the upbringing and development of the child. The best interests of the child will be their basic concern.

2. For the purpose of guaranteeing and promoting the rights set forth in the present Convention, States Parties shall render appropriate assistance to parents and legal guardians in the performance of their child-rearing responsibilities and shall ensure the development of institutions, facilities and services of the care of children.

3. States Parties shall take all appropriate measures to ensure that children of working parents have the right

to benefit from child-care services and facilities for which they are eligible.

Article 19

1. States Parties shall take all appropriate legislative, administrative social and educational measures to protect the child from all forms of physical or mental violence, injury or abuse, neglect or negligent treatment, maltreatment or exploitation, including sexual abuse, while in the care of parent(s), legal guardian(s) or any other person who has the care of the child.

2. Such protective measures should, as appropriate, include effective procedures for the establishment of social programmes to provide necessary support for the child and for those who have the care of the child, as well as for other forms of prevention and for identification, reporting, referral, investigation, treatment and follow-up of instances of child maltreatment described heretofore, and, as appropriate, for judicial involvement.

Article 20

1. A child temporarily or permanently deprived of his or her family environment, or in whose own best interests cannot be allowed to remain in that environment shall be entitled to special protection and assistance provided by the State.

2. States Parties shall in accordance with their national laws ensure alternative care for such a child.

3. Such care could include, *inter alia*, foster placement *kafalah of Islamic law*, adoption or if necessary placement in suitable institutions for the care of children. When considering solutions, due regard shall be paid to the desirability of continuity in a child's upbringing and to the child's ethnic, religious, cultural and linguistic background.

Article 21

States Parties that recognise and/or permit the system of adoption shall ensure that the best interests of the child shall be the paramount consideration and they shall:

a) Ensure that the adoption of a child is authorised only by competent authorities who determine, in accordance with applicable law and procedures and on the basis of all pertinent and reliable information, that the adoption is permissible in view of the child's status concerning parents, relatives and legal guardians and that, if required, the persons concerned have given their informed consent to the adoption on the basis of such counselling as may be necessary;

b) Recognised that inter-country adoption may be considered as an alternative means of child's care, if the child cannot be placed in a foster or an adoptive family or cannot in any suitable manner be cared for in the child's country of origin;

c) Ensure that the child concerned by inter-country adoption enjoys safeguards and standards equivalent to those existing in the case of national adoption;

d) Take all appropriate measures to ensure that, in inter-country adoption, the placement does not result in improper financial gain for those involved in it;

e) Promote, where appropriate, the objectives of the present article by concluding bilateral or multilateral arrangements or agreements, and endeavour, within this framework, to ensure that the placement of the child in another country is carried out by competent authorities or organs.

Article 22

1. States Parties shall take appropriate measures to ensure that a child who is seeking refugee status or who is

considered a refugee in accordance with applicable international or domestic law and procedures shall, whether unaccompanied or accompanied by his or her parents or by any other person, receive appropriate protection and humanitarian assistance in the enjoyment of applicable rights set forth in the present Convention and in other international human rights or humanitarian instruments to which the said States are Parties.

2. For this purpose, States Parties shall provide, as they consider appropriate, co-operation in any efforts by the United Nations and other competent inter-governmental organisations or non-governmental organisations co-operating with the United Nations to protect and assist such a child and to trace the parents or other members of the family of any refugee child in order to obtain information necessary for reunification with his or her family. In cases where no parents or other members of the family can be found, the child shall be accorded the same protection as any other child permanently or temporarily deprived of his or her family environment for any reason, as set forth in the present Convention.

Article 23

1. States Parties recognise that a mentally or physically disabled child should enjoy a full and decent life, in conditions which ensure dignity, promote self-reliance and facilitate the child's active participation in the community.

2. States Parties recognise the right of the disabled child to special care and shall encourage and ensure the extension, subject to available resources, to the eligible child and those responsible for his or her care, of assistance for which application is made and which is appropriate to the child's condition and to the circumstances of the parents or others caring for the child.

3. Recognising the special needs of a disabled child, assistances extended in accordance with paragraph 2 of the present article shall be provided free of charge, whenever possible, taking into account the financial resources of the parents or others caring for the child, and shall be designed to ensure that the disabled child has effective access to and receives education, training, health care services, rehabilitation services, preparation for employment and recreation opportunities in a manner conducive to the child's achieving the fullest possible social integration and individual development, including his or her cultural and spiritual development.

4. States Parties shall promote, in the spirit of international cooperation, the exchange of appropriate information in the field of preventive health care and of medical psychological and functional treatment of disabled children, including dissemination of and access to information concerning methods of rehabilitation, education and vocational services, with the aim of enabling States Parties to improve their capabilities and skills and to widen their experience in these areas. In this regard, particular account shall be taken of the needs of developing countries.

Article 24

1. States Parties recognise the right of the child to the enjoyment of the highest attainable standard of health and to facilities for the treatment of illness and rehabilitation of health. States Parties shall strive to ensure that no child is deprived of his or her right of access to such health care services.

2. States Parties shall pursue full implementation of this right and, in particular, shall take appropriate measures:

   a) To diminish infant and child mortality;

b) To ensure the provision of necessary medical assistance and health care to all children with emphasis on the development of primary health care;

c) To combat disease and malnutrition, including within the framework of primary health care, through, *inter alia*, the application of readily available technology and through the provision of adequate nutritious foods and clean drinking water, taking into consideration the dangers and risks of environmental pollution;

d) To ensure appropriate pre-natal and post-natal health care for mothers;

e) To ensure that all segments of society, in particular parents and children, are informed, have access to education and are supported in the use of basic knowledge of child health and nutrition, the advantages of breastfeeding, hygiene and environmental sanitation and the prevention of accidents;

f) To develop preventive health care, guidance for parents and family planning education and services.

3. States Parties shall take all effective and appropriate measures with a view to abolishing traditional practices prejudicial to the health of children.

4. States Parties undertake to promote and encourage international cooperation with a view to achieving progressively the full realisation of the right recognised in the present article. In this regard, particular account shall be taken of the needs of developing countries.

Article 25

States Parties recognise the right of a child who has been placed by the competent authorities for the purposes of care,

protection or treatment of his or her physical or mental health, to a periodic review of the treatment provided to the child and all other circumstances relevant to his or her placement.

Article 26

1. States Parties shall recognise for every child the right to benefit from social security, including social insurance, and shall take the necessary measures to achieve the full realisation of this right in accordance with their national law.

2. The benefits should, where appropriate, be granted, taking into account the resources and the circumstances of the child and persons having responsibility for the maintenance of the child, as well as any other consideration relevant to an application for benefits made by or on behalf of the child.

Article 27

1. States Parties recognise the right of every child to a standard of living adequate for the child's physical, mental, spiritual, moral and social development.

2. The parent(s) or others responsible for the child have the primary responsibility to secure, within their abilities and financial capacities, the conditions of living necessary for the child's development;

3. States Parties, in accordance with national conditions and within their means, shall take appropriate measures to assist parents and others responsible for the child to implement this right and shall in case of need provide material assistance and support programmes, particularly with regard to nutrition, clothing and housing.

4. States Parties shall take all appropriate measures to secure the recovery of maintenance for the child from the parents of other persons having financial

responsibility for the child, both within the State Party and from abroad. In particular, where the person having financial responsibility for the child lives in a State different from that of the child, States Parties shall promote the accession to international agreements of the conclusion of such agreements, as well as the making of other appropriate arrangements.

Article 28

1. States Parties recognise the right of the child to education, and with a view to achieving this right progressively and on the basis of equal opportunity, they shall, in particular:

   a) Make primary education compulsory and available free to all;

   b) Encourage the development of different forms of secondary education, including general and vocational education, make them available and accessible to every child, and take appropriate measures such as the introduction of free education and offering financial assistance in case of need;

   c) Make higher education accessible to all on the basis of capacity by every appropriate means;

   d) Make educational and vocational information and guidance available and accessible to all children;

   e) Take measures to encourage regular attendance at schools and the reduction of dropout rates.

2. States Parties shall take all appropriate measures to ensure that school discipline is administered in a manner consistent with the child's human dignity and in conformity with the present Convention.

3. States Parties shall promote and encourage international cooperation in matters relating to education, in particular with a view to contributing to the elimination of

ignorance and illiteracy throughout the world and facilitating access to scientific and technical knowledge and modern teaching methods. In this regard, particular account shall be taken of the needs of developing countries.

Article 29

1. States Parties agree that the education on the child shall be directed to:

   a) The development of the child's personality, talents and mental and physical abilities to their fullest potential;

   b) The development of respect for human rights and fundamental freedoms, and for the principles enshrined in the Charter of the United Nations.

   c) The development of respect for the child's parents, his or her own cultural identity, language and values, for the national values of the country in which the child is living, the country from which he or she may originate, and for civilisations different from his or her own;

   d) The preparation of the child for responsible life in a free society, in the spirit of understanding, peace tolerance equality of sexes, and friendship among all peoples, ethnic, national and religious groups and persons of indigenous origin;

   e) The development of respect for the natural environment.

2. No part of the present Article or article 28 shall be construed so as to interfere with the liberty of individuals and bodies to establish and direct educational institutions, subject always to the observance of the principle set forth in paragraph 1 of the present article

and to the requirements that the education given in such institutions shall confirm to such minimum standards as may be laid down by the State.

Article 30

In those States in which ethnic, religious or linguistic minorities or persons of indigenous origin exist, a child belonging to such a minority or who is indigenous shall not be denied the right, in community with other members of his or her group, to enjoy his or her own culture, to profess and practise his or her own religion, or to use his or her own language.

Article 31

1. States Parties recognise the right of the child to rest and leisure, to engage in play and recreational activities appropriate to the age of the child and to participate freely in cultural life and the arts.

2. States Parties shall respect and promote the right of the child to participate fully in cultural and artistic life and shall encourage the provision of appropriate and equal opportunities for cultural, artistic, recreational and leisure activity.

Article 32

1. States Parties recognise the right of the child to be protected from economic exploitation and from performing any work that is likely to be hazardous or to interfere with the child's education, or to be harmful to the child's health or physical, mental, spiritual, moral or social development.

2. States Parties shall take legislative, administrative, social and educational measures to ensure the implementation of the present article. To this end, and having regard to

the relevant provisions of other international instruments, States Parties shall in particular:

a) Provide for a minimum age or minimum ages for admission to employment;

b) Provide for appropriate regulation of the hours and conditions of employment; and

c) Provide for appropriate penalties or other sanctions to ensure the effective enforcement of the present article.

Article 33

States Parties shall take all appropriate measures, including legislative, administrative, social and educational measures, to protect children from the illicit use of narcotic drugs and psychotropic substances as defined in the relevant international treaties, and to prevent the use of children in the illicit production and trafficking of such substances.

Article 34

States Parties undertake to protect the child from all forms of sexual exploitation and sexual abuse. For these purposes, States Parties shall in particular take all appropriate national, bilateral and multilateral measures to prevent:

a) The inducement or coercion of a child to engage in any unlawful sexual activity;

b) The exploitative use of children in prostitution or other unlawful sexual practices; and

c) The exploitative use of children in pornographic performances and materials.

Article 35

States Parties shall take ali appropriate national, bilateral and multilateral measures to prevent the abduction of the sale of or traffic in children for any purpose or in any form.

Article 36

States Parties shall protect the child against all other forms of exploitation prejudicial to any aspects of the child's welfare.

Article 37

States Parties shall ensure that:

a) No child shall be subjected to torture or other cruel, inhuman or degrading treatment or punishment. Neither capital punishment nor life imprisonment without possibility of release shall be imposed for offences committed by persons below eighteen years of age;

b) No child shall be deprived of his or her liberty unlawfully or arbitrarily. The arrest, detention or imprisonment of a child shall be in conformity with the law and shall be used only as a measure of last resort and for the shortest appropriate period of time;

c) Every child deprived of liberty shall be treated with humanity and respect for the inherent dignity of the human person, and in a manner which takes into account the needs of persons of his or her age. In particular, every child deprived of liberty shall be separated from adults unless it is considered in the child's best interest not to do so and shall have the right to maintain contact with his or her family through correspondence and visits, save in exceptional circumstances; and

d) Every child deprived of his or her liberty shall have the right to prompt access to legal and other appropriate assistance, as well as the right to challenge the legality of the deprivation of his or her liberty before a court or other competent, independent and impartial authority, and to a prompt decision on any such action.

Article 38

1. States Parties undertake to respect and to ensure respect for rules of international humanitarian law applicable to them in armed conflicts which are relevant to the child.
2. States Parties shall take all feasible measures to ensure that persons who have not attained the age of fifteen years do not take a direct part in hostilities.
3. States Parties shall refrain from recruiting any person who has not attained the age of fifteen years into their armed forces. In recruiting among those persons who have attained the age of fifteen years but who have not attained the age of eighteen years, States Parties shall endeavour to give priority to those who are oldest.
4. In accordance with their obligations under international humanitarian law to protect the civilian population in armed conflicts, States Parties shall take all feasible measures to ensure protection and care of children who are affected by an armed conflict.

Article 39

States Parties shall take all appropriate measures to promote physical and psychological recovery and social reintegration of a child victim of: any form of neglect, exploitation, or abuse; torture or any other form of cruel, inhuman or degrading treatment or punishment; or armed conflicts. Such recovery and reintegration shall take place in an environment which fosters the health, self-respect and dignity of the child.

Article 40

1. States Parties recognise the right of every child alleged as, accused of, or recognised as having infringed the penal law to be treated in a manner consistent with the promotion of the child's sense of dignity and worth, which reinforces the child's respect for the human rights

and fundamental freedoms of others and which takes into account the child's age and the desirability of promoting the child's reintegration and the child's assuming a constructive role in society.

2. To this end, and having regard to the relevant provisions of international instruments, States Parties shall, in particular, ensure that:

   a) No child shall be alleged as, be accused of, or recognised as having infringed the penal law by reason of acts or omissions that were not prohibited by national or international law at the time they were committed;

   b) Every child alleged as or accused of having infringed the penal law has at least the following guarantees:

i) To be presumed innocent until proven guilty according to law;

ii) To be informed promptly and directly of the charges against him or her, and, if appropriate, through his or her parents of legal guardians, and to have legal or other appropriate assistance in the preparation and presentation of his or her defence;

iii) To have the matter determined without delay by a competent, independent and impartial authority or judicial body in a fair hearing according to law, in the presence of legal or other appropriate assistance and, unless it is considered not to be in the best interest of the child, in particular, taking into account his or her age or situation, his or her parents or legal guardians;

iv) Not to be compelled to give testimony or to confess guilt; to examine or have examined adverse witnesses and to obtain the participation and examination of witnesses on his or her behalf under conditions of equality;

v) If considered to have infringed the penal law to have this decision and any measures imposed in consequence thereof reviewed by a higher competent, independent and impartial authority or judicial body according to law;

vi) To have the free assistance of an interpreter if the child cannot understand or speak the language used; and

vii) To have his or her privacy fully respected at all stages of the proceedings.

3. States Parties shall seek to promote the establishment of laws, procedures, authorities and institutions specifically applicable to children alleged as, accused of or recognised as having infringed the penal law, and, in particular:

   a) The establishment of a minimum age below which children shall be presumed not to have the capacity to infringe the penal law; and

   b) Whenever appropriate and desirable measures for dealing with such children without resorting to judicial proceedings, providing that human rights and legal safeguards are fully respected.

4. A variety of dispositions, such as care, guidance and supervision orders; counselling; probation; foster care; education and vocational training programmes and other alternatives to institutional care shall be available to ensure that children are dealt with in a manner appropriate to their well being and proportionate both to their circumstances and the offence.

Article 41

Nothing in the present Convention shall affect any provisions which are more conducive to the realisation of the rights of the child and which may be contained in:

a) The law of a State Party; or

b) International law in force for that State.

Part II

Article 42

States Parties undertake to make the principles and provisions of the Convention widely known, by appropriate and active means, to adults and children alike.

Article 43

1. For the purpose of examining the progress made by States Parties in achieving the realisation of the obligations undertaken in the present Convention, there shall be established a Committee in the Rights of the Child, which shall carry out the functions hereinafter provided.
2. The Committee shall consist of ten experts of high moral standing and recognised competence in the field covered by this Convention. The members of the Committee shall be elected by States Parties from among their nationals and shall serve in their personal capacity, consideration being given to equitable geographical distribution, as well as to the principal legal systems.
3. The members of the Committee shall be elected by secret ballot from a list of persons nominated by States Parties. Each State Party may nominate one person from among its own nationals.
4. The initial election to the Committee shall be held no later than six months after the date of the entry into force of the present Convention and thereafter every second year. At least four months before the date of each election, the Secretary-General of the United Nations shall address a letter to States Parties inviting them to submit their nominations within two months. The Secretary-General shall subsequently prepare a list in alphabetical order of all persons thus nominated, indicating States Parties

which have nominated them, and shall submit it to the States Parties to the present Convention.

5. The elections shall be held at meetings of States Parties convened by the Secretary-General at United Nations Headquarters. At those meetings, for which two thirds of States Parties shall constitute a quorum, the persons elected to the Committee shall be those who obtain the largest number of votes and an absolute majority of the votes of the representatives of States Parties present and voting.

6. The members of the Committee shall be elected for a term of four years. They shall be eligible for re-election if renominated. The term of five of the members elected at the first election, shall expire at the end of two years; immediately after the first election the names of these five members shall be chosen by lot by the Chairman of the meeting.

7. If a member of the Committee dies or resigns or declares that for any other cause he or she can no longer perform the duties of the Committee, the State Party which nominated the member shall appoint another expert from among its nationals to serve for the remainder of the term, subject to the approval of the Committee.

8. The Committee shall establish its own rules of procedure.

9. The Committee shall elect its officers for a period of two years.

10. The meetings of the Committee shall normally be held at United Nations Headquarters or at any other convenient place as determined by the Committee. The Committee shall normally meet annually. The duration of the meetings of the Committee shall be determined, and reviewed, subject to the approval of the General Assembly.

11. The Secretary-General of the United Nations shall provide the necessary staff and facilities for the United Nations shall provide the necessary staff and facilities for the effective performance of the functions of the Committee under the present Convention.

12. With the approval of the General Assembly, the members of the Committee established under the present Convention shall receive emoluments from United Nations resources on such terms and conditions as the Assembly may decide.

Article 44

1. States Parties undertake to submit to the Committee, through the Secretary-General of the United Nations, reports on the measures they have adopted which give effect to the rights recognised herein and on the progress made on the enjoyment of those rights:

   a) Within two years of the entry into force of the Convention for the State Party concerned; and

   b) Thereafter every five years.

2. Reports made under the present article shall indicate factors and difficulties, if any affecting the degree of fulfilment of the obligations under the present Convention. Reports shall also contain sufficient information to provide the Committee with a comprehensive understanding of the implementation of the Convention in the country concerned.

3. A State Party which has submitted a compre-hensive initial report to the Committee need not, in its subsequent reports submitted in accordance with paragraph 1 (b) of the present article, repeat basic information previously provided.

4. The Committee may request from States Parties further information relevant to the implementation of the Convention.

5. The Committee shall submit to the General Assembly, through the Economic and Social Council, every two years, reports on its activities.
6. States Parties shall make their reports widely available to the public in their own countries.

Article 45

In order to foster the effective implementation of the Convention and to encourage international cooperation in the field covered by the Convention:

a) The specialised agencies, the United Nations Children's Fund, and other United Nations organs shall be entitled to be represented at the consideration of the implementation of such provisions of the present Convention as fall within the scope of their mandate. The Committee may invite the specialised agencies, the United Nations Children's Fund and other competent bodies as it may consider appropriate to provide expert advice on the implementation of the Convention in areas falling within the scope of their respective mandates. The Committee may invite the specialised agencies, the United Nations Children's Fund, and other United Nations organs to submit reports on the implementation of the Convention in areas falling within the scope of their activities;

b) The Committee shall transmit, as it may consider appropriate to the specialised agencies, the United Nations Children's Fund and other competent bodies, any reports from States Parties that contain a request, or indicate a need, for technical advice or assistance, along with the Committee's observations and suggestions, if any, on these requests or indications;

c) The Committee may recommend to the General Assembly to request the Secretary-General to undertake on its behalf studies on specific issues relating to the rights of the child;

d) The Committee may make suggestions and general recommendations based on information received pursuant to articles 44 and 45 of the present Convention. Such suggestions and general recommen-dations shall be transmitted to any State Party concerned and reported to the General Assembly, together with comments, if any, from States Parties.

Part III

Article 46

The present Convention shall be open for signature by all States.

Article 47

The present Convention is subject to ratification. Instruments of ratification shall be deposited with the Secretary-General of the United Nations.

Article 48

The present Convention shall remain open for accession by any State. The instruments of accession shall be deposited with the Secretary-General of the United Nations.

Article 49

1. The present Convention shall enter into force on the thirtieth day following the date of deposit with the Secretary-General of the United Nations of the twentieth instrument of ratification or accession.

2. For each State ratifying or acceding to the Convention after the deposit of the twentieth instrument of

ratification or accession, the Convention shall enter into force on the thirtieth day after the deposit by such State of its instrument of ratification or accession.

Article 50

1. Any State Party may propose an amendment and file it with the Secretary-General of the United Nations. The Secretary-General shall thereupon communicate the proposed amendment to States Parties, with a request that they indicate whether they favour a conference of States Parties for the purpose of considering and voting upon the proposal. In the event that, within four months from the date of such communication, at least one third of the States Parties favour such a conference, the Secretary-General shall convene the conference under the auspices of the United Nations. Any amendment adopted by a majority of States Parties present and voting at the conference shall be submitted to the General Assembly for approval.
2. An amendment adopted in accordance with paragraph 1 of the present article shall enter into force when it has been approved by the General Assembly of the United Nations and accepted by a two-thirds majority of States Parties.
3. When an amendment enters into force, it shall be binding on those States Parties which have accepted it, other States Parties still being bound by the provisions of the present Convention and any earlier amendments which they have accepted.

Article 51

1. The Secretary-General of the United Nations shall receive and circulate to all States the text of reservations made by States at the time of ratification or accession.

2. A reservation incompatible with the object and purpose of the present Convention shall not be permitted.

3. Reservations may be withdrawn at any time by notification to that effect addressed to the Secretary-General of the United Nations, who shall then inform all states. Such notification shall take effect on the date on which it is received by the Secretary-General.

Article 52

A State Party may denounce the present Convention by written notification to the Secretary-General of the United Nations. Denunciation becomes effective one year after the date of receipt of the notification by the Secretary-General.

Article 53

The Secretary-General of the United Nations is designated as the depositary of the present Convention.

Article 54

The original of the present Convention, of which the Arabic, Chinese, English French, Russian and Spanish text are equally authentic, shall be deposited with the Secretary-General of the United Nations.

In Witness Whereof the undersigned plenipo-tentiaries, being duly authorised thereto by their respective Governments have signed the present Convention.

Bibliography

Aguilar, L. M., "The Role of the NGOs in Monitoring Children's Rights", in VERHELLEN, E., Monitoring Children's Rights, The Hague, Martinus Nijhoff Publishers, 1996, p. 503.

Alen, A. et P. Wounter, "The UN Convention on the Rights of the Child's Self-executing Character", in Monitoring Children's Rights, The Hague, Martinus Nijhoff Publishers, 1996, p. 165.

Alston, P. , *The Best Interests of the Child : Reconciling Culture and Human Rights*, Oxford, Oxford University Press, 1994.

Cantwell, N., "Non-governmental Organizations and the United Nations Convention on the Rights of the Child", (1991) 62 Revue internationale de droit pénal 16.

Detrick, S., The United Nations Convention on The Rights of the Child : A Guide to the "Travaux préparatoires", Dordrecht, Kluwer Academic Publishers, 1992.

Eekelaar, J., "The Emergence of Children's Rights", (1986) *Oxford Journal of Legal Studies* 181.

Eekelarr, j., "The interest of the Child and The Child Wishes : The role of Dynamic Self Determinism" in Alston, P. , *The Best Interests of the Child : Reconciling Culture and Human Rights*, Oxford, Oxford University Press, 1994, p. 47.

Freeman, M. et P. Veerman, *The Ideologies of Children's Rights*, Dordrecht, Kluwer Academic Publishers, 1992.

Hammarberg, T., "The UN Convention on the Rights of the Child and How to Make It Work", (1990) 12 Human Rights Quarterly 97.

Himes, J. R., *Implementing the Convention on the Rights of the Child : Resource Mobilisation in Low-Income Countries*, The Hague, Martinus Nijhoff Publishers, 1995.

Jupp, M., "The UN Convention on the Rights of the Child: An Opportunity for Advocates", (1990) 12 Human Rights Quarterly 130.

Lucker-babel, M., "The Rights of the Child to Express Views and Be Heard : An Attempt to Interpret Article 12 of the UN Convention on the Rights of the Child", (1995) *The International Journal of Children's Rights* 391.

Miljeteig-olssen, "Advocacy of Children's Rights-The Convention as More than a Legal Document", (1990) 12 Human Rights Quarterly 148.

Philip Alston (ed.), *The Best Interests of the Child: Reconciling Culture and Human Rights*, Oxford: Clarendon Press/ UNICEF, 1994

Rosenczveig, J. P., "The Self-executing Character of the Children's Rights Convention in France", in Verhellen, E., *Monitoring Children's Rights*, The Hague, Martinus Nijhoff Publishers, 1996, p. 187.

Ruiz-gimenez, J., "The Human Rights of the Child", (1993) *International Commission of Jurists* 81.

Saulle, E., *The Rights of the Child : International Instruments*, New York, Transnational Publishers Inc., 1995.

Index